Anne Perry and the Murder of the Century

Peter Graham

Skyhorse Publishing
A HERMAN GRAF BOOK

Originally published in 2011 under the title of *So Brilliantly Clever: Parker, Hulme and the Murder That Shocked the World* by Awa Press, Wellington, New Zealand.

Skyhorse Publishing books may be purchased in bulk at special discounts for sales promotion, corporate gifts, fund-raising, or educational purposes. Special editions can also be created to specifications. For details, contact the Special Sales Department, Skyhorse Publishing, 307 West 36th Street, 11th Floor, New York, NY 10018 or info@skyhorsepublishing.com.

Skyhorse® and Skyhorse Publishing® are registered trademarks of Skyhorse Publishing, Inc.®, a Delaware corporation.

Visit our website at www.skyhorsepublishing.com.

10 9 8 7 6 5

Library of Congress Cataloging-in-Publication Data is available on file.
Hardcover ISBN: 978-1-62087-630-5
Paperback ISBN: 978-1-63450-518-5
eBook ISBN: 978-1-62636-305-2

Printed in the United States of America

Cover design by Ceri Hurst

EDITORIAL NOTES
1. Honorah Parker's first name was misspelled 'Honora' by the police and in subsequent media reports. The correct spelling has been used here except where quoting reports of the time.
2. In 1955 the Supreme Court was the court where the most serious criminal cases were tried before a jury. Today this is called the High Court, and the Supreme Court is the name of New Zealand's court of final appeal.

ABOUT THE AUTHOR

Peter Graham worked for thirty years in Hong Kong as a barrister before taking up a new career as a crime writer. His first book, *Vile Crimes*, about a notorious double poisoning case, was praised by *The New Zealand Herald* as "murderously good ... a pacy narrative and a study in pathological selfishness". His quest to unearth the whole truth about Pauline Parker and Juliet Hulme has taken him around the world. Peter Graham lives in rural Canterbury, New Zealand.

To Rebecca, Guy, Lucy and Louise

Contents

Author's Note

When Juliet Hulme and Pauline Parker bashed Pauline's mother to death on June 22, 1954, I was seven years old. I don't remember hearing about the murder or the trial, even though I clearly remember the conquest of Mount Everest by Hillary and Tenzing and Queen Elizabeth II's coronation the previous year. It would seem my parents hid the news of the vicious killing from my sister and me: such protection of young minds was normal in those days. Matricide by teenage girls was then an exceedingly rare crime, as it is still. The killing of Honorah Parker, not to mention the talk of a lesbian relationship between the girls, would have made deeply distressing reading for parents everywhere.

I first heard of what is usually called "the Parker–Hulme murder" in 1972, when as a young, newly qualified barrister and solicitor I went to Christchurch to work as an assistant to Brian McClelland, who had been junior counsel for Juliet Hulme. He often talked about the case, and on one occasion Peter Mahon, who had been junior to the crown prosecutor Alan Brown, shared his remembrances with me and others. From Brian McClelland I heard that the two girls had been engaged in a lesbian love affair when they were threatened with separation—although Pauline, he said, also enjoyed regular sex with a male law student. Pauline's parents were not married and several cuts below the Hulmes socially. Her father ran a fish and chip shop in Sydenham and Pauline had been bedazzled by what seemed to her the glamorous social world of the Hulmes. The girls wrote poems and books together, and believing they were geniuses and great beauties made plans to run away to Hollywood and have their books made into films. McClelland firmly believed that Juliet Hulme, who called him "Bambi", was certifiably mad but was not convinced the same was true of Pauline.

The Parker–Hulme murder was somehow embedded in the soil of Christchurch, as much a part of local history as the pilgrims who, a century earlier, had footed it over the bridle path from Lyttelton, the men in frock coats and top hats, the women in crinolines, to found the city. I not infrequently met people who had been friends of Juliet's parents Hilda and Henry Hulme when Henry was rector of Canterbury University College.

The rector's house, generally known then as Ilam Homestead, stood in its magnificent grounds in Ilam Road. You could not go past it—I was not alone in this—without thinking about those two strange girls. It was the same passing the old Girls' High building in Cranmer Square, now sadly demolished after suffering severe damage in the earthquakes of September 2010 and February 2011. And if you went to Victoria Park you could not help wondering exactly where Pauline's mother met her terrible end.

The case so fascinated me that in 1975 I decided to find out as much as I could and write an account of it, as true as I could make it. From what I already knew the facts seemed too good, from a literary point of view, to waste on fictionalisation. I had come to unwittingly share Dr Johnson's belief that "the value of every story depends upon its being true".

With Brian McClelland's support I tried to retrieve the case papers from his old firm, Wynn Williams and Co. I was informed the file had gone missing. For such a cause célèbre it is astonishing how many files, boxes of photographs and exhibits of various kinds have disappeared from solicitors' offices, court registries and police stations. Regrettably, my book was not started in 1975 but in 2008, after I had returned from thirty years in Hong Kong. In the interim a number of people involved had died, but one way and another I was able to find more than enough documentary evidence and people with long memories to piece together a wide-ranging narrative of the death of Honorah Parker, the backgrounds of Juliet Hulme and Pauline Parker, and their lives both before and after the murder.

My research began at the Alexander Turnbull Library in Wellington. At the front desk the librarian told me there was always a lot of interest in the Parker-Hulme case. "Mostly prurient," he added. How could he tell? I tried my best not to look shifty but may not have succeeded. That disapproving "here's another one of them" look from librarians and archivists was something I would get used to. As my research progressed I was, however, frequently rewarded by new discoveries that were interesting in themselves, or shone new light on Juliet, Pauline and the lives of people affected by their crime.

The murder is internationally New Zealand's most famous crime. In part that is due to the success of Peter Jackson's film *Heavenly Creatures*. The trial of Parker and Hulme caught the attention of the world's press from the word go, but to many it is, and will always remain, the "*Heavenly Creatures* murder". A quick search on the internet will disclose that there exists in cyberspace an international cult whose devotees feed on every morsel of information, however small, connected with the crime.

What makes one act of murder and its surrounding circumstances fascinating, where another is merely sordid or banal? Other than the assassination of presidents and other heads of state, no other murder of a single individual anywhere in the world has probably inspired so many works of fiction—novels, films, plays and screenplays—not to mention film and television documentaries. The only possible exception is the 1924 Chicago kidnap and murder of Bobby Franks by Nathan Leopold and Richard Loeb, two outstandingly intelligent teenage sons of millionaires convinced they were Nietzschean supermen.

Surprisingly, though, apart from short lurid accounts in anthologies of crime, the only previously published true account of the Parker-Hulme murder is *Parker and Hulme: A Lesbian View*. The scope and purport of that book, which appeared twenty years ago, is very different from my own, being motivated by the wish to examine the effect of the murder on the lesbian community in New Zealand. *Anne Perry and the Murder of the Century* tells the whole story for the first time.

Peter Graham
September 2011

CHAPTER 1

A Walk in the Park

By eleven o'clock in the morning, hard bright sunlight had melted the last pockets of frost from the rector's expansive lawns and dispelled the mist from the river that glided through the grounds. It was Tuesday, June 22, the winter solstice, but the sky was blue and cloudless. Dr Henry Hulme was at the wheel of his Jaguar in front of the carriage-porch, warming the engine while he waited for his daughter. It was a late start, but Hulme's days at Canterbury University College were all but over. Soon, thank heaven, he would be back home in England.

A tall ectomorphic man in his mid forties wearing good London tailoring and horn-rimmed spectacles, the rector looked every inch the Cambridge boffin. There were women who found his aquiline features and pleasant dry manner rather attractive. His prominent forehead intimated a powerful intelligence, and indeed at the time he took up his appointment in New Zealand he had been rated among the leading mathematical physicists of his generation and one of Britain's foremost authorities on nuclear weapons.

As Juliet slipped into the front passenger seat her father was agreeably surprised by her cheerful smile and inconsequential chatter. Julie could be moody—damned difficult in fact. One way or another the rest of the family was always hostage to her uncertain temperament. She had been delayed in the kitchen, modelling for her mother and Bill Perry the camel skirt she was wearing, bought the day before. Julie loved clothes. Perhaps the new skirt explained her buoyant mood.

Hulme eased the car around the sweep of the drive, past the

stately Wellingtonias and Ilam's famous rhododendrons. Turning into the road, father and daughter headed towards town.

The professorial board had left Henry Hulme no choice but to resign. But he had had it anyway with the endless bickering that had proved an unhappy feature of university administration in New Zealand. The thought of getting down to serious research work again at home appealed greatly.

Still, the college had done things properly: he and Hilda had been farewelled with every token of regard. And Bill Cartwright's valediction had generously praised his contribution to Canterbury College and the University of New Zealand. He had been presented with quite a decent cheque—a collection from the academic staff. Rudi Gopas had applied the final brushstrokes to his portrait, commissioned to hang alongside those of the other illustrious men and women of the college.

In less than a fortnight he and Juliet would be departing. His daughter was still convalescing from tuberculosis. He and Hilda were agreed that it would be best for her health if she stayed with his sister Ina in Johannesburg during the European winter while he looked for a job in England.

Hilda, as always, would do what suited her. The current plan was that she would pack up the house and bring their son Jonty home to England when his school broke up for the August holidays. Bill Perry—officially a close family friend, in truth her lover—might perhaps be in tow. Hilda wanted a divorce and Henry was determined they should all be adult about it.

Unsuprisingly, there had been ructions in the household, with Julie at the epicentre. She was upset about saying goodbye to her great friend and soulmate Pauline Rieper. That was only natural, but she was turning the thing into a tragic opera. She overdramatised everything. Always had. Deborah and Gina the two girls called each other. Julie insisted the family also had to call her Deborah.

Both girls were desperate for Pauline to join Juliet in Johannesburg but of course that was impossible. Pauline's mother would never allow it. He had done everything he could, but that didn't stop dear Julie making herself thoroughly disagreeable whenever she chose. Only when the Rieper girl stayed at Ilam was there anything like peace in the house. Henry was quietly confident all this unpleasantness would resolve itself in eleven days' time, when he and his daughter sailed for South Africa.

On the journey into town, Juliet told her father something of her plans for the day. She was going to have lunch with Gina at the Riepers, after which Mrs Rieper was taking them up to Victoria Park for a walk. That evening she was going to Léon Goossens' recital at the Civic Theatre with Jan and Diony Sutherland. To Henry, who loved good music, the last item was welcome news. The accomplished English oboist's concert was a foretaste of how life would be back in England, when Julie's life no longer revolved around Pauline Rieper.

Henry dropped Juliet in the centre of town, at the intersection of Colombo and Cashel Streets. She was looking beautiful: tall for her age, slender—an English rose, not quite sixteen. Her light brown shoulder-length hair—almost blonde with a little help from a product called Golden Rinse—was parted on the side like one of the wholesome young film actresses of the day. If Juliet were feeling troubled, as would have been natural enough with parental divorce in the air, and the prospect of being shunted off to South Africa looming, no one seeing her march confidently into Beath's department store that morning to make some small purchases would ever have guessed.

Leaving Beaths, Juliet walked down Cashel Street towards the river and on to the Riepers' house at the Christ's College end of Gloucester Street. Number 31 was a large, plain, two-storey Victorian house that backed on to Christchurch Girls' High. The weatherboard exterior was in urgent need of repainting, and there were bicycles all over the place. Pauline's parents, Nora and Bert Rieper, took in boarders, mostly young male university students or trainees from the Teachers' College in Peterborough Street.

Juliet didn't much enjoy spending time at the Riepers. Their frightful furniture and tasteless nicknacks, not to mention the faint pong of fish and gas from the water heater, would put anybody off. And Nora and Bert, although they could not help being who they were, were hopelessly ignorant of anything that mattered: art, great music, literature. *Molto insimpatico*. Pauline agreed entirely. She lived at home only under sufferance.

The girls' first idea had been to have a picnic at Victoria Park, but Mrs Rieper preferred to have lunch—the Riepers called it dinner— at home first. Bert Rieper was already back from work and in his vegetable garden when Juliet arrived. Pauline's sister Wendy turned up not long afterwards. Like Juliet, Pauline was in a happy mood. Not just happy, *excited*. Lunch was a particularly cheerful occasion. Pauline and Juliet cracked jokes, and Bert and Nora joined in the laughter. Wendy, a pretty seventeen-year-old proud of her position in the lingerie section of a nearby department store, may not have found the girls quite so amusing, but Nora was basking in the restored warmth of family life.

For a long time, Pauline—or Yvonne, as the family called her— had been sulky and often downright rude, treating them with a contempt she didn't bother to hide. And the way she usually spoke to Wendy was dreadful. In her eyes her family measured up poorly against the Hulmes. Many harsh words had been exchanged between mother and daughter, and the truth was that Nora could hardly wait for the stuck-up, obnoxious, self-opinionated Juliet Hulme to disappear from New Zealand forever—along with her snooty mother and the rest of the Hulmes. Freed from Juliet Hulme's influence, her daughter would soon get her feet back on the ground, forget all the airs and graces she had acquired over the last two years.

However, since Sunday afternoon, when they had collected Pauline from the Hulmes' house at Ilam, where she had been staying for more than a week, they had noticed a change. She was in a happier frame of mind than they had seen for ages; she seemed to have finally come to terms with Juliet's departure. She had sat in front of the fire that evening, writing an opera she said, but at least making a contribution to the conversation. That was something she hadn't bothered to do for a long time. She had spoken civilly to her father for once. And yesterday she had worked like a demon, helping with housework. Nora had no desire to go walking in Victoria Park or anywhere else, but seeing how Pauline had bucked herself up it would be nice: a mother-and-daughter outing and a sort of farewell to Juliet. Pauline had found a job and was starting the following week, and Nora would probably not see Juliet again before she left New Zealand. The thought cheered her greatly.

After lunch, Bert and Wendy biked back to their places of work—Wendy to her lingerie counter and Bert to Dennis Brothers, Poulterers and Fishmongers, the modest retail business of which he was the manager. As soon as the dishes were washed and dried, Nora Rieper and the two girls set off along Gloucester Street, nipping through Chancery Lane to Cathedral Square to catch the Cashmere Hills bus.

They were an unremarkable trio, although Juliet, half a head taller than Pauline, stood out a little on the streets of Christchurch with her self-assured manner and the unmistakably English cut of her fawn coat. Pauline, who had just turned sixteen, had a stocky frame that no amount of dieting or purging seemed able to change. With her pale waxy complexion, intractable black hair and frequent scowl, she was not as attractive as her friend. Her coat was of a commonplace grey Donegal tweed. And while Juliet carried herself well, Pauline walked with a slight limp, a legacy of childhood osteomyelitis. Both girls toted shoulder bags, as girls their age did when out of school uniform. Nora, a buxom woman with grey-brindled hair and muscular legs, was turned out in a matronly matching jacket and skirt with hat, gloves and handbag. It was a lovely afternoon but the pullover around her shoulders was there in reserve for the drop in temperature to be expected later on.

Victoria Park in the Port Hills above Christchurch is five miles south of Cathedral Square. Barging down Colombo Street, a river of bicycles and cars, the number two bus that had only recently replaced the tram service passed Dennis Brothers at number 668 and carried on over Moorhouse Avenue and the railway line. With frequent stops and starts it juddered past Sydenham, then on through dreary Beckenham to Thorrington at the foot of the Cashmere Hills. Here the road tacked west, tracing the Heathcote River around to Hackthorne Road, before climbing uphill past the affluent houses of Cashmere. The bus reached its terminus outside the Sign of the Takahe, a large, incongruous building that sought to emulate an English manor house of the fifteenth or sixteenth century. The vision of a conservation-minded eccentric named Harry Ell, it had taken an army of masons, wood carvers, heraldic painters and other craftsmen more than thirty years to complete.

From the Sign of the Takahe a rough-metalled roadway led about a mile up a rise into Victoria Park. A couple of hundred acres of reserve land, the park had been opened to the public fifty-seven years earlier to the day—June 22, 1897—as Christchurch's tribute to the great queen on the occasion of her diamond jubilee. For the most part it was a wilderness of tussock grass and scrubby trees, pierced in places by outcrops of volcanic rock.

The three trudged up the hill to the park. None was much used to exercise and the light westerly had produced a warm afternoon. At the top, the girls unbuttoned their coats and caught their breath outside the tea kiosk that adjoined the caretaker's house. The view over Christchurch and across the Canterbury Plains to the snow-licked foothills of the Southern Alps, milky-blue in the soft afternoon light, was spectacular. Not the sort of woman to venture into untamed wastes without fortification, Nora Rieper led the way into the tearooms. It was shortly after half past two.

The caretaker's wife was in charge. Nora ordered a pot of tea with cakes and scones, and suggested the girls might like soft drinks. Both said they preferred still and Agnes Ritchie brought the bottles of drink, orange for one, lemon for the other, with straws to their table. She chatted a little to Nora and the girls responded politely when she addressed them. They were a quiet group, she thought. Nothing out of the ordinary. The bill was paid and they left just before three o'clock.

Pauline had been to Victoria Park before: when Juliet was away in the North Island with her parents in the Christmas holidays, she and another girl had gone there. She took the lead, heading down a steep track that started at a gap in the stone wall near the caretaker's house. The east side bush track, as it was known, descended to "a delightful sylvan setting of native and English trees with young pines, ribbonwood and lemonwood predominating", as a reporter from *N.Z. Truth* would later describe it. Another journalist would more theatrically call it "a lonely ravine". Either way, a more secluded spot within a bus ride and short walk of central Christchurch did not exist.

CHAPTER 2

State of Shock

At half past three, give or take a few minutes, Agnes Ritchie was in the servery making ice creams for two small children. Half a dozen stone steps led up to the serving window. While busy scooping the ice cream she saw the two girls who had been in the tearooms earlier dashing up to the foot of the steps, breathless, greatly agitated, with bloody hands and clothing. One girl's face was splattered with blood and the other's finely speckled. Both were shouting. One was calling out, "Please, could somebody help us? Mummy has been hurt! It's Mummy—she's terribly hurt! She's *dead!*" The other yelled, "It's her mother—she's hurt! She's covered with blood! Please, somebody help!"

Agnes Ritchie sent her two young customers to fetch her husband, who was burning rubbish nearby, and rushed out through the tearooms to the girls. She asked them to show her where it had happened. One gasped, "Down in the bushes—down the track." Agnes went through the gap in the stone wall and peered down the track, but couldn't see anything. She went back to the girls and told them they would have to show her. They begged her not to make them go down to that horrible place again. Assuring them she wouldn't, Agnes took them into the kiosk. One, whom she later learned was Juliet Hulme, was bordering on hysteria; the other, Pauline Parker, was quieter, white as an aspirin, perhaps in shock.

Kenneth Ritchie, the caretaker, knew only that a woman had been injured in an accident. Seeing the two girls, he took the one with the blood-splashed face through the gap in the stone wall to the edge of the bush. Her left hand was coated with gore. He demanded to know where the accident had happened. The girl gestured vaguely towards the vegetation below. Ritchie could get from her only that her mother had slipped and hit her head on a rock. Thinking he might have to staunch some heavy bleeding, he raced into the house to grab a towel. The second his assistant, Eric McIlroy, showed up the two men hotfooted it down the track.

Agnes Ritchie took the girls back into the tearooms and phoned for an ambulance. Juliet kept saying, "Don't go away! Don't leave us!" She was definitely the more upset of the two. Next, Agnes phoned Donald Walker, a doctor whose Beckenham surgery was not far away. Juliet, in particular, was worried about the blood on her hands and clothes and wanted to wash urgently. There was no hot water in the house that day; Agnes took them into the servery to clean themselves as best they could at the sink. She gave them towels and left them to it. "Oh dear, isn't she *nice*?" Juliet said and both girls dissolved in giggles.

When they were slightly more presentable, the girls asked Agnes Ritchie if she would ring their fathers. Pauline said she didn't want to go back to her house as no one would be there. The phone at Bert Rieper's fish shop was engaged but Agnes got hold of Henry Hulme at the university. He would come immediately and collect them both. While they waited, Agnes gave them a cup of tea. Pauline gulped hers scalding hot, not pausing to add milk.

Agnes asked repeatedly how the accident had happened. Juliet shrieked, "Don't talk about it! I can't bear to talk about it!"

Pauline said in a slow, husky voice, "She slipped on a plank and hit her head on a brick. ... Her head kept bumping and banging as it fell."

Juliet chimed in, "Don't think about it. It's only a dream. We'll wake up soon. Let's talk about something else."

Agnes thoughtfully moved on to more general topics. Which school did they go to? They weren't at school any more, they said. During a lull in the conversation, Pauline groaned loudly, "Mummy—she's dead." Agnes suggested she might not be hurt that badly. Pauline just stared at her.

After a long silence, Pauline volunteered that they had tried to pick up her mother and carry her, but she was too heavy and they had dropped her. "Perhaps we didn't do the right thing," she suggested. Both kept saying they wanted to go home. "Will my Daddy be long?" Juliet plaintively asked no one in particular. "I wish he would hurry." She wanted to get away at once from "this horrible place". Pauline said she just wanted to go to bed, although she was very calm, Agnes Ritchie observed.

Kenneth Ritchie and Eric McIlroy had run a quarter of a mile down the rough track when they came upon a woman lying on her back near a ramshackle bridge of wooden planks. Her legs, splayed indecently, lay towards them; her head, smashed and bloody, was downhill. The woman's eyes were closed and bulging. Her mouth gaped and her hair was matted with globs of blood. Blood smeared her face and was caked in her mouth and nostrils. Jets of blood from her head had travelled in rivulets, now clotted twelve feet down the track. Her skirt was around her thighs. Instinctively protecting the woman's modesty, Kenneth Ritchie pulled at the hem to cover her knees. It didn't look like an accident, he thought. There were no rocks anywhere near, and on the ground a foot from her head there was a half-brick with blood and bits of hair on it. McIlroy remained at the scene while Ritchie shot back up the hill to call the police.

A St John's ambulance was pulling up as Ritchie got to the top. Harold Keys, the driver, asked him about the woman who had fallen down a bank. Not a man to waste words, Ritchie tersely informed him she was down the track—dead. Keys went to have a gander, leaving his offsider Ray Edmonds to wait by the ambulance. At her husband's instruction, Agnes Ritchie phoned the police. By then it was ten to four.

Shaken by what he had seen, Kenneth Ritchie called the girls into the sitting room but got nothing out of them. That was when he saw the large patch of blood on the front of the girl Hulme's skirt. He made a brief report by telephone to Morris Barnett, the superintendent of reserves. Barnett was worried the woman might have tripped on the planking of the bridge: they both knew it was overdue for repair. Out of caution Barnett phoned Ross Lascelles of Weston Ward and

Lascelles, the council's solicitors, alerting him to a potential legal problem.

When Henry Hulme arrived at Victoria Park, Juliet and Pauline sank happily into the aromatic upholstery of the Jaguar. Relieved that the police had not yet arrived, Hulme paused only to leave his name and address with Edmonds before accelerating away in the direction of Ilam. At a quarter past four, he and the two girls arrived at the house. Bill Perry, who lived in the self-contained flat at the back of the house, had arrived seconds earlier and was collecting his newspaper at the gate when Hulme's car turned into the drive. The men did not speak.

As the girls, pale and trembling, entered the panelled entrance hall Hilda was on the telephone. She stared at them horror-struck and crisply brought her phone call to a close. "I have to go. Juliet's just come in and she's covered in blood!"

There had been an accident, Henry told her. Julie and Pauline had seen Mrs Rieper fall on some rocks at Victoria Park. She had been very badly injured—was possibly dead. Even as he spoke, an accident sounded hardly plausible considering the state the girls were in. Fearing a ghastly crime had been committed, he was stunned into inertia.

Hilda was made of sterner stuff. Both girls appeared to be in shock. While running them a bath, she summoned Bill Perry. Henry was hopeless: Bill would prove much more resourceful in a crisis. After instructing Hilda how to treat shock, Perry took charge. For a start Henry should phone Nancy. All he had to do was tell her there had been an accident at Victoria Park and Julie would not be able to go to the Léon Goossens recital with Diony and Jan. That was all he needed to say.

While Hilda was bathing the girls—in water as hot as they could stand—Perry left cups of very sweet hot tea on a tray outside the bathroom. The two bloodstained coats were on the landing. The left sleeve of Pauline's coat was sodden with blood six inches up from the cuff. Her mother's blood—God almighty! He roared off to the nearest dry-cleaning depot, Hicks' Drapers at the corner of Clyde and Fendalton Roads, which closed at five o'clock. He hadn't yet spoken to the girls; he took their coats to be cleaned—or so he would later claim—only because he thought it wouldn't be good for them to see their bloodied clothing while in a state of shock.

While Perry was away, Hilda washed the girls' underwear. After her bath Juliet became excitable, flushed and talkative, but remained reluctant to discuss the accident. Hilda put the girls to bed together in Juliet's room. They told her they were hungry and she brought them a light supper. When Perry returned, he looked in on them. A wireless was playing music. Pauline was very quiet, very white, almost in a coma. Juliet was flushed, perspiring, and extremely animated. He gave each of them a sedative. Best they got to sleep as soon as possible. He did not discuss Mrs Rieper's accident but chatted quietly about books and music, hoping to keep their minds off unpleasant thoughts.

Dr Donald Walker was the first to arrive at Victoria Park after Henry Hulme had taken the girls away. Kenneth Ritchie told him he was wasting his time if he thought he was going to give the woman medical help. The doctor decided he might as well wait at the tea kiosk for the police.

Constable Donald Molyneaux, on duty in the watch house at Central Police Station in Hereford Street, received the call at ten to four. Molyneaux drove Sergeant Robert Hope up to the park, arriving at twenty past four. The two police officers spoke briefly to Dr Walker and Harold Keys and then, guided by Eric McIlroy, they all descended the track. Kenneth Ritchie and Ray Edmonds were gazing in reflective silence at the body. It was as utterly motionless as anything could be—stone, stone dead. It was eerily quiet down in the bush, where the east side of Latters Spur fell away steeply to Bowenvale. Night was falling fast: not a sparrow's peep disturbed the intense silence. It was hard to imagine the corpse at their feet had been as alive as them only an hour ago.

As Dr Walker confirmed what they already knew, Sergeant Hope's eye was drawn not only to the half-brick, but to a stocking lying on the bank beside the track. He instructed Constable Molyneaux to make sure no one touched the body or anything else, then hared back up the hill to contact the Criminal Investigation Branch office on his patrol-car radio.

Detective Sergeant Archie Tate and Detective Ferguson Gillies of the CIB and Constable Audrey Griffiths of the Women's Division were dispatched to Victoria Park. Being the shortest day of the year, it was getting dark by the time they arrived at five-fifteen. Sergeant Hope led them down the zigzag. They were joined soon afterwards by Inspector Duncan McKenzie and Senior Detective Macdonald Brown of the CIB, Ted Taylor, the coroner, Dr Colin Pearson, the police pathologist, and the police photographer Bill Ramage. The huge gibbous moon that rose in the sky as darkness fell cast hardly a glimmer under the trees, where the body of Nora Rieper lay on a dirt track, surrounded by bloody pine needles.

The experts studied the scene by torchlight: the body, still warm; the half-brick; the lisle stocking, knotted at the ankle and broken at the toe. It turned chilly as they poked and probed, took photographs, made measurements, drew sketch plans, and wrote careful notes. The abject details were all recorded: the woman's muddied stockings, the shoe cast off her right foot, her lower denture half-buried in gritty clay to the left of her jaw, her trampled hat and gloves, the brooch squashed beneath her left leg. Nearby were a handbag and white cardigan—lost or discarded as the first blows thonked into her. A placenta-like pudding of clotted blood lay near her feet on the grass beside the track. It suggested her body had been moved from where it first lay oozing blood. Marks around the neck indicated that the woman had been held down by the throat while being bashed on the head.

The wounds to her hands escaped no one's attention. The tip of the little finger of her left hand was hanging by a piece of skin. She had clearly tried to ward off blows to her head. She had put up a fight. Her death had been neither quick nor painless.

The death scene sickened them all. Violent killings were rare in Christchurch, and as Detective Sergeant Tate would say, "The deceased had been attacked with an animal ferocity seldom seen in the most brutal murders." That this savagery was the work of two teenage girls who might have been their own daughters was a thought too shocking for words. Tate's own daughter Lesley was the same sort of age.

They now knew that one of the girls was the daughter of the rector of Canterbury College. Her mother, the rector's wife, was often on the wireless, dishing out advice about family things on *Candid Comment*. Station 3YA, for crying out loud. It was beyond comprehension how or why two young girls—girls like that—anyone—could have done such a thing. It was something people would puzzle about for a long time to come.

When the detective work at the scene was finished, the woman's body was humped up to the top of the track, where Constable Griffiths was deputed to escort it to the Christchurch Public Hospital morgue—"the dead house" as it was unceremoniously known. Hers would be the grim task of undressing the corpse, and wrapping and labelling items of clothing that might be needed as evidence. She would have to tie the upper joint of the left-hand little finger to the lower in case it became detached and lost. When she was finished, a mortuary attendant would come and shear the dead woman's head and get everything ready for Dr Pearson in the morning.

At seven-thirty, Inspector McKenzie ordered Brown and Tate to get cracking and interview the girls. Up at the tea kiosk the two men came across Bert Rieper. Agnes Ritchie had telephoned Dennis Brothers again later in the afternoon and Bert had finally got her message at half past four. A friend had driven him to Victoria Park, where Sergeant Hope had given him the bitter news. He had been hanging around since then, stunned, transfixed, unable to bring himself to venture down the track yet powerless to leave. Crushed by grief, he had all but lost the power of speech. The detectives sought his permission to question Pauline, whom they believed was at the home of Dr and Mrs Hulme. With a mute nod he agreed.

Some time after eight o'clock, Senior Detective Brown and Detective Sergeant Tate arrived at the imposing Ilam home of the rector of Canterbury University College. They pressed the bell with a sense of unease. Behind these daunting doors was a world unknown to policemen. The two CIB men had hardly needed Inspector McKenzie's anxious enjoinder to go easy in their dealings with Dr and Mrs Hulme. These people weren't just anybody.

CHAPTER 3

The Investigation

On June 22, 1954, sunset was officially at 4.59 p.m: the shortest day of the year was followed by the longest night. It would be a very long night at 87 Ilam Road.

After Henry Hulme phoned their family friend Nancy Sutherland to say Juliet wouldn't be able to attend the Léon Goossens recital, he did something odd: he telephoned Harold Norris, vicar of Saint Peter's Anglican Church in Upper Riccarton. Although Henry and Hilda were parishioners, they were hardly regular churchgoers. Norris was more a social acquaintance, a sympathetic ear who could be relied upon to keep confidences entrusted to him. It was obvious Henry was upset about something: the vicar readily agreed to come and see him. After he arrived, the two talked for some time, closeted together where they could not be overheard.

Later, people would wonder why Henry Hulme had not instead talked to his friend Terence Gresson, a prominent Christchurch barrister and solicitor whom he had known since Cambridge days. What could Harold Norris offer but words of comfort: Be of good heart ... trust in the Lord? Gresson, on the other hand, was a lawyer experienced in criminal cases. He could have given the practical advice the Hulmes needed there and then. What should they do if—when—the police came and wanted to interview Julie? Should she make a statement? Was it best to cooperate? Or was it in her interest to say nothing, claim the right of silence?

Henry and Hilda knew little about what had happened up at Victoria Park. The girls hadn't said much, other than that Mrs Rieper had fallen and hit her head on some rocks. Perhaps they were leaping to conclusions—perhaps it *was* an accident. Perhaps Mrs Rieper wasn't too badly hurt. They were clutching at straws, trying not to think the very worst.

It is possible, of course, that Henry Hulme did try to contact Terence Gresson but was unable to reach him—possible but not particularly likely. He, Hilda and Bill Perry probably thought it would be jumping the gun to get a lawyer involved at that stage. Standing on their rights might look bad to the police. If the situation turned out to be not as serious as they thought, the fact Henry had suspected his daughter of being involved in a bloody murder would be an embarrassment. It would overhang his friendship with Gresson for ever.

With the two girls in bed, in their nightwear, bathed, fed, lightly sedated, with soothing music on the wireless, Hilda, Henry and Bill waited downstairs in the drawing room to hear from the police. They were bound to come. Perhaps they would leave it until the morning? Probably not.

At seven-thirty the telephone rang. Henry answered. The police! They had been examining the scene of Mrs Rieper's death. She was dead. A *full* investigation—the emphasis was unmistakable—would follow.

Deciding there was something she had to attend to, Hilda went upstairs to Juliet's untidy bedroom and gathered up her scribblings: the two novels she had written in a pile of school exercise books, her poems, her scrapbooks, her letters from Pauline ... her diary. She knew Juliet kept a diary and with a rush of panic worried about what it might contain. The last few entries gave her a heart stab. Flipping the pages, it was immediately clear the diary was terribly embarrassing and *dreadfully* incriminating. On no account could it be seen by the police. She tucked it away in a safe place, to be destroyed in the morning. The rest of Juliet's writings, papers, and bits and pieces she stuffed into a suit box, to be handed to the police if they should ask to see such things.

A second phone call alerted the household that CIB officers would be arriving shortly to interview the girls. Perry proposed that in whatever time was available they should find out more about what had happened at Victoria Park, and, if they could, prime the girls a bit before the police questioned them. While Hilda talked to Juliet, Perry spoke with Pauline, who had been moved to the bed in the verandah room. He gently apologised for having to discuss the accident with her. As the police were grown-ups and she was a child, it would be best if she told him all about the accident so he could speak to them on her behalf. He trod delicately, not mentioning that her mother was dead; he thought she probably knew that already.

Pauline was very distressed. He had to pause at intervals to comfort her and allow her to recover her composure. Her mother, she said, had tripped on a piece of wood, and in falling had banged her head repeatedly on a stone. She demonstrated this with vigorous movements of her head.

"What sort of stone was it?" Perry asked.

"I don't know," she answered. "I think it was a brick, or half a brick."

"Was she having a fit?"

"It might be. I don't know. She kept hitting herself."

At that she became very distressed again. Perry asked if her mother had fallen down a steep ravine.

"No," she said. "It wasn't very steep but very slippery. ... We tried to pick her up but she was too heavy and we dropped her."

She was worried they might have hurt her when they dropped her. That was when they ran up to the tea kiosk to get help. Perry asked whether her mother was alive when they left her. She didn't know. Her mother was making gurgling noises. She had felt for a heartbeat but couldn't feel anything.

Unconvinced by much of what he heard, Bill Perry tried another tack. "We must make quite sure we've got everything right. Policemen have all sorts of ways of looking at these things, and if a quarrel was the cause of the accident you must tell me about it. For instance, if your mother had been quarrelling with you and tried to hit you—"

"Oh no. My mother never struck me."

Bill Perry went downstairs to rejoin Henry and Hilda in the drawing room. They both begged him to stay and help them deal with the police.

*

As Senior Detective Macdonald Brown and his detective sergeant stood beneath the colonnaded carriage porch waiting for the doors of Ilam to be opened to them, they held little hope of making any progress with their investigation that evening. Most likely Dr and Mrs Hulme would tell them the two girls could not be interviewed until they had obtained legal advice. That would be understandable. Considering the girls' ages, there could be no argument. They were not out to take any unfair advantage of the Hulmes or their daughter—or the other girl. They just wanted to get on with the job as quickly as they could. Tate, in particular, had a reputation among defence lawyers as being straight as a die, incapable of pulling a fast one. Big and fair-haired, he was a good-humoured bloke who played rugby for Christchurch Police. Brown was a tall well-built Scotsman, a high-flyer. He was a Brethren but no wowser: he enjoyed a whisky off duty.

The way it went, the Hulmes couldn't have been more pleasant. Dr Hulme was distinguished-looking, professorial. Mrs Hulme was attractive, immaculately groomed, stylish in her way. *A lady*. Both were welcoming and courteous. Although Hilda Hulme could be—as Terence Gresson's wife Eleanor would say—"cold as the Arctic circle", that evening her inner turmoil was well concealed. Both she and Henry were urbane enough to know how to be charming when charm was called for. The detectives were promised their fullest cooperation. And the Canadian, Bill Perry, was a likeable man's man: burly, handsome in a worldly Clark Gable sort of way, a natural diplomat.

Brown took Perry to one side and described the horrific injuries suffered by Mrs Rieper. Pauline's story about slipping or tripping and banging her head on a brick or half-brick that happened to be lying on the ground couldn't possibly be true. Perry provided the information that he had taken the girls' coats to Hick's Drapers for drycleaning. They could pick them up in the morning.

Henry Hulme opened the batting by quietly announcing that his daughter Juliet had not been there—not actually *there*—when Mrs Rieper fell. She hadn't seen what happened. She had been walking well ahead of Pauline and her mother, and when someone called out she went back to look for them. She found Mrs Rieper on the ground, unconscious, blood everywhere.

Brown decided they should interview Pauline first. Hilda took the two policemen up to the verandah room. Pauline was tucked snugly in bed but, as Archie Tate observed, awake and attentive. Hilda remained as Pauline recounted how she and Juliet and her mother had taken the bus to the Sign of the Takahe and then walked up to Victoria Park, where they had afternoon tea in the kiosk. Afterwards, she said, they walked down a path almost to the bottom of the hill before turning back. On the way back Juliet was leading, about six feet ahead of her. Her mother, at the rear, was immediately behind her.

As they were walking, Pauline continued, her mother slipped or stumbled, twisted sideways and fell, hitting her head on rocks or stones. Her head seemed to toss up and down convulsively, hitting stones or rocks or something. Pauline saw half a brick there. She and Juliet tried to restrain her mother but couldn't. They tried to lift her up but they dropped her. They ran back to the tea kiosk to tell someone she was dead.

"How did you know she was dead?" Archie Tate asked.

"The blood! The blood! There was a lot of it!" Pauline replied with feeling.

Brown asked if she had seen a stocking at the scene. She looked taken aback. "We didn't take Mother's stockings off. I didn't have stockings on, I was wearing sockettes." She thought a little. "I had a stocking with me. I usually carry an old one in my bag. I used an old one to wipe up the blood."

Brown called Bill Perry into the room and Pauline repeated her account. It was not what he and Hilda were expecting or wanted to hear: the girl's story placed Juliet right on the spot at the moment of Mrs Rieper's death.

Bill, Hilda and the two policemen now trooped down to the drawing room, where the fire was well stoked. Hilda fetched Juliet to be questioned. All four listened intently as Juliet described the expedition to Victoria Park, and how, coming up the path, Pauline's mother had slipped.

To their despair her story was practically identical to Pauline's. Brown, reluctant to believe Juliet had been involved in the attack on Mrs Rieper, questioned whether she was telling the truth. They had reason to believe she was not present when the tragedy occurred, he told her. At this Juliet hesitated. Perry quickly intervened to ask if he might speak to her on her own. The detectives obligingly left the room. So did Henry and Hilda.

The police suspected it was murder, Perry told Juliet. From what he knew of Mrs Rieper's injuries it could not possibly have been an accident. Juliet, grasping at that moment the seriousness of her situation, grabbed the lifeline being thrown to her. She would, she said, tell the truth as she had told it to her mother earlier.

Perry called Brown and Tate back into the room. Juliet wished to make a statement. This time it would be the truth. Archie Tate began to take it down on his portable typewriter.

She had, Juliet said, been to Victoria Park only once before, five years earlier. She had never been there before with Gina. After Mrs Rieper had tea and they had soft drinks and cakes and scones, they walked down a track through a plantation on the side of a hill. She thought it had been decided before they left the Riepers' house to go down that track but it was not her idea. They went quite a long way down the track, the three of them walking together. She found a small pink stone on the ground. She still had it. Before they reached the bottom Mrs Rieper decided she had walked far enough. Gina and she went on a bit further, then decided to turn back and rejoin Mrs Rieper. She herself was in front nearly all the way. At some point she left the other two and went on ahead to the place where she had found the pink stone, thinking she might also find the ring it had come from. She spent some minutes looking for a ring. While she was looking she heard someone call out back down the track— Gina or her mother, she couldn't be sure. She shouted back that she was coming—something like that—but didn't go back immediately. After an interval she turned back to look for Gina and Mrs Rieper. She had no idea how far back she walked until she came upon Mrs Rieper lying there. There was blood all round her head and Gina was hysterical. Mrs Rieper seemed to be unconscious. She cradled Mrs Rieper's head in her lap. Gina said her mother had slipped and banged her head against a stone. She believed it at the time. She didn't remember seeing a stocking with a knot in it, nor did she notice a brick.

When they rushed back to the tea kiosk, she went on, they said they had been together when Mrs Rieper got her injuries but it wasn't true. She only said it because she thought Gina and her mother might have quarrelled. She thought it would be better for Gina if she said she was there and supported her story that Mrs Rieper had been injured as the result of an accident. They didn't have any quarrel in her presence. She only said she was there when it happened because she wanted to be loyal to Gina, didn't want to see her in any trouble.

The two detectives were convinced they were now hearing the truth. Obviously Juliet Hulme had played no part in the crime. They felt only sympathy for this lovely girl whose eyes filled with tears as she recounted in her beautiful English diction the gruesome events of the afternoon. It was understandable—forgivable—that out of misplaced loyalty to her friend she had at first spun the yarn that she was there when Mrs Rieper was injured. Young Pauline was definitely a queer one, but Juliet was obviously a decent type of girl whose upbringing had been very sheltered. It was impossible to believe that a girl brought up here, by parents like these, in this house, would have willingly taken any part in the brutal murder of a defenceless woman.

While Tate was hammering on his typewriter taking down Juliet's statement, Brown, escorted by Hilda, went back upstairs to confront Pauline. They had reason to believe Juliet was not there when her mother was attacked, he told her. At this she looked surprised. Brown cautioned her: "You are suspected of having murdered your mother. You need not say anything. Anything you do say will be taken down and may be used in evidence."

Pauline quickly realised Juliet had told the police she wasn't there when her mother was killed. She knew nothing more than that, but if she could support Deborah she would—and Mrs Hulme. Mrs Hulme called her her foster daughter, said how wonderful it would be when *we*—including her, Gina—were all back in England. She always called her Gina. And dear Dr Hulme was the dearest man she had ever met. She was one of the family. They would be grateful to her if Deborah could be kept out of it.

"You ask me questions," she had the wit to say when Brown asked if she would like to tell him what happened: it would give her a better chance to tailor her account to whatever it was Juliet had told them. In answer to Brown's questions she admitted she had assaulted her mother using a half-brick in a stocking. She was carrying both the half-brick and the stocking in her shoulder bag when she went to Victoria Park.

Brown asked her why she had killed her mother.

"If you don't mind, I won't answer that," she coolly responded.

"What did she say when you struck her?"

"I should rather not answer that question."

"How often did you hit her?"

"I don't know. A great many times I should imagine."

Bloody little madam! *I don't know. A great many times I should imagine*. It was staggering. She was a different person from the distraught child he and Tate had found on their arrival. Once she had abandoned the lie that her mother's death had been an accident, there was no need for her to pretend she was in shock and grief-stricken. But she was still steadfastly insistent that Deborah knew nothing about it, that she was somewhere else and did not see her attack her mother.

Brown helpfully rendered this into police verbiage. "I wish to state that Juliet did not know of my intentions and did not see me strike my mother. I took the chance to strike my mother when Juliet was away."

A handwritten record of the interview was read back to Pauline, and the second she signed it as correct she was arrested for murder.

If Hilda Hulme was not brimming with joy, she was profoundly relieved. Juliet had been rescued from a very nasty situation indeed. Bill had been wonderful. Even her ridiculous husband hadn't cocked things up too badly. She was fairly sure Pauline wouldn't let them down. She was a strange little thing but she loved them and would want to protect Julie come hell or high water. Anyhow, she could hardly back-pedal on the statement she had just signed.

Hilda found Pauline something to wear and the girl was escorted downstairs. At the foot of the staircase it occurred to Brown to ask her where she had got the half-brick. Hilda jumped in. "She didn't get it here."

"No," Pauline said, taking her cue, "I took it from my own home."

Brown asked where she had left the bag in which she carried the brick, and there it was, hanging on the banisters at the foot of the stairs. The police took it away with them. It contained only a purse with one pound seven shillings and three and a half-pence, and a small handkerchief.

As Pauline was driven in the back of the patrol car to Central Police Station, Juliet was frantic. Gina would be alone in a dark dungeon living on bread and water. She would have to face being done for murder alone. Juliet paced about the house excitedly, reciting much-loved poems to herself, as a Buddhist chants a mantra to block negative thoughts:

"We travel not for trafficking alone;
By hotter winds our fiery hearts are fanned:
For lust of knowing what should not be known
We make the Golden Journey to Samarkand."

James Elroy Flecker was one of her favourite poets, along with Rupert Brooke, Byron, Shelley, and Edward FitzGerald, translator of *Rubáiyát of Omar Khayyám*.

Hilda slept with Juliet that night. Her daughter seemed elated, Hilda would say. She was still reciting poetry as she eventually fell asleep, her mind far distant from Victoria Park.

CHAPTER 4

Taking the Blame

Central Police Station, a large grey stone building, occupied
most of the south side of Hereford Street between Cambridge
Terrace and Montreal Street. Two-storey and bay-fronted,
with Romanesque windows and entranceway, it dated from 1897.
Surprisingly harmonious red brick wings had been added in 1906,
giving the whole thing the look of a large gloomy house sequestered
behind heavy railings.

Behind the station a spacious yard backed on to King Edward
Barracks, a large structure used for military drills. Black police cars
came and went from the yard: Chevrolets, Plymouth Specials, Ford
Consuls, Wolseleys, and four Humber Super Snipes that had been
especially bought for the visit of the newly crowned Queen Elizabeth
and the Duke of Edinburgh five months earlier. The yard also contained the lock-up, a squat stone building with two cells reserved
for female prisoners, in one of which Pauline Rieper would spend her
first night in police custody. As a prisoner charged with murder, she
would be under suicide watch, observed throughout the night—
as regulations required in the case of female prisoners—by two
constables, one male and one female.

First, though, she had to be formally charged with the murder of
her mother. While Detective Sergeant Tate was fiddling about with the
paper work, Senior Detective Brown was interviewing poor Bert
Rieper. The Riepers' house was only a few hundred yards from the
police station and Bert had walked over at Brown's invitation. In the
course of the interview, Bert delivered some unexpected news: he and
Honorah—the deceased—had lived together as man and wife for

twenty-five years but never married. He knew he had to tell them, painful as it was to do so: they would find out anyway, sooner or later. The only other living soul who knew was Nora's mother Amy Parker, who lived at 13 Churchill Street, off Bealey Avenue. Their daughters had no idea in the world.

This was something of a bombshell. Brown called Tate into his office to discuss the matter. If Honorah Rieper had not been lawfully married to Herbert Rieper, legally speaking her name was Honorah Mary Parker and the girl—the illegitimate girl—they were about to charge was Pauline Yvonne Parker. Nora Rieper was there and then expelled from the league of decent married women. Archie Tate later recalled that Pauline was "genuinely astonished to learn her surname was not Rieper".

While Pauline was in Tate's office, Tate noticed her scribbling on a piece of scrap paper. She was writing her diary entry for June 22, 1954. She recorded that she had successfully committed her "moider" but "found herself in an unexpected place". To call it "moider", like a Brooklyn gangster, was one of the girls' private jokes.

Pauline was delighted with the attention she had been receiving. "All the Hulmes have been wonderfully kind and sympathetic. Anyone would think I'd been good. I've had a pleasant time with the police talking nineteen to the dozen and behaving as though I hadn't a care in the world." She ended, "I haven't had a chance to talk to Deborah properly but I am taking the blame for everything."

When she finished, Tate seized the piece of paper and read it with disgust. "I am taking the blame for everything": clearly he and Brown had been taken for a ride. They had been completely sucked in by Juliet Hulme's tearful insistence she had not been there when Pauline Rieper killed her mother. On that little piece of paper Pauline had made it clear that both girls had been in it together.

More than that, Archie Tate was alerted to the fact the Rieper girl may have kept a diary. Obviously such a diary would be of the greatest interest. Tate asked Bert Rieper, who was still at the station, if he knew whether Pauline kept a diary. She did: he had given her a diary himself for Christmas 1953. And Christmas the year before. He had never looked at her diary: that wouldn't be honourable.

Tate pointed out that things were different now. The diary might contain evidence pertinent to a murder investigation. Bert said if they came over to the house they would probably find it. Tate and Brown went with him to search his daughter's bedroom. Pauline had made no attempt to hide her diaries. The current one was in full view on her dressing table. They took them away, together with fourteen exercise books filled with writing, and two scrapbooks containing photographs of film actresses.

There were some chilling entries in the 1954 diary, such as the one for the previous day, Monday, June 21: "I rose late and helped Mother vigorously this morning. Deborah rang and we decided to use a rock in a stocking rather than a sandbag." The whole thing had obviously been planned and carried out by the pair of them. They would visit Miss Hulme again in the morning.

Bert Rieper was now left with the task of telling Nana Parker that her beloved and only daughter had been bashed to death by one of her granddaughters. How, too, would he break it to Rosemary, the mongoloid child at Templeton Farm, that neither her mother nor her sister Yvonne would ever be visiting her again?

The city's crime reporters closely followed the comings and goings at Central Police Station. In the morning a brief item appeared in *The Press*: "The body of a middle-aged woman was found in a hollow in Victoria Park below the tearooms about four p.m. yesterday. An arrest has been made and a charge of murder will be preferred in the magistrates' court this morning. The woman was Honora Mary Parker, aged forty-five, of 31 Gloucester Street. Her body was found by the caretaker…" Like the police, and the Crown when it launched the prosecution for her murder, *The Press* omitted the final "h" from the dead woman's name.

In the same edition of the newspaper, the celebrated oboist Léon Goossens was awarded plaudits for his "stupendous technical mastery and … flawless musicianship". The perfect timbre of his "great crescendi and diminuendi" put him "among the immortals". Juliet was unfortunate to have missed this musical treat.

That same morning Nancy Sutherland was preparing breakfast for her family at their house in Ashgrove Terrace. She and the twins, Diony and Jan, were listening to the news on the wireless. Some woman's body had been found at Victoria Park. It was murder and an arrest had been made. Jan, who sometimes experienced flashes of prescience, said, "It's the girls. I bet it's the girls."

"Girls?" her mother inquired.

"Juliet. Julie Hulme and Pauline, her friend. I'm certain. She couldn't go to the recital because there was an accident in Victoria Park. Remember?"

Nancy told Jan in no uncertain terms how ridiculous she was being. She was shocked a daughter of hers could say such a dreadful, silly thing.

At ten o'clock Pauline Yvonne Parker appeared before a magistrate, Rex Abernethy S.M., charged with murder and was remanded in police custody. Nancy, by now put in the picture by a distraught Hilda, drove to Christchurch Girls' High to tell Jan she had been right. Juliet *was* involved in the death of the woman in Victoria Park. Pauline Rieper had been arrested. She and Diony were not to discuss it with anyone.

Also that morning, Bert Rieper was escorted by Detective G.F. Gillies to the morgue at Christchurch Public Hospital. He had an unpleasant duty to perform: the dead woman had to be formally identified before Dr Pearson could get started on his post-mortem.

Honorah's body was a sickening sight. People who saw the police photographs, too disturbing to be produced in court, would still remember that battered head more than fifty years later. The hair was shorn to the scalp, the better to examine numerous head wounds. The woman was unrecognisable from her pallid face, disfigured by hideous bruises and deep gashes around the eyes, ears, forehead and scalp, a good many down to the bone, exposing the smashed skull. Her jaw lay at a crooked angle, obviously broken. In Archie Tate's words, "her head had literally been battered to pieces".

With the head and face in that condition you couldn't in all honesty say who she was. But the sturdy, womanly body, the strapping legs—Bert was sure. He had fallen in love with her when she was a twenty-two year old, not long arrived from England with her mother. He had been thirty-six and trapped in a miserable marriage. A formulaic statement was signed for the coroner: "It is the body of Honora Mary Parker. ... I last saw [the] deceased at about one p.m. yesterday when I left home after lunch. She was then in good health."

Further indignities awaited the remains of Nora—now, for official purposes, Honora Mary Parker—at the scalpel of Dr Pearson. After removing and examining her heart, lungs, stomach, kidneys and the rest of her innards, he felt confident to pronounce that the cause of death was shock associated with the multiple wounds of the head and fractures of the skull. In his professional opinion these wounds were inflicted by a blunt instrument applied with considerable force.

Pauline was escorted to and from her first appearance in the magistrates' court by Margaret Felton, the police matron. Afterwards, Mrs Felton returned her to Tate's office. The morning was frosty and she and Pauline sat chatting by the coal fire. Tate entered the room with an envelope in his hand. He removed from the envelope the piece of paper taken from Pauline the previous night. "I am taking the blame for everything," he read to her. That meant, did it not, that Juliet Hulme was as much involved in the attack on her mother as she was?

Pauline asked if she could she talk to Juliet. "Let Deborah and me get together and have a discussion. I am sure Deborah will say whatever I say. She will think it's right, whatever I say."

Absolutely not, Tate thought. The girl was dippy, seemed to think it was a game. But thanks to her they would now arrest Juliet Hulme as well. He and Brown departed for Ilam.

Pauline realised perfectly well what Detective Sergeant Tate was getting at. "I am taking the blame for everything" of course implied Deborah was in on it. She had written it realising that impulsively accepting sole responsibility for her mother's death had been a mistake. That was what she needed to talk to Deborah about. She would end up stuck in New Zealand, in borstal or jail or something, while Deborah went tootling off to South Africa. That wasn't the idea at all. She intended that Tate would read what she had written. Her plan had succeeded brilliantly. But now they were off to arrest

Deborah, Pauline wasn't sure she wanted her to see the scrap of paper.

Tate's desk was on the other side of the room from the fireplace where Pauline and the police matron were keeping themselves warm. About ten minutes after the two officers left, Pauline got up and wandered over to it. The hawk-eyed Mrs Felton growled that there was nothing there to interest her. On the desk Pauline spotted the envelope containing her diary entry. She snatched it and threw it into the fire. It started to burn but the matron swiftly rescued it. It was only a little damaged. Pauline went back to the cells in disgrace.

At Ilam, Hilda and Henry Hulme had risen early from their respective beds. As soon as the gardener turned up for work, at Hilda's instruction Henry gave him some household bits and pieces, among which was the lethal diary. He was to burn the lot in the incinerator. There was nothing odd about that as far as Merv was concerned. The Hulmes were leaving New Zealand any time and it was hardly surprising they should have a clean-out. Having got the gardener, via Henry, to do the dirty work, if Hilda were ever asked whether she had destroyed Juliet's diary she could totally deny it—on oath, if necessary.

Henry Hulme and Bill Perry were on hand to meet Brown and Tate when they arrived at Ilam, but not Hilda, who was at the hairdresser's. Although her daughter had eluded arrest, she knew that, as the mother, she was bound to come in for attention. Her hair required regular styling; there was no reason for her to go about looking like the wreck of the *Hesperus*. Good grooming was part of the armour with which Hilda would confront the unfriendly citizens of Christchurch in the cruel months ahead. Later she would be criticised for it. One of the university wives called her "hard as nails".

The two detectives talked to Henry Hulme and Bill Perry. Perry took Brown up to Juliet's bedroom. She was in bed, calm and composed. Brown told her they had reason to believe her written statement taken the night before was incorrect. She had been present when the assault took place. He formally cautioned her: "You are suspected of murdering Mrs Rieper. You are not obliged to say anything. Anything you say may be taken down in writing and used in evidence."

Juliet was full of questions. She wanted to know what Gina had told them. Brown told her he wasn't prepared to say anything, other than that they had reason to believe she was present when Mrs Rieper was killed, and Pauline had said that if she and Deborah had a discussion she was sure Deborah would agree with whatever she said. Was she willing to give some explanation? She was not, just at that moment.

Brown and Perry left the room. After talking to Henry Hulme, they decided to wait until Mrs Hulme returned. A short time after she appeared, Perry told the detectives Juliet would like to see them. She had come to the conclusion that the present situation—Gina under arrest for murder and herself off scot-free—was intolerable. Tate went up to her bedroom first. Juliet sweetly apologised, saying the statement she had signed the previous night was untrue. Now she wanted to tell the truth and was sorry for misleading him before. He cautioned her and she confirmed her willingness to make a further statement. Tate took it down in longhand.

Macdonald Brown, Hilda Hulme and Bill Perry were all present when he read the statement back and Juliet signed it. She hadn't exactly made a clean breast of it but had said more than enough. Hilda's thoughts as her daughter confessed to her part in the killing of Honorah Rieper can scarcely be imagined. Henry absented himself. He could not bear to listen.

"Pauline wanted to come with me to South Africa," Juliet stated. "I wanted her to come too. My father and I were booked to go on 3 July next. Pauline and I had discussed this matter. We both thought Mrs Rieper might object. We decided to go with Mrs Rieper to Victoria Park. We decided that it would be a suitable place to discuss the matter and have it out. I know that it was proposed we should take a brick in a stocking to the park with us. … I left my home with my father about 10.30 yesterday. I had part of a brick which I wrapped in a newspaper. I had got it from near the garage. My father left me near Beaths. I made some personal purchases and walked to the Riepers' house. I arrived there still carrying the brick. I gave it to Pauline. I know the brick was put in the stocking at the Riepers' house. I did not put it there. Mrs Rieper, Pauline and I left their place after lunch to go to Victoria Park. Pauline carried the brick and stocking in her shoulder bag. … After the first blow was struck I knew it would be necessary for us to kill her…"

Underneath Archie Tate's fluent scrawl, Juliet had signed 'J.M. Hulme' in a scratchy schoolgirl hand. She was arrested and later that afternoon taken to Central Police Station where she Pauline were reunited. The first chance they had for a proper talk was at nine-thirty in the evening, when they were taken to the old stone lock-up for the night. P.C. Wallace Colville was watch-house constable on duty. He and a female police constable were posted to suicide watch over the two prisoners. Pauline and Juliet, in their pyjamas, were in one cell while Colville and the other constable sat in the other, separated by a narrow passageway.

The two constables were absolutely dumbfounded. Suicide was far from the girls' minds. One in the top bunk, one below, they chatted to each other as though they hadn't the slightest concern about anything. They weren't talking about the murder, just this and that—two normal girls having a good gossip session. At one stage the Hulme girl got out of her bunk and in a cheeky sort of way called out through the bars, "Can I have a cup of tea?" "No. Get back to bed," Colville said firmly.

The girls talked for about an hour and then went to sleep. They slept sound as a bell. Wally Colville couldn't believe it. He would later hear they were "sort of involved with each other a bit". There were rumours about things that went on between them when they were in police custody, like fondling each other in a sexual way. Well nothing like that happened on P.C. Colville's watch—for absolute certain.

Deborah and Gina were happy. Together again. Whatever happened next, one thing was sure: Deborah would not be going to South Africa, leaving Gina behind. In April, when they had first heard Deborah's parents were leaving New Zealand, were probably going to divorce, and South Africa was mentioned, the two girls had made a pact: they would sink or swim together. Even if they were now sinking, they were still together and would remain together. Nothing else mattered.

The following morning, Thursday, June 24, Juliet Marion Hulme, four months short of her sixteenth birthday, stood before Raymond Ferner S.M., jointly charged with the murder of Honora Mary Parker. She was represented by Mr T.A. Gresson. Henry and Hilda Hulme sat to the left of the dock. By then the whole of Christchurch had got wind of it. All the public seats in the No. 1 Courtroom were taken and a capacity crowd craned their necks at the back. The *Christchurch Star-Sun* reported that the prisoner looked pale but showed no sign of emotion. Nora Rieper was cremated that same morning at the Bromley Cemetery, after a funeral as miserable as they come.

CHAPTER 5

A Suitable Man

When Dr Henry Hulme applied for the position of rector of Canterbury University College, Lord Snow—the great C.P. Snow, scientist, novelist and Whitehall mandarin—informed the selection panel he "knew few men more suitable for the position of principal of a university college". Another of Hulme's supporters declared him "really too good for such an intellectually isolated country". His wife Hilda, the panel was assured, showed loyal devotion to her husband and family; she would "grace any function she attended, whether in a public or private capacity". Her "good appearance ... charm, presence and dignity, fitted her perfectly for a principal's wife". Even little Juliet fitted the bill: Dr and Mrs Hulme had a "charming daughter (nine in October) who inherits her mother's good looks".

Henry Rainsford Hulme was born in 1908 in Ormskirk, a village a few miles from Southport, Lancashire, and twenty odd miles north of Liverpool. His Manchester-born father James Hulme was a director of Hulme Brothers Limited of Southport, manufacturers and distributors of fancy goods, leather and aluminium trunks and portmanteaus. Hulme Brothers had two shops in elegant Lord Street, another in the ultra-smart Leyland Arcade, and manufacturing works in King Street. Henry was brought up in a substantial but by no means grand semi-detached house in Belmont Street, within an easy walk of Lord Street: a comfortable middle-class home.

Displaying outstanding brainpower from a young age, Henry won a scholarship to Manchester Grammar, the most famous of the great grammar schools of England. Founded in the reign of Henry VIII, the school was, and still is, an intellectually élite establishment. Bright young minds were worked hard, and to no one's surprise Henry Hulme won a place reading mathematics and physics at Gonville and Caius College, Cambridge. In 1929 he graduated with honours in mathematics; two years later he won both the Smith's Prize and a Rouse Ball Studentship, the most coveted awards for young mathematicians at Cambridge, and was elected to the Isaac Newton Studentship in astronomy. His particular interest was quantum mechanics, the revolutionary branch of mathematical physics that dealt with the motion of sub-atomic particles.

After receiving a Ph.D. in 1932, Hulme went to Germany to study at the University of Leipzig under Werner Heisenberg, who had just won the Nobel Prize in Physics for the discovery at the root of quantum theory: that Newtonian dynamics did not apply to the behaviour of electrons and nuclei within atoms and molecules. Nineteen thirty-two was a momentous year for physicists, with the discovery of the neutron and the positron making it possible, for the first time, to produce nuclear transmutations in large quantities using artificially accelerated protons. Nuclear physics had arrived.

Returning to Cambridge the following year, Hulme was elected a fellow of Gonville and Caius. He had unquestionably made the grade as a young mathematical physicist with a specialist interest in astronomy. While lecturing in mathematics, he continued to study quantum theory, especially the effect of light on the orbits of inner electrons of atoms, and became friendly with a fellow mathematical physicist who would come to play an important part in his later career. Bill Penney was the son of a sergeant-major in the Royal Army Ordnance Corps. A brilliant student, he had had a stellar career at Imperial College, London, and been awarded a senior studentship at Trinity College, Cambridge. Still in his mid twenties, he had an international reputation for applying quantum mechanics to the structure and behaviour of metals.

In 1936, Hulme accepted an appointment as lecturer in mathematics at the University of Liverpool. The previous year, James Chadwick, who had worked with Ernest Rutherford to develop the nuclear theory of atoms at Cambridge's Cavendish Laboratory, had accepted the Lyon Jones chair of physics at the university. Chadwick needed first-rate mathematical physicists such as Henry Hulme, and Hulme saw opportunities under his patronage that did not exist for the time being at Cambridge.

In Liverpool, Hulme met and married twenty-five-year-old Hilda Reaveley. Three years younger than him, Hilda was coolly elegant, beautiful, outspoken, theatrical in temperament and sexually out-going. To a man more worldly-wise than Henry Hulme, such an exciting combination might have spelt trouble.

Hilda's ancestors, the Reaveleys, were an old Northumbrian family who, in the fifteenth century, had occupied a manor house in the Breamish Valley at the foot of the Cheviot hills. By the sixteenth century they had become substantial landowners in their own right, as well as hereditary bailiffs of Chatton to the earls of Northumberland in the barony of Alnwick. A Major William Reveley, married to a niece of the earl of Stafford, was killed in the royalist cause at the battle of Naseby of 1645. By the nineteenth century the most distinguished branch of the family was the Reaveleys of Kinnersley Castle, Herefordshire, although the Reverend John Reaveley, born in Spennymore, County Durham, was sufficiently notable to be included in the 1938 edition of *Kelly's Handbook of Distinguished People.*

Hilda's connection with these distinguished Reaveleys was real but distant. She was born in Alnwick, where her father, Joseph Reaveley, was the minister of St James's Presbyterian Church. He, too, had been born in County Durham, only a short hop from Spennymore, but he was the son of a coal miner.

Hilda did not, as far as anyone knows, have a university education and indeed, as one of two daughters of a Presbyterian minister who was a coalminer's son, it is unlikely she received anything out of the ordinary in the way of schooling. What she did after leaving school, or what took her to live in Birkenhead, is not known. The best guess is that she became a schoolteacher. Somewhere along the way she acquired a self-confident and polished manner: Hilda could hold her own in any company in a cut-glass accent that bore no trace of the north of England.

Not long after he and Hilda were married in 1937, Henry Hulme was presented with a wonderful opportunity when the position of chief assistant to the Astronomer Royal became vacant and he was appointed. He was the perfect man and it was the perfect job. Hilda must have been delighted. Living in London, the wife of the chief assistant to the Astronomer Royal—it was a thrilling prospect. But just before the move to London took place she found she was pregnant.

One of the joys of being chief assistant to the Astronomer Royal was having the run of Christopher Wren's delightful red-brick Royal Observatory in Greenwich Park, overlooking the Thames. The original part, Flamsteed House, had been built in 1675 at the command of Charles II in the hope of finding an astronomical solution to the problem of determining longitude at sea. The Hulmes bought a two-storey brick semi-detached house at 79 Foyle Road in the Maze Hill area east of Greenwich Park. From the house it was a short walk to the observatory.

Although Harold Spencer Jones, the Astronomer Royal, would become little more than a footnote in the history of astronomy, his thirty-year-old chief assistant was as ambitious as he was able. Hulme set himself to a theoretical study of the spectra of stars— the electromagnetic radiation produced by rearrangements of the innermost electrons of atoms. Had he continued to devote himself to astronomy, he may in a few years have attained the Plumian chair at Cambridge, and even in time become Astronomer Royal himself.

Henry and Hilda Hulme's first child, Juliet Marion, was born at Greenwich on October 28, 1938, as ominous clouds were massing over Europe. At Munich a month earlier the Sudetenland region of Czechoslovakia had been handed to Germany, after Hitler's assurance that it would be his last territorial claim in Europe. Fortunately, the British government's preparations did not falter. The month Juliet was born Sir John Anderson took charge of air raid precautions: the bombing of Guernica by the Luftwaffe in April 1937 had left few illusions in official circles about what the civilian population of Britain was in for in the event of war. Expenditure on civil defence increased from nine million pounds in 1937 to fifty-one million in 1938. Millions of gas masks were issued, with instructions for making blackout curtains, and how to tape up windows to prevent their being shattered by bomb blasts.

At 79 Foyle Road, Henry and Hilda acquired, at a cost of six pounds and fourteen shillings, an Anderson shelter. These structures consisted of arched sheets of corrugated steel sunk into the ground. Sandbags were stacked on top and around the small entrance and the whole thing was dug into four feet of soil. The shelters were no protection against a direct hit but could withstand the blast of a 250-kilogram bomb landing as close as ten feet away.

On September 3, 1939 war was declared. Juliet was not quite a year old.

Hilda did not take naturally to motherhood. In her book, babies had to learn their place and not be pandered to and fussed over. And the war made things difficult: it was impossible to get nursing help. While everybody else had exciting and glamorous war work, Hilda was stuck at home with a baby. It cannot have been the life she had imagined for herself when they moved up to London.

Greenwich was badly affected by bombing: the oxbow bend in the Thames enfolding the Isle of Dogs created a landmark conspicuous from high altitude. German bombers crossing the channel from their bases in France to attack London would establish their positions visually from the Isle of Dogs before making their runs. The Luftwaffe's major navigation point over London was just a mile from the Hulme's house.

At half past four on the afternoon of September 7, 1940, 350 German bombers escorted by 600 fighter aircraft flew up the river. Woolwich Arsenal took a terrible hammering and the Royal Victoria and Surrey Docks were flattened. At the Surrey Docks—in Rotherhithe, just upriver of Greenwich—bombs set vast stacks of Norwegian timber ablaze, creating a beacon that guided in further waves of bombers throughout the night. Four hundred and thirty people were killed and 1,600 seriously injured in that first major raid, effectively the start of the Blitz.

Bombs fell around Greenwich noon and night. Even in the comparative safety of a dank Anderson shelter the experience would have been terrifying. The corrugated steel walls amplified the racket outside: the unending drone of aircraft, the high-pitched whine and express-train roar of falling bombs, the thunderous crashes of walls collapsing, the clashing of splintering glass, the "boom-ker-boom" of ack-ack guns, and wailing sirens hour after hour after hour. Like many other children, two-year-old Juliet suffered bomb shock. For a month afterwards she had nightmares so severe she would wake up screaming. Hilda would later suggest this had scarred her deeply, perhaps permanently.

The Blitz went on for nine months until the end of May 1941. In seventy-one major raids, the Luftwaffe succeeded in killing nearly 20,000 Londoners, and wounding 72,000 more, but after that first big raid hundreds of thousands of children were evacuated from London to safer parts of the country. Although the government organised a scheme for the children of the poor, the better-off were expected to make private arrangements to billet their offspring with friends or relatives.

Hilda would later reveal little about the comings and goings of Juliet and her during the war years. She resided in London "some of the time", she said, implying she was mostly elsewhere. Her health was "very indifferent" and after her second child was born she was seriously ill for some months. That and "war conditions" caused periods of separation from Juliet. Evacuees under school age were usually accompanied by their mothers. It is possible some part of Juliet's early years were spent in northern England, perhaps with her grandmother in Alnwick.

Hilda had difficulty controlling her "very demanding and sensitive daughter", who resisted discipline and resented correction. Juliet was excitable and lived in a world of fantasy. She found it difficult to stop playing games and re-enter the family circle, always wanting to remain a fairy or some other imaginary creature. Although she was quick to laugh and often enchanting, she had a strong will and temper. There was an incident in the wartime streets of London when

Hilda wished to go one way and Juliet insisted on going the other. Hilda stood debating the point with her for half an hour before the child was persuaded to do as her mother wanted.

When Jonathan was born on March 22, 1944, there was serious trouble. At first things seemed to go well: Juliet, then aged five and a half, was taken to visit her mother and new brother in the nursing home and seemed to accept the baby. Unfortunately, however, soon after arriving home Hilda became ill in the night, and as Henry was otherwise engaged she left Juliet home alone in bed while she and the baby returned to the nursing home. Juliet was deeply distressed to wake and find her mother and the baby gone, and to be told for days afterwards that her mother was too ill to be visited. From that time on, Hilda would say, she "definitely resented" Jonathan and was a problem to her parents.

Soon afterwards, supposedly because of Hilda's continuing ill health, Juliet was sent away. She must have felt cruelly rejected by her mother, in whose affections she had been displaced by the hated baby. Where was Juliet packed off to? Hilda would later give an account of the period to her friend Nancy Sutherland. With Hilda the truth was always malleable and open to embellishment—someone who knew her well in New Zealand went as far as to say she was a chronic liar—but the story may well be true in its main particulars. Hilda described being pregnant with Jonathan during the dreadful English winter of 1944. As German bombing intensified, she said, she and Juliet had to run down to the Anderson shelter at the bottom of the garden in all weathers. There they would take refuge until the all-clear siren sounded. If a stick of bombs was falling close by, Hilda would go on ahead, leaving Juliet to follow. Juliet would lie under a bush or shrub until the immediate danger had passed and her mother called her.

One particularly atrocious night towards the end of her pregnancy, Hilda opened the shelter, called Juliet, and then, because of her size, got stuck in the entrance as the bombs began to rain down. Left lying in the snow until her mother extricated herself, Juliet contracted pneumonia. A mobile X-ray unit found she had shadows on both lungs, and doctors advised Hilda they must get her to a warmer climate at once if they were to save her life. It was decided she would go to Barbados in the care of a nurse. The little girl was sent, as Nancy Sutherland put it, "with a stranger to a strange land" until the war ended. When she was reunited with her family "she found she had a small brother who took all her mother's attention, and hardly saw anything of her nuclear scientist father".

Although the Blitz was over by early June 1941, bombing was briefly resumed by the Luftwaffe in February 1944 in retaliation for the Allies' "Baedecker raids". If Nancy Sutherland accurately recalled what Hilda told her, Juliet must have been dispatched to Barbados early in 1944 and remained there until the end of the war.

The damage caused to infants by inadequate attachment to, or prolonged separation from, their mothering figures was little understood at the time, although as early as 1939 the psychiatrists John Bowlby and Donald Winnicott had warned about the psychological dangers of evacuation programmes that involved separating infants and young children from their mothers. It was hardly surprising that Juliet became an even more difficult child who escaped the profound hurts of her everyday existence—sibling jealousy and the sting of maternal rejection—by retreating into an imaginary world.

CHAPTER 6

Strains of War

E ven Henry Hulme, although distracted by his work, could hardly fail to notice he had an unhappy wife and troublesome little daughter, both in poor health. These problems, he might have thought, could be readily ascribed to the stresses and strains of the war. His mind was on other things—important things—at the Admiralty. At the outbreak of war he had been transferred on loan from the Royal Observatory, and in 1940 he had become head of the degaussing section of the mine design department, in charge of fifty tweedy bespectacled scientists incongruous among the suave naval officers and glamorous Wrens.

The future of Britain depended on the ability of Hulme and his team to find the solution to a serious problem threatening British sea lanes. By September 1939, forty-one ships had been sunk by German U-boats, but an even greater menace to shipping were the thousands of electromagnetic mines the enemy had dropped around the British coast. In the course of being built, a steel-hulled ship becomes charged with magnetism—in effect a floating magnet. The mines, dropped by parachute, lay on the sea bed. When a ship passed overhead, the needles inside these mines would be pulled upwards by magnetic force, complete a circuit and touch off a detonator. Degaussing is the technique for demagnetising an object by passing through it a decreasing alternating current. Henry Hulme's degaussing section at the Admiralty would succeed in devising equipment that, when fitted to individual ships, effectively protected them against magnetic mines. It was a development of the most critical importance to both the Royal Navy and merchant shipping.

In 1942, the distinguished physicist Patrick Blackett was appointed director of operational research at the Admiralty and Henry Hulme became his deputy, at the same time maintaining his credentials as an astronomer by becoming secretary of the Royal Astronomical Society. The great challenge now facing the Admiralty was how best to protect merchant ships crossing the Atlantic to bring back the material of war and food on which Britain's survival depended. The navy's resources were badly stretched and U-boats were picking off British shipping with appalling frequency. It was essentially a mathematical problem: how to optimise the use of the available escort vessels to maximise protection for the convoys? Hulme and a small group of mathematicians were set to the task.

These human computers, known as "Blackett's circus", established that there was no relationship between the size of a convoy and the number of ships sunk in any one attack. By doubling the size of a convoy it would be possible to halve the overall loss rate: with fewer convoys to escort, the protective screen could be twice the usual size. Conventional wisdom had been that forty ships in a convoy was ideal, and more than sixty dangerous in the extreme. By the end of the war, as a result of the work of Hulme and his colleagues, convoys often comprised as many as one hundred and sixty ships. The importance of this to the war effort cannot be exaggerated. The Battle of the Atlantic was won and in 1945 Hulme's contribution was recognised when he became director of operational research as Patrick Blackett moved onwards and upwards.

Around June 1944, Hulme travelled to the United States. The Normandy landings took place on June 6. What mission was so important it required the presence in America of Britain's deputy director of naval operational research at such a critical time? The answer, almost certainly, was the nuclear fission bomb: Hulme was closely connected with a number of the British scientists involved with the Manhattan Project, including Blackett, his mentor from Cambridge University James Chadwick, and Bill Penney. Penney had become the recognised expert on the mathematics of blast waves, and been enlisted as a member of the small British team that went to Robert Oppenheimer's Los Alamos laboratory just before D-Day, along with Chadwick and German scientist Klaus Fuchs, later unmasked as a Soviet spy. Penney went to New Mexico in June 1944 and it is likely Hulme accompanied him. Hulme's rare knowledge of quantum theory and mathematical physics would certainly have been of great assistance to Penney in his work there.

On his return to England in 1945, Hulme was promoted to director of operational research at the Admiralty. He did not return to the Royal Observatory at Greenwich and soon resigned as secretary to the Royal Astronomical Society. The electromagnetic radiation of the spectra of stars had lost its fascination. The chief assistant to the Astronomer Royal was now a nuclear weapons scientist, known in the corridors of Whitehall as a leading expert on the military use of atomic energy. In 1946 he accepted a new appointment as scientific adviser to the Air Ministry on an annual salary of two thousand pounds, in charge of a staff of around eighty, including sixty-five scientists.

After the short-lived euphoria of victory, London was a sad, dispirited place. There were shortages of everything: rationing would be a disagreeable feature of life until June 1954. Driving daily between Greenwich and Parliament Square in Whitehall, Henry Hulme was better placed than anyone to survey the damage the city had suffered. His route through Rotherhithe, Bermondsey, the Borough, and across the river to the City of Westminster was an almost unrelieved picture of ruin and rubble. At his desk in Whitehall he was required to ponder the future development and deployment of atomic weapons that would have a destructive capability a thousand times greater than anything that had caused the devastation he witnessed daily. It was not a pleasant prospect.

On May 30, 1947 an advertisement appeared in leading newspapers in the United Kingdom, Australia, New Zealand, Canada and South Africa: "Applications are invited for the position of full-time rector. Salary £2000 per annum (New Zealand currency). Schedule of duties, etc obtained from any University or University College or from the undersigned. Applications close in London on 15th September, 1947." It was signed "C.C. Kemp, Registrar, Canterbury University College."

Higher education in New Zealand was provided by the University of New Zealand, an amorphous body of six colleges, one of which was Canterbury College, located in the southern city of Christchurch. Settled by English immigrants from the 1850s onwards, Christchurch was thought of as New Zealand's most English city. The college was housed in a collection of grey stone buildings in neo-Gothic style: there were cloisters, turrets, crockets, mullioned windows, emerald-green quadrangles, and a clock tower. It was easily the finest complex of Victorian architecture in New Zealand.

Canterbury University College had gone into decline during the war years, but by 1944 "rehab students"—ex-servicemen—had begun to arrive in large numbers. It was apparent that Canterbury, like all the university colleges, was in for a time of unprecedented growth.

Since 1921, when the position of rector was established, it had been held by one of the senior professors as an addition to his everyday teaching responsibilities. In practice, the college was run by the chairman of the council in cahoots with the registrar. A professorial board existed but it was consulted only on matters that were strictly academic. The rector was little more than a figurehead, trotted out for ceremonial occasions.

In November 1945 a proposal was revived that each of the colleges of the University of New Zealand should have a full-time rector, who would not only be the academic head of the college, but would sit as a member of the council, chair the professorial board, and collaborate in the work of the university as a member of the senate. Such a person would have to be an outstanding academic with administrative skills and experience. Qualities of vision, leadership, diplomacy and some social graces would be a distinct advantage. In January 1946 the senate gave its approval, and after approaches to the minister of education and the prime minister the necessary funding was secured. The Universities Bureau of the British Empire in London was appointed to vet the applications and make recommendations.

Dr Henry Hulme was a strong candidate for the Canterbury College post. There could be no doubt about his academic credentials

—indeed there was surprise that a man of his calibre was interested. His work had been described as one of the great successes of the scientific war and he was praised for his "outstanding contribution to the theory of convoy protection". And he certainly seemed to have the necessary experience in high-level administration. J.H. Barnes, permanent under-secretary to the Air Ministry, testified to his considerable organising ability, his manner—"pleasant, yet not lacking in force when force was required"—and his lucidity in oral and written communications. And of course, as a former director of operational research at the Admiralty, he would be well used to smoothing out personnel difficulties. Everybody knew how difficult scientists were to manage.

The five-man selection committee sitting in London comprised a former governor general of New Zealand, two principals of United Kingdom universities, and two Cambridge dons. They were informed in confidence that Dr Hulme had modestly toned down his part in winning the Battle of the Atlantic. The fact he bore no honours for his great service was simply because neither he nor his chief, Professor Patrick Blackett, were of the type to accept the honours that had been offered to them. (Blackett overcame any aversion he may have had to honours, accepting the American Medal for Merit in 1946, the Nobel Prize in Physics in 1948, the Companion of Honour in 1965, the Order of Merit in 1967, and a life peerage in 1969, while Hulme remained unaccountably unhonoured.)

Lest the selection committee was left wondering why this exceptionally able man would wish to take up an appointment at a not especially distinguished university college on the other side of the world, they were informed that he was keen to go to New Zealand partly for domestic reasons connected with the health of his children. His friend L.M. Comrie, a New Zealander, explained that Dr Hulme "had always wanted to go to New Zealand" and often questioned him and borrowed books about New Zealand.

Hulme was recommended highly to Canterbury University College. The secretary of the Universities Bureau of the British Empire reported on his "good presence", mentioning that he was a polished speaker with a direct but not abrupt manner. The college's staff appointments subcommittee swiftly concurred with the recommendation from London and on November 25, 1947 the senate of the University of New Zealand, sitting in Wellington, approved his appointment. On December 22 Hulme replied with a cablegram: "Confirm acceptance—expect to sail late June—Hulme."

On January 30, 1948 the New Zealand Department of Labour and Employment was requested to grant priority passages for Dr and Mrs Hulme and their two children—wartime red tape yet to be eradicated. A sum of two hundred pounds was telegraphed to the New Zealand Shipping Company in London to cover the passages, but a delay ensued. It was finally reported that Dr and Mrs Hulme and their two children had embarked on the *Ruahine* and sailed for New Zealand on September 2.

The *Ruahine* docked in Auckland on October 13. Whatever Canterbury College, the University of New Zealand—or, for that matter, the Department of Labour and Employment—might have believed, the Hulme's daughter Juliet was not on board.

Things had gone badly for Juliet since the birth of her brother in March 1944. She had contracted life-threatening pneumonia and bronchitis. She had been evacuated from London to live with strangers, possibly some of the time in Barbados, and had barely seen her parents for long stretches of time. Finally, in the middle of 1947, she had been despatched to live with friends of her parents in the Bahamas. She was then eight years old. After several months she was moved once more, this time to the Bay of Islands in the north of New Zealand. If poor health were the reason, the cure was extreme, prolonged and cruel.

Hilda Hulme later gave a brief resumé of this period. "When we arrived [in New Zealand] Juliet was already here. She had come on ahead. Because of Juliet's health my husband and I had been apart from her for thirteen months. Juliet had been staying with friends in the Bahamas and later the Bay of Islands in New Zealand. ... She was in the Bahamas for seven or eight months and the Bay of Islands, New Zealand, for six to seven months."

Juliet had been apart from her parents for well over a year before the family was reunited in October 1948.

The names of the friends, or foster parents, in the Bahamas have never been mentioned, but from Hilda's account they must have taken Juliet to New Zealand some time between February and April 1948—several months after Henry was offered the position at Canterbury University College. Most parents of a young child sent abroad for health reasons would want to be reunited with her as soon as circumstances permitted, but the Hulmes remained in England for nearly a year and appear to have made no move to have Juliet rejoin them.

It is hard to avoid the conclusion they were in no hurry to re-gather Juliet to their bosom. Was Juliet's health even the real reason for her being dispatched to the Bahamas? A doctor had advised them their daughter should not live in England during winter 1947, but why was she sent abroad in high summer, July or August, or at the latest in September? And why did she not return to England in the spring—say April 1948—instead of going to New Zealand? It seems that Hilda and Henry Hulme were happy to forego for as long as they could the company of their daughter, whose "defects in temperament and personality" made her difficult and troublesome to handle.

CHAPTER 7

Cathedral City

A visitor to Christchurch in the spring of 1851 noticed that the expectations raised by the Canterbury Association, the body set up in England to promote settlement in the colony, had "caused a higher and somewhat different class of persons to emigrate than is usually found in an infant colony". There was a shortage of labourers and tradesmen.

Another early observer recorded that Canterbury was regarded by New Zealand's other provinces as "a very aristocratic settlement". The prospect of making fortunes growing wool had attracted an invasion of gentlemanly adventurers. They were public-school men: younger sons of landed families; offspring of admirals, baronets and bishops; Oxford scholars; retired army officers. Some, fortunately, brought with them wives and daughters.

In 1879 a Miss C.L. Innes, who had arrived as a girl in 1850, noted that strangers often remarked, "Canterbury is so English." This she attributed to "those early days when we all did our best to keep up the standard of morality and manners and to create pure types of English homes". Her remark showed how deeply the values of the founding father, John Robert Godley, had been imbibed. To Godley, a product of Harrow and Oxford, Englishness equalled civilisation. To lose one's Englishness—to become colonial—was to become coarse and degenerate.

The Englishness of Christchurch and Canterbury was both an article of faith and a source of pride for many who lived there. When Queen Elizabeth and the Duke of Edinburgh visited in January 1954, a local newspaper boasted that in Christchurch they found "a city more like an English one than any other they would see in their six months away from home". When the young couple alighted from their train at the railway station, they were met by the "greatest crowd of welcome to line any route in the whole royal tour, surpassing even those of Auckland and Wellington". Some of these loyal subjects had waited for more than ten hours.

When two Australian journalists, Tom Gurr and Harold Cox, with other representatives of the world's press, arrived in Christchurch in August 1954 to report on the trial of Pauline Parker and Juliet Hulme for the murder of Honora Mary Parker, the city moved them to flights of lyricism: "In the spring," they wrote under their shared byline, "crowds of daffodils dance on the green banks of a winding little river called, inevitably, the Avon, a river so English you suspect it of being an art director's creation. ... under the oaks, the willows, the planes and the beeches, the roses riot. You will see houses and shops similar to those of New Zealand's Christchurch in many an English provincial city, and when you are walking along the flat, tree-lined streets in the twilight, with the starlings twittering sleepily in the branches, you will experience the peace which you have felt in cities like Salisbury and Cambridge and Exeter."

In Cathedral Square they observed the descendants of the well-bred gentlemen who had cut Canterbury into huge sheep-grazing properties in the 1850s; they were prospering after the 1951 wool boom driven by the Korean War.

"English cars," Gurr and Cox noted, "are parked neatly in the square, across which falls the pointed shadow of the soaring spire of the cathedral. From the cars step red-faced hearty men wearing tweed trout-fisherman's hats and expensive but sagging suits of hairy-looking tweed. They hand out their ladies, who wear cashmere jumpers and tweed skirts and sensible shoes, and they walk into the hotels, the United Service and Warner's, talking together in accents so entirely English that no county in all England can rival them for English purity."

It was, of course, a caricature: the inhabitants of Christchurch were no more typified by rich, jolly, anglified sheep farmers than Londoners were by Beefeaters and duchesses in tiaras. The United

Service Hotel was a lively place to stay for show week in November, but the red-faced hearty men were most likely heading to the Christchurch Club for a sherry before lunch while their wives shopped at Ballantynes.

Even the famously English appearance of Christchurch was not without qualification. While in expensive suburbs, such as Fendalton and Cashmere, large Arts and Crafts-style houses sat among wide lawns and spreading trees, in the humbler parts of town—Linwood, say, or Richmond, or Phillipstown, or any of the sprawling post-war suburbs—it took a good deal of wishful thinking to see anything much of old England. Nevertheless, the more prosperous and attractive parts of Christchurch were certainly agreeable places to live, and until the late 1950s the city was New Zealand's cultural capital, a magnet for artists, poets, writers and musicians.

On Saturday, October 16, 1948, when the new rector of Canterbury University College and his family—including his young daughter, who had finally rejoined her parents in Auckland—arrived by DC3 at Harewood Aerodrome to be whisked to a garden party in their honour, Christchurch was looking its best. Spring flowers—daffodils, wisteria, lilac, clematis, camellias and rhododendrons—were in their glory. The air was full of the delectable scent of freshly mown lawns.

The garden party, hosted by Sir Joseph Ward, third baronet and chairman of the college council, at his house in Merivale Lane was remarkably civilised, the Hulmes thought. In a city with a population of 186,000 there were bound to be a few people with whom they had things in common. Although Juliet was being extremely trying, it was something she would get over. Henry had a challenging new job ahead of him, one he was looking forward to immensely. He was certain they could all be happy in Christchurch. Why should they not be?

Henry and Hilda Hulme cut something of a dash in Christchurch. As rector of the university, Henry was a prominent figure in the community, and Hilda dressed smartly, if often with a flamboyance some thought unsuitable. They made many friends, were in demand for dinner parties, dances and cocktail parties, and entertained regularly, both privately and officially.

Henry Hulme was considered dry and a bit of an odd fish, but his detractors were mainly those who disliked his handling of university affairs and came to despise his shortcomings as rector. With Hilda it was more complicated. More than a few found her cool demeanour off-putting. Her studied lack of enthusiasm smacked of superiority. A number of college wives objected to the way she queened it over them, and certainly she made no secret of her impatience with the provincialism of most New Zealanders who crossed her path. She was inclined to compare almost everything in New Zealand unfavourably with England. Her closest friends tended to be English, educated in England, or well-travelled New Zealanders whose artistic inclinations or liberal views on sexual matters acquitted them of the crime of small-mindedness.

The family leased a house in Hackthorne Road in Cashmere and in November 1948 Juliet, then aged ten, was enrolled as a day-girl at St Margaret's College Junior School in Papanui Road. St Margaret's had been founded by an order of Anglican nuns, and was favoured for educating the daughters of Christchurch's professional men and well-heeled Canterbury sheep farmers—*nice* girls. It was quite close to the university: Henry could drive her in each morning and she could take the tram home after school. Juliet would remain at the school until the end of 1949. A beautiful little girl, she was remembered by a fellow pupil for her lanky legs and enviable blonde plaits, as well as her aloofness. Perhaps the latter was not surprising: by Juliet's own reckoning, St Margaret's was the tenth school she had attended.

While living in Cashmere, Hilda became friendly with a woman called Nancy Sutherland, who lived nearby. Nancy's husband, Ivan Sutherland, held the chair of philosophy at the university; during the war years he had been in the awkward position of being head of department to Karl Popper, an outstandingly brilliant Vienna-born philosopher, whose inspirational lectures drew crowds of students and staff. While Henry Hulme got on well with Sutherland, notwithstanding his colleague's strong left-wing views, Hilda and Nancy became extremely close friends and confidantes. It was a surprising friendship—the two women were not at all alike—but they had no secrets from each other. Hilda would remember Nancy with heartsick fondness years later, after things had gone so badly wrong.

Nancy had grown up on a remote farm in Marlborough, at the top of the South Island. She was athletic, sporty, a great swimmer. Loud, with a deep, booming voice, she was warm, motherly and generous, giving much of her time to good causes, especially to do with early childcare and the welfare of mothers and infants. She was also, a friend would recall, "frightfully frank talking about sex". It was one thing she and Hilda had in common.

Nancy would later remember her friend as "a very pretty woman … physically attractive, gay and vivacious, caring, considerate and egotistical". But, she added, "I thought her somewhat irresponsible for a woman of her position in the university."

The remark referred to Hilda's sexual escapades. By the time she arrived in New Zealand, Hilda was unenamoured with the bloodless Henry and openly seeking sexual satisfaction, or at least pleasure, wherever she could find it. A younger woman who knew her at the time said she attracted men like bees to a honeypot. A distinguished New Zealand diplomat and writer who met her when he was a young man vividly remembered her siren-like presence. She was "a very sexy woman. I have never seen a woman so … steaming".

A psychiatrist, James Walshe, has given an amusing account of his first meeting with Henry and Hilda Hulme at a *conversazione* held by the headmaster of Christ's College, a prestigious boys' school in the city. Ngaio Marsh was the guest of honour. The celebrated writer of popular crime novels, Christchurch born and bred, was equally well known in her hometown as the producer of Shakespearean plays for Canterbury University College's drama society. Walshe, a young master teaching English and history at the school, had been invited to the select gathering as one of Marsh's former prodigies: he had played Claudius in her acclaimed wartime production of *Hamlet*.

Walshe recalled that Marsh swept into the room with her usual panache, in the role of the Cantabrian grande dame. The Hulmes arrived later. There had obviously been an argument in the car and

Henry Hulme, "a tall, thin and distinguished figure in … a well-cut suit", said scarcely a word all evening. Hilda, on the other hand, "a comely woman used to getting her own way, forceful, fun-loving, style-conscious … [flashed] smiles at those who carried clout, cutting dead anyone who didn't matter, ignoring academics' wives".

Walshe was fascinated by Hilda's body language, "sinuous, pelvic, live and unplugged. I couldn't help thinking of a black panther in its cage, prowling, prowling, until the business of introductions was over and she could be prevailed upon to sit: there was no divan on which to stretch out *en Odalisque*".

Hilda was determined not to be upstaged by Ngaio Marsh. At some point Noël Coward's name was mentioned. "I have met him. I do know him," Marsh said in answer to an inquiry from Hilda.

"Ah yes, he's a dear isn't he?" Hilda said knowledgeably.

"No," Marsh said firmly, "he's a bit of a shit actually."

This exchange was greatly enjoyed by all present. It was game, set and match to Marsh, who rolled her eyes heavenward as the Hulmes made an early departure.

After further acquaintance with the Hulmes, Walshe observed that "how Dr and Mrs Hulme had ever managed a cessation of hostilities long enough to get married was always an intriguing puzzle to the social worker in all of us". He was not the only one to appreciate the rich irony of Hilda becoming a "founding sister" of the Christchurch Marriage Guidance Council.

From time to time Hilda made vague attempts to be a good rector's wife, but her ill-concealed contempt for her husband made this impossible. There was a faction of staff wives who admired her, but at least an equal number, mostly the more senior wives, could not abide her. Some of the younger women found her kind and helpful. Renee Stockwell's husband was a post-graduate student. The couple lived near the Hulmes, and although Renee was a little in awe of what she saw as Hilda's "controlled and austere character", she appreciated her invitation to use the Hulmes' telephone whenever she liked, and was grateful for Hilda's attentiveness when her son contracted pneumonia.

Helen Garrett, married to the professor of English, John Garrett, was very much in the other camp. To her, Hilda was "hard as nails" and less than truthful. She was even at fault for having brought a wringer-mop from England, complaining loudly that such a simple thing was unprocurable in "this God-forsaken country".

Juliet seems to have made no friends at St Margaret's. One of her classmates who was invited to play at her house was refused permission by her mother because of "goings-on" in the Hulme household. Rumours were obviously rife. Juliet sometimes played with the Sutherland twins, Diony and Jan, who were a year older. Jan Sutherland remembered her as tall and very lovely-looking, but strange in some undefinable way, "rather a lonely child". Juliet's mother seemed "not very warm—not to children", and her father "aloof", wanting nothing to do with children.

There is no doubt that the young, lovely-looking English schoolgirl *was* a strange child. She was happiest in a world of her own imagination—a world where she was at all times the centre of attention, a dream land of lords and ladies, castles and caparisoned chargers, milk-white palfreys and damsels in distress. Nancy Sutherland noticed that Juliet was always a princess or some other form of superior being. Her little brother Jonty was sometimes forced to wait on her as a pageboy or groom but she resented him and played with him only when prevailed upon, never by her own choice.

Hilda had hoped that in New Zealand her daughter might stay put in one school, make real friends, forget the past, and forsake her fantasy world, but the loneliness and isolation of her early years had made too deep an impression. The Hulmes were not a happy family.

CHAPTER 8

A New Residence

Although by October 1948 Canterbury University College was at bursting point, acceptable accommodation had been found for the new rector in the clock tower building. The study, with its magnificent baronial fireplace and richly glazed oriel window, was the former meeting room of the professorial board but, splendid though it was, it was a little distant from the centre of power—the registrar's office. The initiative to recruit a full-time rector had come from the board, which hoped to reestablish academic control over the affairs of the college. However, Sir Joseph Ward, the chairman, and Charles Clifford Kemp, the registrar, were used to running the show. They were not at all keen on being meddled with by some new appointee.

Hulme tried valiantly to immerse himself in the life of the college. He mixed freely with students and staff and frequently dropped into the senior common room. But even those well-used to the eccentricities of academics found him a very odd fellow. For one thing, there was his way of lounging with his feet on the desk, or legs slung over the arm of his chair, when receiving visitors. He had his feet on the desk when Archie Stockwell, a lecturer in English, first met him. Stockwell was even more appalled when Hulme suddenly thrust a chocolate bar in his face. Perhaps informality carried to such extremes was a habit Hulme had acquired during his time in America, or perhaps he just hoped to appear approachable, unstuffy and forward-thinking. For many, it seemed not the way to behave and was intensely annoying. His support in January 1949 for a proposal that a new school of forestry should be located in Auckland rather than Christchurch added fuel to the fire: it was seen as a rank betrayal of his own college.

In November 1949 Kemp resigned, and at a council meeting the relationship between the rector and the registrar was redefined. The rector was confirmed as chief executive officer of the college, while the registrar would act as secretary to the council and professorial board and, "under the general direction of the rector", supervise and be responsible for the office staff and its work, the caretakers, cleaners and ground staff and their work, and the upkeep of buildings and grounds. The registrar's wings had been clipped. It seemed to be a victory for Hulme, but there was a condition: as CEO the rector had to have the confidence of both council and professorial board. It was a stipulation that would return to haunt him.

Hulme's dealings with the new registrar, James Logie, were much easier than they had been with Charles Clifford Kemp, but by the council meeting the seeds of animosity planted in January had already started to sprout. A question was tabled: Was there any truth in the rumour that the rector, when visiting Wellington, had made statements concerning the council or individual members that were in any way disloyal to the council?

It became clear that Henry Hulme had little aptitude for personnel management and was tactless, intellectually arrogant, and remarkably slow to learn that New Zealand was a small pond in which gossip travelled at the speed of a sonar pulse. At a meeting of the senate of the University of New Zealand, he may have spoken—as he often did—of certain members of the college council as "city buggers" or "Hereford Street mafia", with a disdain those included found intolerable when they heard about it. There was talk that he had been a complete dud in operational research at the Admiralty in London and been kicked upstairs to the Air Ministry, although there was no truth in this.

Hulme's relations with the professorial board were hardly any better. His idea of paying enhanced salaries to professors and senior lecturers who were singled out as particularly able or worthy, approved by the government in October 1949, proved contentious. Those who did not receive the bounty were outraged. Even those who gained an additional two or three hundred pounds a year were unhappy with the rector for creating a most unpleasant hoo-ha.

Meanwhile, Hilda Hulme had found her new avocation. A member of the college council most definitely not a "city bugger" was Alwyn Warren, the dean of Christchurch. New Zealand-born, Warren had been educated in England, at Marlborough College and Magdalen College, Oxford. A physically commanding presence, he had won a Miltary Cross in the Italian campaign while serving as chaplain to the New Zealand Divisional Cavalry. In February 1948 Warren and his wife Doreen had helped found the Christchurch branch of the New Zealand Marriage Guidance Council. An off-shoot of an altruistic movement started in Britain, the council was supported by the government and the principal churches: among its local leading lights were the magistrate Rex Abernethy, Maurice Bevan-Brown, a psychiatrist, and Francis Bennett, a well-known doctor. Its aim was to curtail marital breakdown and divorce.

Hilda must have impressed this muscular Christian as the right type to become a marriage counsellor. Like the other volunteers she was sent to training courses in Wellington, conducted by the Department of Justice, on topics such as "Sexuality". The stated goal of the Marriage Guidance Council was "to encourage and assist individuals in their striving to relate happily and fully to one another, particularly within the social institution of marriage". Counsellors would "facilitate the endeavours of couples to understand, respect and love one another". It was an odd mission for a woman who seemed to lack empathy, and who placed little stock on marital fidelity. Despite her obvious lack of suitability, Hilda rose to become vice-chair of the Christchurch branch.

Towards the end of 1949, the Hulmes' short-term lease on their house in Cashmere expired and the family moved to Rapaki Road in the Port Hills. It was a less convenient location: in Hackthorne Road Juliet had been able to get herself home from school and the tram had stopped virtually at their gate. But this was only a small inconvenience. In the New Year Hilda planned to send her twelve-year-old daughter to Queenswood, a private girls' boarding school in the North Island.

Travelling to Queenswood was no small endeavour. Juliet would have to take an overnight ferry from Lyttelton to Wellington and then travel for a good six hours by train. It was unlikely she would have any other Christchurch girls as travelling companions. Most of the girls at Queenswood were the daughters of prosperous Hawke's Bay sheep farmers. Few parents in Canterbury would contemplate sending young children so far to preparatory school.

In 1949 Erica Hoby, Queenswood's longtime proprietor and head-mistress, had retired and sold the school to the Anthroposophical Society, whose members wanted to establish a school run along the lines advocated by the Austrian philosopher Rudolf Steiner. The prime movers and financial backers, Edna Burbury and Ruth Nelson, had visited Waldorf School in Stuttgart, which operated according to Steiner's ideas, and been inspired by what they had seen.

Steiner believed there was a spiritual world that was compre-hensible to pure thought, but accessible only to the highest faculties of mental knowledge. These faculties of knowledge, he believed, were latent in all humans. Enhanced consciousness, enhanced spiritual perception—dreamlike, independent of the senses—could be taught. Access to the spiritual world could be gained by those trained in the "knowledge produced by the higher self in man". To all but a few this seemed at best eccentricity and at worst outright lunacy, but fortunately for Queenswood the wool-rich farmers continued to send their daughters there.

Perhaps Hilda was interested in anthroposophism and Rudolf Steiner's ideas on education. She was the type of person attracted to modish ideas that would set her apart from the common herd. Perhaps she believed the Rudolf Steiner method might be of benefit to her troublesome daughter. Many years later she made only a cryptic and brief mention of this sorry new turn in her daughter's life: "She attended a private school, Queenswood School in Hastings. ... She was happy at first but became very unhappy later at this school and we brought her home."

A few days before Christmas 1950, while Christchurch was celebrat-ing the centenary of the arrival of the first four ships of the Canterbury Association in 1850, the Hulmes had a party at Ilam. It was both a house-warming and a belated birthday for Juliet, who was back from

Queenswood for the long summer holidays. Henry and Hilda had rounded up the children of friends and university staff as playmates for the occasion.

The birthday girl was, as usual, self-contained and self-absorbed, wanting little to do with other children. Hilda, though, was in spanking form. She stood on the upstairs verandah throwing down sweets and small gifts to the children gathered on the lawn below. The adults, drinks in hand, looked up at her, laughing appreciatively. She was in her element—the focus of attention, the gracious hostess admired by all. How well the big house and its delightful grounds became her. In later years, she may have looked back on this moment as her finest. She seemed to be juggling sure-handedly the components of her life: mother, rector's wife, enchanting hostess, and sexually alluring woman.

The Hulmes had only recently moved to Ilam. The house and its surrounding fifty-three acres had been bought by the government from the estate of Edgar Stead, a passionate plantsman and ornithologist, and vested in Canterbury University College as part of the site for the university's future relocation. At the same time as it acquired the Ilam block, the university purchased land on the other side of Ilam Road and with it another fine old house, Oakover. In February 1951, the government also expropriated Avondale, a large, elegant relic of the 1880s, and its surrounding lands under the Public Works Act, making one hundred and twenty-six acres in all available to the university.

Once the big house at Ilam had been earmarked as the rector's residence, Dr Hulme was urged to occupy it as soon as possible. It would be a symbolic hoisting of the flag, a demonstration that the move to Ilam was really going to happen. Henry and Hilda needed little persuasion. The place would not be ideal for Juliet's health—the house was on the flat and with the upper waters of the Avon flowing through the grounds it would be damp and foggy in winter—but with Juliet away at school in Hawke's Bay, Ilam, surrounded by fields and paddocks, would be a wonderful place for Jonty to live. Hilda was delighted. It was a very suitable place for her to entertain and hold court.

*

The Hulmes' new residence came with a colourful history. The original home on the site had been built in the early days by John Charles Watts Russell, late of the 17th Lancers, and his Irish wife Elizabeth, and been a centre of the social life of Canterbury's self-styled aristocracy. Later it had been bought by Leonard Harper, an Eton-educated barrister and solicitor, member of the House of Representatives and notable explorer—the first white man to journey from the east coast of the South Island across the Southern Alps. There had been an almighty scandal when, in July 1891, Harper had absconded, leaving £200,000 of his clients' funds unaccounted for. After being briefly occupied by Patrick Campbell, the son of a colonel in the Madras Army of the East India Company, the property had been sold to a mysterious woman who went by the title Countess de Fresnado. In August 1910 it had burned to the ground.

The house occupied by the Hulmes was designed by J.S. Guthrie, the leading Christchurch architect of the day, and completed in 1914. Large, handsome and slate-roofed, it was one of the showplaces of Christchurch. The lower storey was red brick and the upper stucco. A *porte-cochère*, the dominant feature of the front of the house, was supported by four elegant columns. The hall and other ground-floor reception rooms were panelled with burnished native timbers.

The house's previous owner, Edgar Stead, had established an outstanding woodland garden. On a trip to Britain in 1925, he had collected and shipped out hundreds of rhododendrons from English and Scottish gardens, including the latest hybrids, his main sources being Lionel de Rothschild's garden Exbury in Hampshire, and the Earl of Stair's collection at Castle Kennedy in Wigtonshire, Scotland. He had experimented with hybridisation himself and produced Ilam Cornubia, Ilam Alarm, Ilam Canary, Ilam Violet, and others. His favourite hybrid, IMS, was named for his wife, Irene Mary Stead. Through what became a firm friendship with Lord Rothschild, Stead had been appointed a judge of the rhododendron exhibits at the Chelsea Flower Show and acquired an international reputation as a grower.

During the thirty-five years Stead had lived at Ilam, the gardens had always been opened to the public in late spring, with an admission charge donated to the Christchurch Horticultural Society. From time to time there were also garden parties to raise funds for the Red Cross; these were attended by anybody who was anybody in Canterbury, and sometimes honoured with the presence of the governor general. In a modest way Canterbury University College maintained the tradition, employing a full-time gardener and opening the gardens to the public each spring. Because there was a shortage of space in the college library, Henry Hulme also encouraged students to use the garden as a place to study for end-of-year exams; he would wander around offering them glasses of lemonade.

Latvian refugees from displaced persons' camps in Germany had begun to be resettled in New Zealand, and the Hulmes employed one as a housekeeper. Mrs Grinlaubs lived in the flat at the back of the house with her husband and two young children. She was flabbergasted when one morning, over a cup of coffee, Hilda Hulme confided, "Of course, we belong to the top of the tree." The housekeeper was able to observe Juliet's behaviour from close range. The girl, she thought, was "in a class of her own—very spoilt, precocious and very arrogant. She was rude at times to everyone, including her parents". Hilda would defend her daughter by explaining how gifted she was. Mrs Grinlaubs was never convinced.

At Ilam the Hulmes held frequent dinner parties, as well as memorable Sunday lunches and receptions for university staff and visiting VIPs. Lady Rutherford, the widow of the New Zealand's Nobel Prize-winning physicist Ernest Rutherford, came for dinner one evening, but perhaps the greatest coup was the English actor Anthony Quayle, whom the Hulmes entertained in March 1953. Quayle was in Christchurch leading the Shakespeare Memorial Theatre Company in *Othello* and *As You Like It* at the Theatre Royal. The thirty-nine year old was forging a successful career as a Shakespearean actor and manager—later he would branch into films, playing virile, stiff-upper-lip officer types—and he and the exquisitely beautiful Barbara Jefford, who was playing Desdemona to his Othello, were hugely in demand. Hilda must have been in heaven.

CHAPTER 9

"Sapienta et Veritas"

The novelist Fay Weldon, then Fay Birkinshaw, attended Christchurch Girls' High School between 1944 and 1946 while living in New Zealand with her mother and sister. She would later remember it as a "deeply serious and miserable place … [at] the wrong end of Cranmer Square, where the building shook with every earth tremor". The place was "uneasy … Classrooms would darken for no reason: no one ever wanted to be alone in the locker room". The panelled walls were "redolent with doom" and the pupils sometimes felt like "extras in some kind of horror film". There were places in the playground where nobody ever played and which everyone avoided. The school, she claimed, was haunted by the yet-to-occur murder of Honorah Parker, and there was a "hum of repressed lesbianism … a heavy atmosphere of unexplored passions".

These moody recollections prove only that memory is unreliable and even distinguished novelists are capable of foolishness. The red-brick neo-Gothic building stood at the sunny end of Cranmer Square. Former pupils fondly remember pleasant strolls around the square at morning interval and the sight of towering chestnut trees in Rolleston Avenue, bright green against the clear blue sky from the Montreal Street gate. Earthquakes were not regular occurrences in the 1940s, when Weldon attended the school. The cloakroom is remembered with nostalgic affection for the smell of damp felt hats on rainy days, implanted in the mind forever, along with the taste of acid drops in small white paper bags from Proudlock's tuck shop. And Weldon's contemporaries deny the hum of lesbianism, repressed or otherwise. "There may well have been some very good solid friendships," one said, "but if any lesbianism went on I am sure it was extremely well concealed."

Girls' High was a great place for rules. The headmistress, Jean Isobel Stewart, who lived in the school's boarding establishment, was a traditionalist who issued an unrelenting stream of directives. Prefaced with the words "No girl at any time will", they governed virtually every aspect of human behaviour. There were places you couldn't run, places you couldn't walk, couldn't eat, couldn't talk, couldn't sit. There were places in town where no girl at any time could be seen. There were rules about the wearing of hats, the wearing of gloves, and the polishing of shoes. Gym tunics had to cover the knee, and hair could be no longer than two inches above the collar, unless secured in a plait or ponytail.

Miss Stewart's prescriptive code was enthusiastically enforced by the teaching staff. When the Latin teacher, Miss Waller, was taking a third-form class one day, she glanced out the window and announced in a tone of horror, "That is something I hope never to see any girl of this school do!" The girls rushed to the window, eager to see the nature of the offence. The young woman standing below in Montreal Street was putting on her gloves in the street.

That was Girls' High. You sat up straight in assembly, recited the Lord's Prayer, and stood, chest out, shoulders back, to sing "Gaudeamus Igitur", "Jerusalem", "Nymphs and Shepherds", and "Among the Leaves So Green-O". The school motto—in Latin, naturally—was "Sapientia et Veritas", "Wisdom and Truth", and the school song, lively, in marching time, was of the usual banality:

> High School forever!
> Sing, girls, that never
> Our hearts shall sever
> From her dear rule!
> Years ring their fleeting chime,
> Still at our meeting time
> Raise we this greeting rhyme
> God speed the School!

In England Juliet might have attended a private, fee-paying school.

In New Zealand, however, there was nothing unusual about the daughter of a senior academic attending a state school. Diony and Jan, the twin daughters of Professor Sutherland, also went to Girls' High. The school had a reputation for scholastic excellence unrivalled in Christchurch. Its private counterpart, St Margaret's College, was content to produce well-mannered, nicely spoken young ladies, versed in the rituals of the Anglican Church, not over-burdened with learning, and certainly not expected to earn their own living.

In her Form Two year at Ilam School, which she had briefly attended after Queenswood, Juliet had been given an IQ test and scored 170 on the Stanford-Binet scale. The average was 110, so 170 was exceptionally high. Intelligence was thought to be both measurable and immutable—something doled out unequally at birth. Given the brilliance of Henry Hulme, it was considered not surprising that Juliet, too, should have great ability. Her imaginative stories and plays had made a great impression on her teacher and classmates at Ilam. The Hulmes considered their daughter far too gifted for the type of education St Margaret's offered.

Some of their friends and acquaintances saw things differently. To many, it was unthinkable to send a girl anywhere other than St Margaret's or another private school, Rangi Ruru, or to Craighead Diocesan School in Timaru. Girls' High was perfectly decent in its way but there were all sorts of girls there, from who knew what backgrounds. Wasn't it more important for a girl to make the right friends than worry about what marks she got in School Certificate? After the murder plenty of people said Henry and Hilda Hulme had made a shocking mistake. If only they hadn't been such inverted snobs. If only they had sent her to St Margaret's, where she would have mixed with her own sort, not got tied up with the fish shop girl whose people weren't even married, the whole thing would have been avoided.

On February 4, 1952, Juliet Hulme began her secondary schooling in Form 3A. She was turned out in the summer uniform: a cotton frock with a cream panama hat, fawn gloves and white ankle socks. Two days later King George VI died. In Britain his death was announced at 10.45 on the morning of February 6, late in the evening New Zealand time. Next day Christchurch Girls' High, like schools all over New Zealand, closed for the day. It was as though everyone had lost a distant but much-loved uncle.

Form 3A was in Room 9, first on the landing up the stairs with the polished brass rail. The class was made up of the bright girls on a fast track to sit School Certificate in the fifth form; less able students would take the exam in the sixth. The curriculum included Latin, French, English, mathematics, general science and social studies. There was also physical education, music, sewing and, in the fourth form, cooking.

"We all loved Juliet," one of the 3A pupils recalled. The girl who had arrived in New Zealand four years earlier gangly and awkward was now willowy and graceful, with a self-composure that set her apart. She was clever and knowledgeable, good at English, French and maths particularly. She spoke with a beautiful English accent, wore her hat with the brim pulled down all around, in defiance of school rules, and was much admired. "We all looked up to her and wanted to be her friend," a classmate remembered.

Juliet, though, was somehow unattainable. She treated her classmates with an airy bemused dismissiveness: it was as if they were barely to be taken seriously as human beings. One day when Form 3A had, for some reason, congregated in the cloakroom, she walked in and in her imperious voice proclaimed, "You girls look so positively mid Victorian." No one was exactly sure what she meant, but it was tremendously impressive. So funny and so like Juliet! It would be remembered forever.

Then, as the year progressed, something utterly unexpected happened: Juliet became friendly with a girl in the class called Pauline Rieper. A strange girl and something of a misfit, Pauline liked to be called "Paul", like George in Enid Blyton's *Famous Five*, who wanted to be a boy and was hot-tempered, brave and adventurous. Also like George, Paul Rieper had curly black hair cut shorter than most girls'.

She was stockily built. A scar, a legacy of childhood osteomyelitis, ran down her right leg from just below the knee to the ankle. She walked with a slight shuffle, pitched forward, with her hands thrust into her blazer pockets. Her face bore a perpetually cross expression; she was bolshie, hated discipline, and at times seemed to crackle with anger. She spoke sarcastically to her teachers, some of whom seemed a little afraid of her. She was, as one classmate put it, "a bit creepy".

Not everyone saw Pauline Rieper that way. One 3A girl thought her better-looking than Juliet. "I loved her wild gypsy look. ... Her dark flashing eyes would knock you dead."

It was obvious the Riepers were not well off. One of the girls who visited their home just over the back fence from Girls' High found it scruffy, and was shocked by how rudely Pauline spoke to her mother, who was "so nice to us—a little care-worn, hard-working woman".

Like many, she was mystified by the attachment between Pauline and Juliet. "They were a very unlikely pair. There was definitely some attraction between them but what the heck was it?"

CHAPTER 10

Family Secrets

When, on the night of the murder, Bert Rieper told Senior Detective Brown he and Nora were not married he had said a few other things too, but he hadn't really been thinking straight. When Brown and Detective Sergeant Archie Tate talked to him again later they got more information. About twenty years earlier he had been an accountant with his own firm in Feilding, a small country town, and married to Louisa McArthur, a woman he had met when on service with the New Zealand Expeditionary Force in Cairo during the war. Louisa was a widow, eight years older than him, and had been born in India.

He and Louisa had no children, he said, and she had made his life living hell. One night he woke up to find she had a strap around his neck and was trying to throttle him. Shortly after that he found a cut-throat razor under the mattress. Fearing for his safety, he moved to another room. She broke the panels of the door. That was when he decided to leave for good.

Intending to drive to his office, he got his car out of the garage, but she rushed at it with a broom and smashed the windows. Then she lay down in front of the car so he couldn't drive away. He got out and walked to his office. He was so disturbed by all this that he decided to end his life. Luckily, though, his confidential secretary Miss Parker returned to the office to finish some typing and found him about to top himself. After calming him down, she suggested they go away together. She would look after him, she promised, and they decided there and then to leave Feilding. They fled to the South Island and began living as husband and wife. Louisa would not give him a divorce, and he had paid maintenance to her ever since he left. Now she was dying of cancer.

It was an extraordinary story, and for the most part it was lies. Bert Rieper had never lived in Feilding. He lived in Raetihi, a small town one hundred miles away. He was not a public accountant—as chartered accountants were then called—and did not have his own firm: he had a job looking after ledgers. Honorah Parker worked in the same office, but Bert's position was unlikely to have been senior enough to require a "confidential secretary". And far from having no children, he and Louisa had two sons, Kenneth and Andre. Kenneth lived in the Hawke's Bay city of Napier with his wife, Marie, and was a motor mechanic. Andre was on his way to becoming a public accountant in Lower Hutt, near Wellington. Louisa, who had lived in Napier since 1941, was not dying of cancer. There is no way of knowing if there was any substance to Bert's account of her violent and threatening behaviour. It could have been the instinctive reaction of a wife who learned her husband was having an affair with a younger woman from the office and was about to abandon her.

Why did Bert concoct this story? Quite obviously he had not been paying maintenance for Louisa and his sons. This was a serious matter: it explained why he had never been able to get a divorce from Louisa and marry Nora—and why, as it turned out, their houses were always registered in Nora's name. Now, because of Nora's death, he had come to the police's attention, and adding to his misery was terror that his guilty secret might be uncovered. He seems to have been trying to enlist the sympathy of the police and discourage them from contacting Louisa—a dying woman—to investigate whether or not he had been supporting her. If they were of a mind to do so, the mention of Feilding might put them off the track.

It was a shabby thing to have done, abandoning his wife and sons in the depths of the Great Depression, and Bert knew it. The sorrow that now afflicted him must have seemed like retribution. There were secrets in the Rieper household. The family had not had a lot of luck from the word go.

*

Herbert Detlev Rieper had been born in 1893 in Strahan, on the west coast of Tasmania. His father, a shop assistant, had emigrated to Australia from Holstein on Germany's southern Jutland Peninsula. As a young man, Bert had left Tasmania and made his way to New Zealand. By 1915, when he enlisted as a private in the New Zealand Expeditionary Force, he was working in the office at Merson's Mill in the small alpine settlement of Ohakune. In army records his mother, Mrs Claude Rieper of Bellerive, Tasmania, was named as his next of kin.

Today Ohakune has a certain chic. Close to the southern slopes of Mount Ruapehu in the central North Island, it attracts well-heeled Aucklanders for skiing. Many buy holiday homes. Modish cafés supplying basic necessities such as pinot noir and café latté prosper. The town's bright orange, ten-metre-tall, fibreglass carrot honouring the area's thriving market gardens is justly famous. But before the First World War Ohakune was a tinpot little place, scarcely a town at all, in the middle of nowhere. Until the Main Trunk railway connected it to Wellington in 1908, the only access was up the Whanganui River to Pipiriki, then overland by dray or Royal Mail coach.

The Main Trunk brought a new industry, the logging and milling of vast stands of native forest. Thirty sawmills, one of which was Merson's, stood within an eight-mile radius of the town. The amusements of the bushmen, mill hands and farm boys in the public bar of the Ruapehu Hotel were as wild and boozy as anywhere in the young country.

On August 23, 1915, Bert enlisted with the Second Battalion of the New Zealand Rifle Brigade at Trentham Camp near Wellington. On November 12 he was shipped on SS *Willochra* to Egypt, where he was attached to brigade headquarters. Bookkeepers were harder to come by than fighting men. Bert—twenty-one years old, five foot six, nine stone ten pounds, Germanic-looking, with fair complexion and fair hair—became a base wallah. He must have impressed someone with his usefulness: when the Rifle Brigade was shipped to France as part of the newly formed New Zealand Infantry Division, he remained in Egypt, having been transferred to the New Zealand Army Service Corps. He missed the action on the Western Front—the

Somme, Messines Ridge, Passchendaele and the other battles in which the Rifle Brigade would distinguish itself—seeing out the war in Egypt and rising to the rank of corporal in the Pay Corps.

According to some accounts he married Louisa McArthur, née Mackrie, in Cairo in 1915. The 1915 date is almost certainly incorrect: the *Willochra* did not disembark at Suez until December 20 that year, rather late for Bert to form an attachment and get married. The following February the troops were transferred to Ishmailia, a city ninety miles southwest of Cairo. Leave to Cairo was strictly rationed, particularly for privates.

At some stage, though, he did marry Louisa. Eight years his senior, she was most likely a nurse attached to one of the base hospitals. She may also have been pregnant with his child: she was dispatched to New Zealand, took a house at 107 Marine Parade, Napier, and gave birth to Kenneth Roy Rieper on July 17, 1917. It would be nearly two more years before Corporal Herbert Rieper marched out of Cairo to Suez and sailed for New Zealand on the troopship *Devon*.

Not long after Bert returned to New Zealand, flush with his overseas war service gratuity of £97.14.6, he took Louisa and his young son Ken from the pleasant coastal city of Napier to Raetihi, a dreary inland town near Ohakune, where the main economic activities were sawmilling and dairy farming. Here Louisa gave birth to the couple's second son, Andre, but whatever prospects Bert and Louisa had for a long and happy marriage came to an end with the arrival in the town of a young English woman.

Honorah Parker's family came from Moseley, a pleasant Worcester village long since absorbed by the southward expansion of Birmingham. When Nora was born on December 18, 1907, the family was prosperous. Their home at 12 Alcester Road—one of a terrace of nine houses known as St Leonard's Place—was a substantial two-storied red-brick dwelling with double bay windows and a large garden, a suitable house in a desirable location for a professional man whose practice was thriving.

Nora's father, Robert Parker, came from Preston in Lancashire, and had moved to Birmingham at the age of twenty-two. Birmingham was "the workshop of the world" and the second largest city in Britain. Robert qualified as an associate of the Institute of Chartered Accountants and practised on his own account in St Philips Chambers, near the great St Philip's Cathedral and Bullring, the city's commercial heart. On February 14, 1907 he married Amy Blakemore, a young Moseley woman, at the Moseley parish church. His background seems to have been securely middle class: his uncle Richard Parker, an Anglican vicar, assisted with the marriage service. Ten months later the couple's first and only daughter was born. Christened Honorah Mary, she was affectionately called Nora by her family. A son, Robert Clive, soon followed.

Amy had every reason to anticipate a comfortable life with the usual assortment of servants to fetch and carry, but early on there was a calamitous change in the family's fortunes. When Nora was two, her father was admitted to the City Asylum. The house in Alcester Road had to be sold, and Amy and the children moved to a more modest dwelling in Strensham Road, Balsall Heath. It was a major downward step—the first of many—from genteel Moseley. In January 1921 Robert died in the asylum. He was thirty-nine. The cause of death, certified by the attending physician, was "general paralysis". It was the usual euphemism for tertiary syphilis.

Robert's estate yielded the sum of £567.8.11, a fortune to the slum-dwellers of Birmingham but not enough to generate an income on which Amy and her children could lead a respectable middle-class life. It could merely postpone an inevitable slide into penury, worry, and the need to work for a living. It was a bitter blow for an intelligent woman bred to a life of ease, a music lover who delighted in choral singing. Amy was forced to acquire typing qualifications and get a job.

In 1926, three years before the Wall Street crash, a general strike in Britain drew attention to the plight of the country's workers. Markets for British manufactures were disappearing and the coal industry, one of the country's biggest employers, was being ruined by the importation of cheap coal from Germany. The Conservative prime minister, Stanley Baldwin, argued that to save British industry all workers would have to take a cut in wages. The middle classes worried about a communist revolution. Amy and Nora, now nearly twenty, decided there was no future in England.

The family's troubles were far from over when they arrived in New Zealand. Problems affecting the British economy rapidly infected New Zealand, which was totally dependent on exports to Britain. Unemployment rose as the Depression took hold.

Soon after arriving in New Zealand, Nora moved to Raetihi. Most born and bred New Zealanders would have found the backblocks town bleak and soulless; for a young woman from Birmingham it must have been unimaginably awful. There was little in the way of entertainment. The pride of the Dominion Cafe was "hot luncheons", finished off with bananas and cream or fruit and jelly. Respectable women steered clear of the one bar in the Waimarino Hotel that admitted females.

Nora was reasonably attractive. Well built and buxom, she had dark wavy hair and smooth olive skin. Coming from Birmingham set her apart: she was not likely to be interested in the monosyllabic mill-hands whose idea of fun was to get drunk and knock someone's teeth out. Nor were the clerks at the Co-op Dairy, Rangatana Timber Company and Raetihi Dairy Factory more inspiring company. But there was one man who appealed to her. Bert Rieper was neatly made, a good dancer and as smartly dressed as anyone who ever stepped out of A.G. Laloli, Gent's Tailor and Outfitter in Seddon Street. Such men were a rarity in Raetihi: there weren't many who wore a suit and tie. Bert made her laugh. And he had seen a bit of the world, if only Tasmania and Egypt. He knew there was life outside New Zealand and didn't mind Nora sometimes talking about "Home". He was ambitious too. He hoped to have his own accounting firm one day.

Nora was delightfully youthful, fourteen years younger than Bert and twenty-two years younger than his wife. He was, he let her know, very unhappy at home. His vile-tempered wife made his life miserable. Bert, Nora thought, deserved better than that. He deserved his share of happiness. He deserved her!

It was impossible to conduct a secret romance in Raetihi. Everyone knew everything that went on. Even if the two of them went out in Bert's little Austin looking for a quiet place to be together, someone was bound to see them. "Working late at the office" was a handy excuse for moments of intimacy, but Louisa was sure to get wind of the affair sooner or later. It was sad he would have to leave Ken and Andre, but it was the only way. It was tough on Andre, but at least Ken was thirteen, old enough to stand on his own two feet, as he had at that age. Louisa, for all her faults, would look after them both like a mother hen. And of course Nora wanted a family of her own.

In July 1931, after Bert had stuck around for Ken's fourteenth birthday, he bought Nora a wedding ring at Ashwell's Jewellers and the pair of them took off. Driving south, they left the past hundreds of miles behind. Free of Louisa and free of Raetihi, they crossed Cook Strait by ferry and finally arrived in Christchurch, where they found a comfortable villa to rent in a peaceful tree-lined street in St Albans.

The love-nest was soon rudely interrupted. On September 23 a policeman came to arrest Bert for failure to maintain his wife and children. Louisa had taken out the warrant on August 10, and was obviously the source of the descriptions published in the *New Zealand Police Gazette*. The apprehension was sought of Herbert D. Rieper, formerly of Ameku Road, Raetihi, "age thirty-five, height 5'5", accountant, native of Tasmania. Slight build, fair complexion, curly fair hair going bald, blue-grey eyes, thin features; usually dressed in a navy-blue suit and grey overcoat tinged with red (seldom wears a hat) ... accompanied by his former office assistant Nora Parker (age twenty-three, height 5'7", stout build, sallow complexion, brown eyes, full, round face) and may be in possession of a dark-blue five-seater Austin Sedan motor car, registration No. 77–732."

Magistrates normally imposed a term of imprisonment of six months or a year in lieu of arrears. Bert presumably came up with the money because there is no record of a court appearance. He was not the only one to leave a wife and children to fend for themselves in those Depression years: one of the first measures implemented by the new Labour government in 1935 was a benefit for deserted wives. The new benefit, and the fact the boys had left school, meant that later, when Bert stopped paying maintenance for good, Louisa no longer had the same incentive to set the police on him.

By July 1934 Bert and Nora had scraped together the deposit for a small house. Twenty-one Mathesons Road in Phillipstown was a less desirable address than their rented house in St Albans but it was their own. To avoid any future claims Louisa might have against Bert, the property was registered in the name of "Honorah Mary Rieper, wife of Herbert Rieper of Christchurch, accountant". It was a falsehood: the couple were not married and Louisa was still Bert's legal wife.

Bert and Nora had three children in quick succession. The first, born in 1936, was a "blue baby" suffering from a heart malformation and lived only a day. In March 1937 a second child, Wendy, was born. She was a delight: happy, healthy, affectionate, adorable, everything a parent could wish for. Just over a year later on May 26, 1938, Pauline Yvonne entered the world at St Helen's Hospital.

Yvonne, as they called her, was an "an average, normal child", her father would remember, until just before she turned five, when she developed osteomyelitis in one leg. An inflammation of the bone marrow due to infection, osteomyelitis, most common in children, is an intensely painful illness and was then, before antibiotics became freely available, life-threatening. At one point it was touch and go whether Pauline would live. Several operations were needed to drain the infected site, and the young girl spent eight or nine lonely months in hospital. For the next two years she went through the daily agony of having her leg dressed.

It would take almost three years for Pauline to get better and she would be left with a permanent limp. Even twelve years after the illness she still experienced terrible nights when her leg ached mercilessly and she would need aspirin and A.P. codeine to relieve the pain. Doctors advised her parents she should not play sports or games. She took up modelling in plasticine and wood, and became particularly adept at making plasticine models of horse. She would carry this enthusiasm through to high school. She also, her sister Wendy remembered, went through a period of religious mania.

*

Fortunately for the Rieper family medical care was paid for by the state. In 1944 Bert and Nora were able to sell the house in Matheson Street and buy a larger villa at 18 Wellington Street in Linwood, another working-class neighbourhood. This was also registered in the name of "Honorah Mary Rieper, wife of Herbert Rieper of Christchurch, Business Manager". Most likely that business was Dennis Brothers, Poulterers and Fishmongers.

After two years the family moved again, this time to a large old house in the centre of the city. Later, Gloucester Street at the Cranmer Square end would become a highly sought-after place to live, with the Christchurch Art Gallery, Christ's College and Hagley Park all close by, but in 1946, when the Riepers moved in, the houses, while mostly big and imposing, were distinctly run down. There were a few exceptions. Across the street stood the childhood home of the Second World War hero Charles Upham, winner of the Victoria Cross and Bar. It was still occupied by his widowed mother Agatha Upham, a woman of impeccable social standing. A few doors along was Orari, the handsome town house of south Canterbury runholders, the Macdonalds, and nearby was the home of an orthopaedic surgeon, Keith Davidson, and his family. But most properties in the street had been converted into boarding houses or cheap flats for students. In 1940s' New Zealand there was no cachet in central-city living: most people preferred to live in a suburb with decent-sized lawns, large well-ordered flower beds and less traffic. For the Riepers it was different: Bert was fifty-four and they needed to think about his retirement in the not-too-distant future. In the new house they could take in boarders.

Pauline was nine when she started at Christchurch Normal School, which was housed in a forbidding neo-Gothic building on the north side of Cranmer Square. For two years she was the only pupil in her class, a reflection of the small number of children then living in the central city. Outside school hours she sometimes played with the doctor's daughter, Rosemary Davidson, who attended St Margaret's Junior School. Rosemary preferred Pauline's older sister Wendy, who was pretty, blonde and quiet. She was rather scared of Pauline, who had a "filthy temper" and would yell and scream if she did not get her own way.

Even as a young girl Rosemary was shocked at the conditions in which the Riepers lived. An air of poverty hung about the place. The house was "shabby and shambolic, nothing was tidy". The family seemed to spend most of their time in one big room which had a coal range for cooking and always smelled of fish. Mr Rieper was shorter than his wife, with small beady eyes and sandy hair. He seemed scared of Mrs Rieper, "a big, raw-boned woman, with very black hair and an angry face", whom Rosemary did not remember ever smiling.

The house had been converted into flats and the Riepers lived upstairs. To get to their flat it was necessary to walk along a dark, dank path lined with trees, then climb a wooden outside stairway. Rosemary Davidson made sure she always went home from the Riepers in plenty of time; she would have been terrified to walk along the "creepy" path in the dark.

Although in 1954 Christchurch was scandalised to discover that Pauline Rieper's parents were living in sin, in reality Bert and Nora lived irreproachably dull lives. With both daughters at school, Nora went back to work, finding a position as secretary to a solicitor. Bert rode his bicycle to his job at the fishmongers and spent his spare time in his workshop and vegetable garden. They listened to the wireless, walked to the library once a week to change books, and sometimes ventured out to see a film. They might go to a music concert if Nora's mother was involved. They dutifully attended parent–teacher meetings. Nora sometimes went to church, but not as regularly as her daughters. The car stayed locked in the motor shed until Sundays, when the family went for a drive. In summer they occasionally had a picnic or went to the beach. There was no money for holidays. A small circle of friends came for afternoon tea, dinner or the occasional "spot", although little alcohol was drunk in the house.

In March 1949 Nora gave birth to a third daughter. The pregnancy was unplanned: she was forty-two and Bert fifty-six. The child, whom they named Rosemary, had Down Syndrome. Although not understood at the time, this is a genetic disorder caused by the presence of an extra chromosome 21. The physical features, which gave rise to the description "mongol", are a round head with a wide flat nose, slightly obliquely slanted eyes, and abnormally short stature. Down Syndrome children have a mental capacity unlikely to exceed that of a five year old.

The new baby was a source of anxiety, stress and guilt to a family saddled with more than enough of all three already. The age at which Nora had conceived Rosemary was thought to be the root cause of the problem. It was a matter of embarrassment to have produced such a child and a daily struggle for Nora to take care of her. She had to give up her job and forgo the income that went with it. When Rosemary was just under four, Bert and Nora sent her to Templeton Farm, a residential institution for intellectually disabled children nine miles outside the city. Many parents treated Templeton Farm as a place to dump their impaired offspring and wipe their hands of them, but the Riepers never did. They visited Rosemary almost every Sunday afternoon and brought her home for weekend visits from time to time, and always at Christmas.

Pauline was eleven when Rosemary was born. Whatever her faults, she was always kind and thoughtful to her little sister.

CHAPTER 11

Indissoluble Bond

According to Bert Rieper, until Pauline went to Girls' High and met Juliet Hulme she was "quite happy in the house" and "very good friends with her father and mother. ... If ever she did anything wrong she would always say she was sorry, she knew she was wrong and would try to do better." As far as he could remember, she was never given physical or corporal punishment. His depiction of a compliant happy child does not square with the girl who, in February 1952, arrived at the school angry and rebellious, felt different from the other girls, resisted discipline, and spoke sarcastically to teachers.

Bert painted a similarly rosy picture of life in the Rieper household, but the truth was that, while Nora was kind and well-meaning, she was frequently overstretched and worn out, and Pauline got under her skin. Nora could be irritable and critical; she would nag Pauline and try to control every aspect of her life. She would fly off the handle for no apparent reason, only to regret it afterwards and try to make up with little gifts or favours. Much of this conflict made its way into the diary that Pauline started to keep in January 1953, but there was nothing to suggest the fourteen year old was dissatisfied with the limitations of her social world. All this changed when she got to know Juliet Hulme.

When she arrived at Christchurch Girls' High in the third form, the daughter of the rector of Canterbury University College presented an image of supreme self-assurance. Juliet Hulme was as sure of her beauty as she was of her outstanding mental ability and many talents. The importance of her father as head of the university and brilliant nuclear physicist, the glamour of her mother, and the social prominence of her family, living in their beautiful house at Ilam, all contributed to her sense of self-importance and made her stand out from the more awkward, self-effacing New Zealand girls.

If anyone called her a "pom" or a "homey", who cared? What did it matter what *they* thought? Juliet had no need for friends. Nobody her own age she had ever met was worth wasting time on. Nobody had shown any interest in the things that were important to her. She knew no one with whom she cared to discuss her triumphs over adversity, her brushes with death, the beautiful world of chivalry and romance that filled her thoughts, her amazing ideas for books to write, her love of grand opera. Nobody had ever appreciated quite how brilliant, how truly special, she was.

Then in the second term of school she became friendly with Pauline Rieper. This development, so surprising to the girls of 3A, came about because she and Pauline were the only pupils in the class exempted from games—in Pauline's case because of osteomyelitis and in Juliet's a weak chest, the legacy of her pneumonia and bronchitis. The two girls could hardly avoid conversing during the hours they sat around while their classmates had sessions of physical education, basketball, hockey, tennis and swimming.

Pauline's sharp-tongued defiance of authority might have impressed Juliet, and she would certainly have risen in Juliet's estimation when she let it be known how much she admired her—her cleverness, her beauty, her wonderful ideas. Pauline, too, was interested in books and poems, and a world of fantasy no one except girls like them could imagine. Both had suffered debilitating childhood illnesses, known loneliness, and grown to love solitude. Almost at the time Juliet had gone into hospital in London with pneumonia and bronchitis, Pauline had been hospitalised for the nine months in Christchurch. Both had come within a whisker of dying. It was as though they had been marked out by fate for some special purpose. Hilda Hulme later claimed that when Juliet became friendly with Pauline she said, "Mummy, I've met someone at last with a will as strong as my own," although this may not be true: Hilda was always keen to portray the girls as equal partners.

Pauline was desperate to have a close friend, especially one like Juliet Hulme, poised, beautiful and sure about everything—and someone with whom everyone, whether they admitted it or not, wanted to be friends. She was spellbound, willing to pay homage— willing to *be* whatever Juliet might wish her to be. It is easy to imagine Juliet realising for the first time the thrilling possibilities of friendship with another girl, a girl who understood her, saw how unique she was, and would do whatever she asked in order to please her. And Paul Rieper shared many of her interests and ideas. In fact she soaked up all her ideas as fast as Juliet's fertile imagination produced them.

Mrs Grinlaubs, who worked for the Hulmes until Christmas 1953, watched the friendship develop to the point where the girls became inseparable. When Pauline first started coming to the house, Mrs Hulme was happy for the two girls to be friends—even though, she felt it necessary to explain to the housekeeper, "Pauline is not from our social strata." Grinlaubs observed Juliet's domineering character. "Juliet," she said later, "could only love herself. Her main consideration was to completely take over someone." Pauline was "a shadow person following in Juliet's footsteps".

This was not surprising. When Pauline first rode her bicycle up the sweeping driveway to Ilam, she discovered a new and wonderful world. The house was like something you only ever saw in films. And she had never met people so *upper class* as Dr and Mrs Hulme. Mrs Hulme was lovely, beautifully dressed, and spoke to her in a friendly way without asking a lot of embarrassing questions. Dr Hulme said less but was also very welcoming. They even had a housekeeper!

According to Hilda, the friendship seemed at first "quite normal", but early on something happened that was perhaps not quite so normal. Juliet and Pauline left Ilam on their bicycles, found a quiet bit of countryside, took off their shoes and socks and windcheaters and danced around madly, working themselves into a state of ecstasy. According to Pauline, that afternoon their friendship became an indissoluble bond.

As their friendship blossomed Pauline came to spend nights, days and even whole weekends at Ilam. Everything about the Hulmes impressed her. Dr and Mrs Hulme drank wine at the table. They had boxes of French wine in a cupboard under the stairs, shipped out from England and with wonderful names like Châteauneuf-du-Pape and Nuits Saint Georges. Sometimes they would have a sherry in the drawing room before supper, in tiny crystal glasses no bigger than an egg cup. "Drawing room" and "supper" were what they said. Mrs Hulme would often have several more generous glasses of sherry as she sat smoking cigarettes and talking to Mrs Sutherland in the late afternoon. The Hulmes had beautiful paintings, and more books than Pauline had seen in anyone's home before. She hungrily observed and absorbed all the minutiae of life in a household so different from her own, so greatly more sophisticated, so much better *in every way*.

For her part, Hilda Hulme regarded Pauline with the patronising kindness of a social worker. "When she came out to Ilam she was obviously happy to be with us," she recalled. "She told Juliet and me many times that she was very unhappy at home. She felt her mother did not understand her and did not love her. She felt happier at Ilam among our family than she had ever felt before. Sometimes after a ... quarrel with her mother she would be in great distress. Juliet would then be upset, often to the point of weeping, and that is one of the reasons Pauline was invited to come to Ilam, I always understood with her mother's permission, as often as she wished. Pauline gave me to understand quite clearly that her mother often subjected her to severe corporal punishment."

In general the account was probably true, even the part about corporal punishment. Nora's stressful life, together with Pauline's rudeness, may have led her to vent her frustration and anger by walloping her willful daughter on a reasonably frequent basis, at least until Pauline began attending Girls' High. This would help explain the girl Pauline became, and the feelings she had about her mother.

Much of the fun the two girls had in the first year of their friendship was innocent enough. Both loved riding: Juliet kept a horse in a paddock over the river from her home and Pauline took regular lessons. At Ilam they loved dressing up and performing plays, even if, as Nancy Sutherland observed, Pauline was usually in a subordinate role—an attendant, or a maid-in-waiting. Juliet had to be the star, the centre of attraction.

As the school year came to an end their amusements became wilder. Pauline would sneak away from her home at night and cycle over to Ilam, Juliet would steal wine and food, and they would picnic outside in the dark, shimmying unseen in and out of the house via the upstairs verandah. Sometimes they would saddle up Juliet's horse and go for midnight gallops. One night they rode their bikes to the beach at New Brighton. By the end of their third-form year, they were going off the rails. They were now Nigel and Philip.

CHAPTER 12

Two Beautiful Daughters

Henry Hulme joined the Christchurch Club in 1951, probably put up for membership by the barrister Terence Gresson, who lunched there every day when not in court. Increasingly, it became a place of refuge. Most of the university council were now openly hostile and Henry's relations with the professorial board ever more strained. Nor could he any longer count on a friendly reception in the senior common room. His social contacts with his university colleagues were mostly on formal occasions or compulsory parades.

When he was in no hurry to rush home to the unwelcoming arms of Hilda and the histrionics never far away when Juliet was around, Henry could enjoy smoking his pipe, reading *Punch, The Illustrated London News*, or two-month-old issues of *The Times* over a peaceful whisky and water. The atmosphere in the smoking room, with its Thorburn gouaches of grouse and ptarmigan and its mildewed prints of almost forgotten Derby winners, was pleasantly nostalgic. Apart from newspapers and magazines, the only reading matter was leather-bound volumes of *New Zealand Turf Register*.

The members were mainly businessmen from old Canterbury families and convivial sheep farmers. These decent uncomplicated men, fond of a drink and an amusing story, were a blessed relief from the academic world where people were forever plotting and planning, forever discontented, always wanting things. Henry even became a member of the Agricultural and Pastoral Society, which allowed him access to the members' tent at the annual show.

The wives of the men at the club were not really Hilda Hulme's cup of tea. She thought them stuffy, insular, cliquey and afflicted with

deplorable clothes sense. Among their sins was most likely an unwilling-
ness to kowtow to the rector's wife. Who was she to *them*?

Hilda had her own set of friends. As well as Nancy Sutherland, she
was drawn to women who were active in the arts, broadcasting and
theatre. She became friendly with Eileen Saunders, who was the same
age. Both, with a few exceptions, "despised colonials", as one acquaintance put it. Another friend, Helen Holmes, was a trim, pretty young
woman who had made a name in amateur dramatics and become
involved in radio broadcasting. Her husband, Lyall Holmes, lectured
at the School of Civil Engineering.

By 1951 Hilda, Helen and Eileen had become radio personalities
on *Candid Comment*, a regular women's radio programme on the local
radio station, 3YA. Listeners wrote in with domestic problems and the
panellists proffered advice. Hilda, by then a prominent member of the
Christchurch branch of the Marriage Guidance Council, spoke as an
expert on marital relations and raising children. Not everyone was
persuaded. Christchurch's old guard regarded the three women, as well
as Nancy Sutherland and others of their coterie, as a fast crowd who
were far too modern in their ideas. They were known to read risqué
books and talk a lot about sex and self-fulfilment. For some it was more
than just talk. People were shocked to hear there was sunbathing in the
nude at Nancy's family farm in the Marlborough Sounds.

In 1952 a tragedy befell Nancy and her family. Nancy's husband
Ivan, who suffered bouts of depression, went missing. Days passed
and a search was mounted. While Nancy stayed at Ilam with Hilda
and Henry, the five Sutherland children were billeted with various
family friends. The search continued until all hope was gone. After
nearly three weeks Sutherland's body was found near a lonely beach.
He had taken his own life.

Jan Sutherland, then fifteen, would never forget what happened
next. After her father's body was found, she and her sisters and brother
were taken to Ilam, where Henry Hulme broke the news. Jan was
desperate to go to her mother to comfort her and be comforted, but
Hilda insisted that Nancy was resting and could not be disturbed. Jan
never forgave her. Hilda was not wilfully unkind, but where children
were concerned she could be heartless and clueless.

Through *Candid Comment* Hilda became friendly with a well-known Māori broadcaster, Airini Grennell. Airini was a grand-daughter of Teone Taare Tikao, a high-born member of the southern tribe Ngāi Tahu. On her father's side, she was descended from an American whaler who had been shipwrecked on the remote Chatham Islands in 1859. Soon after World War I, Airini's family had moved from the Chathams to Port Levy, a small coastal settlement twelve miles south of Christchurch on Banks Peninsula known to Māori as Koukourarata. Airini had attended Christchurch's Sacred Heart College and Canterbury University College. She had a glorious singing voice: she and her sister Hinemoa were members of the famous Waiata Methodist Choir that toured New Zealand, Australia, England, Ireland and Wales during the 1930s, even singing for King George VI at Buckingham Palace.

In 1953 Airini Grennell had returned to live in Christchurch, accompanied by a struggling expressionist painter called Rudi Gopas, whom she would eventually marry. Gopas came from a town on the Baltic coast that had been part of east Prussia but was later annexed by Lithuania. He called himself Lithuanian: had it been known he had served in the German army in the Second World War he would never have been allowed into New Zealand as an immigrant.

Like a lot of painters, Gopas had to paint portraits for a living, something he resented. Perhaps as a way of preserving his artistic self-respect, he sometimes painted two portraits: one a fairly agreeable likeness that would be acceptable to the sitter, and another, expressing his true vision of the person, for himself. He would in time paint portraits of Hilda, Henry and Juliet Hulme. When Helen Garrett, the wife of one of Henry Hulme's colleagues, saw Gopas's second, secret portrait of Hilda, she was shocked to see how successfully the painter had captured on canvas Hilda's "rather ruthless character".

Airini Grennell's father, Harry Grennell, lived in Port Levy, where he ran the post office and skippered a launch that provided the fastest connection between the bay and the nearby port of Lyttelton. The Hulmes learned that next to Harry's place on the shorefront was an unoccupied bach. Harry told them they could use it as a holiday place whenever they liked.

Port Levy is separated from Lyttelton by Adderley Head and a dusty potholed road winding across the Purau Saddle. It is a beautiful place. The narrow bay that probes four miles inland is enfolded by rugged hills. "The hills iron, the quiet tides below" was how the poet Denis Glover described it. Unlike Akaroa or Church Bay, other settlements on the peninsula, Port Levy was not at all fashionable. The scruffy dwellings clustering around the head of the bay housed an assortment of down-to-earth Europeans such as Dirty Mick, a deserter from the Royal Navy, full of salt-flavoured yarns and advice about fishing. Most of the small Māori population lived in or about Puari, a settlement on the eastern side of the bay, on land reserved for them by the Crown in 1849.

Port Levy had an interesting past. In about 1700, when Ngāi Tahu conquered Banks Peninsula, its chief, Moki, had kept his prisoners there to be devoured at leisure, or used as slaves if they were lucky. In the 1820s, during what came to be called the kai huanga—"eat relation"—feud, a war party stole over the hill from Little River and killed a number of people, including an elderly chief. For a time in the 1840s, Port Levy was the most populous settlement in Canterbury, and a favourite place for whaling captains to get wood and water and rest their men. The first Anglican church in the South Island was built there.

At the end of 1952 the Hulmes spent their summer holiday at the Port Levy bach, which Hilda dubbed "Christmas Cottage". Pauline Parker was having a rather different holiday: two weeks at a bible class camp in the north Canterbury countryside. The young Methodists mustered sheep and sang around the campfire. Pauline endured it with surprisingly good humour.

When the school holidays ended, Nora Rieper announced that now Rosemary was living at Templeton Farm the family was going to start taking in boarders. The first intake consisted of four young men, Harry, Ross, Ron and John, also known as Nicholas, all students at the university or teachers' training college. Pauline was enthusiastic. "I do hope Ross turns out to be nice," she wrote in her diary. "I have been looking forward to his coming so much that I will probably be disappointed."

The flurry of excitement was shortlived and life returned to stultifying normality. "This evening after tea we decided to go to the beach," she recorded. "Mother and Nana did the dishes. Ron came with us. Ross was out to tea so naturally he did not come. We went to Brighton. Ron, Wendy and I went for a swim. Mother bought some chocolate and biscuits which we had in the car on the way home…"

Pauline made a resolution to work hard in the fourth form, but for the more academically gifted Juliet success that could be achieved only by hard work was not worth bothering about. She preferred to display her dramatic talent, making a big impression as a murderess in a production of *Ghost Train*. Jill Taylor, who produced the play, remembered that "you couldn't read what was on her face … she was very self-contained, and dismissive of other people".

She was not dismissive of Pauline; the pair were now inseparable, walking around the school hand-in-hand and sitting together having long conversations in low voices. "You were allowed to have a special friend," Jan Sutherland remembered, "as long as it was kept within bounds." But what were those bounds? Whenever they could, Pauline and Juliet withdrew from school activities. At the annual sports day in March, when the entire school marched to nearby Lancaster Park, they found a quiet place under the grandstand where they could sit and write poetry together. Juliet composed a sonnet while Pauline wrote three songs to Carmelita, one of her fictional characters.

The intensity of their involvement with each other was so obvious it was talked about, but for one of their classmates "it was considered normal for girls to have crushes on each other. It was all part of life at a single-sex school … Lesbians were something we didn't know or think about."

The headmistress, Miss Stewart, was less relaxed and had a talk with Hilda Hulme. She was concerned the girls' relationship might be going beyond normal healthy friendship. Hilda, the liberal-minded expert on child raising, reportedly replied that she was not prepared to interfere with her daughter's friendships. This would surely have infuriated Stewart, who was trying to tread gently in a delicate matter, made even more delicate by the fact that Hilda Hulme was now a member of the school's board of governors.

By this time Pauline was blissfully proclaiming Juliet and herself geniuses. "We have decided," she wrote in her diary, "how sad it is for other people that they cannot appreciate our genius. But we hope the book will help them do so a little, though no one could fully appreciate us."

"The book", a proposed collaboration, didn't get far but the girls continued to produce poetry. The one surviving example, Pauline's "The Ones That I Worship", was puerile yet strangely disturbing:

There are living among two beautiful daughters
Of a man who possesses two beautiful daughters
The most glorious beings in creation;
They'd be the pride and joy of any nation.

You cannot know nor try to guess,
The sweet soothingness of their caress.
The outstanding genius of this pair
Is understood by few, they are so rare.

Compared with these two, every man is a fool.
The world is most honoured that they should deign to rule,
And above us these Goddesses reign on high.

I worship the power of these lovely two
With that adoring love known to so few.
'Tis indeed a miracle, one must feel,
That two such heavenly creatures are real.

Both sets of eyes, though different far, hold many mysteries
    strange.
Impassively they watch the race of man decay and change.

Hatred burning bright in the brown eyes, with enemies for fuel,
Icy scorn glitters in the grey eyes, contemptuous and cruel.

Why are men such fools they will not realise
The wisdom that is hidden behind those strange eyes?
And these wonderful people are you and I.

*

Hilda encouraged the fantasy swirling around pleasantly in Pauline's brain that she and Juliet were sisters, "beautiful daughters of a man who possesses two beautiful daughters". Pauline did everything she could to win favour with Juliet's mother, and was overcome with happiness when Hilda kissed her twice in thanks for a gift of cigarettes. Hilda, for her part, seems to have got mischievous pleasure out of making remarks that were so dearly prized.

Pauline was invited to stay at the Port Levy bach for the Easter holidays. These days, she wrote, were the most heavenly she had ever experienced. "Mrs Hulme did my hair. She calls me her foster daughter." And a few days later: "Mrs Hulme says she wished I was her daughter too." It was unfair: she would have traded her mother for Mrs Hulme without a second's hesitation. She was besotted with Juliet, in love with Mrs Hulme, in love with Dr Hulme, in love with the whole world of the Hulmes. Even the little beast Jonty was, by association, bathed in a golden light.

The two girls wandered the beach and hills day and night, not wanting to sleep, thinking thoughts that grew more and more bizarre. On Good Friday, April 3, they rose before dawn and walked up the hill behind the cottage. Pauline described in her diary a "queer formation of clouds" underlit by moonlight reflected off the sea, and a vision appearing as the sun rose: "Today Juliet and I found the key to the 4th World. We realise now that we have had it in our possession for about six months but we only realised it on the day of the death of Christ. We saw a gateway through the clouds. We sat on the edge of the path and looked down the hill out over the bay. The island looked beautiful. The sea was blue. Everything was full of peace and bliss. We then realised we had the key. We now know that we are not genii as we thought. We have an extra part of our brain which can appreciate the 4th World. Only about ten people have it. When we die we will go to the 4th World—but meanwhile on two days every year we may use the key and look into that beautiful world which we have been lucky enough to be allowed to know of on this Day of Finding the Key to the way through the Clouds." There were echoes of Queenswood, of Rudolf Steiner and anthroposophism, of a spiritual world accessible only to the initiates, the enlightened, the chosen few.

The daily entries in Pauline's 1953 diary were interspersed with her fiction. As early as March she was writing a piece described by someone who read it as "bedroom scenes ... highway robberies and often more than one violent death a day". No doubt it owed something to *The Highwayman*, a film screening at the time, starring Philip Friend as the romantic masked bandit. Posters heralded it as "Nobleman Turned Outlaw! Adventure from the black hell of torture dungeons to the sweet aroma of scented boudoirs!"

Pauline was creating a cast of violent characters. In April, she had Roland slapping Carmelita's face when Carmelita turned down his marriage proposal on the grounds she was engaged to Roderick. In a fit of black rage, Roland shot Roderick. A horse called Vendetta killed Gianina on the eve of her marriage to Nicholas. On the ledge of Satan's Hollow, Vendetta's crashing hooves trampled Nicholas to death.

The main inspiration for the girls' subsequent novels—and, for a time, a large part of their imaginative world—was the 1952 MGM film *The Prisoner of Zenda*, which opened at the Majestic in Christchurch on April 17, 1953. The setting is the fictitious Mitteleuropean kingdom of Ruritania at the close of the nineteenth century. An Englishman, Rudolf Rassendyll, layabout brother of the Earl of Burlesdon, is the spitting image of Prince Rudolf of Ruritania. Stewart Granger plays both Rassendyll and Prince Rudolf. The two men's striking resemblance is explained best in the book. Rassendyll's great-grandmother, an earlier Countess of Burlesdon and a great beauty, gave birth to a child illicitly fathered by King Rudolf III of Ruritania when he was on a visit to England. Every so often the blood of the royal house of Ruritania surfaces in the Rassendyll family.

Rudolf Rassendyll, one of its inheritors, goes to Ruritania for a spot of quiet fishing. It turns out that Prince Rudolf, soon to be crowned king, is being held captive in the castle of Zenda by Black Michael, Duke of Strelsau, who is keen to get his hands on both the throne and Princess Flavia (Deborah Kerr), the prince's betrothed. He is abetted by his evil, handsome henchman Count Rupert of Hentzau (James Mason).

Lurking about is a woman of mystery, Antoinette de Mauban (Jane Greer), recently arrived on the train from Paris. A year or two over thirty, tall, dark and of rather full figure, she is attached to the wicked duke Black Michael, but not as permanently as she would like.

To thwart the treacherous plot against the prince, Rudolf Rassendyll is forced to impersonate the missing king at his coronation. Princess Flavia is astounded by how much her intended has changed for the better— the Rudolf she remembers was overfond of the bottle and lacked any sort of way with women. She falls deeply in love with the new Rudolf, as he does with her. In pursuance of his plan, Black Michael is prepared to forsake Antoinette de Mauban and marry Princess Flavia, by force if necessary. Rupert, meanwhile, has plans of his own for Antoinette...

Rassendyll manages to free the prince from the castle of Zenda after a showdown with Rupert of Hentzau, featuring some of the finest swordplay ever seen on film. Rupert, the devil incarnate, lives to fight another day by diving into the moat as the king's cavalry thunders across the drawbridge into the castle. Being an upright fellow and the brother of an English peer, Rassendyll restores the lovely princess to the real king with her virtue safely intact. The princess's sense of duty obliges her to forsake Rassendyll, the man she loves, to remain in Ruritania as queen.

Juliet had adored James Mason as the oily, treacherous valet of the British ambassador to Turkey busy selling military secrets to the Nazis in *5 Fingers*, which had screened in Christchurch a few months earlier, but *The Prisoner of Zenda* was the beginning of her intense adulation of Mason—"the dark young god", as the director, Michael Powell, called him—and her fascination with the ruthless cold-blooded characters that were his specialty. After seeing Mason as Field Marshal Rommel in *The Desert Fox* and *The Desert Rats*, she was captivated by Rommel and what one English journalist called "the suggestion of romantic evil" attached to the German army. She began to side with masterful villains: men not tied, like lesser beings, to petty morality and the tedious path of virtue.

So enthralled were she and Pauline with the film version of *The Prisoner of Zenda* that they read Anthony Hope's swashbuckling novel on which it was based and its sequel, *Rupert of Hentzau*. The girls' imaginary empires, Borovnia and Volumnia, owed much to the fictional kingdom of Ruritania, but in them violence was incomparably more rife and moral standards practically non-existent. Other books firing their imaginations were *Dark Duet* by Peter Cheyney, Robert Graves' *I Claudius*, *Lord Hornblower* by C.S. Forester, *These Old Shades* by Georgette Heyer, *Cage Me a Peacock* by Noel Langley, and the Scarlet Pimpernel novels of Baroness Orczy.

Where Juliet led Pauline followed, but Pauline's writings showed she was more than a match for her friend. As might be expected of the girl with "hatred burning bright" in her eyes, she was preoccupied with her own fantasies of blood-letting and violent revenge.

CHAPTER 13

Charles and Lance

The great excitement generated by *The Prisoner of Zenda* sparked another round of midnight sprees, mostly in and around the grounds of Ilam. Summer was over and the nights were now cool and damp. When she was not at Ilam, Pauline was at home writing into the early hours of morning. She calculated that she slept four and three-quarter hours a night on average during the week of April 20. Juliet was living a similarly sleep-deprived existence.

Around this time it was decided that Henry Hulme would represent Canterbury University College at the 1953 Congress of the Universities of the British Commonwealth in London. Hilda was desperate to accompany him. Neither had been back to England since they arrived in New Zealand five years earlier. They decided to combine the trip home with a short visit to the United States. They would be away for three months, leaving on May 28 and returning at the end of August.

There was no difficulty about Jonathan, who could become a boarder at Medbury. The problem of what to do with Juliet was solved in early May when Nora Rieper contacted Hilda and offered to have Juliet stay with them. The offer was accepted gratefully. Evidently none of the parents had any great concern about the girls' relationship at this time. Nor, it would seem, did Nora regard Juliet as an objectionable presence in her house or an unwelcome influence on her daughter.

Within a week or so it became clear that Juliet would not be staying with the Riepers after all. The late nights capering about outdoors in early winter had proved disastrous for her health. On May 15 Pauline wrote in her diary: "Mrs Hulme told me they had found out today that

Juliet has tuberculosis on one lung. Poor Guilietta! It is only now I realise how fond I am of her. I nearly fainted when I heard. I had a terrible job not to cry. It would be wonderful if I could get tuberculosis too!" The romantic appeal of the consumptive—the pallid, ethereal young girl destined to die, Violetta in *La Traviata*—was not lost on Pauline.

On May 21 Juliet was admitted to Cashmere Sanatorium for treatment. The sanatorium was on Huntsbury Hill in the Port Hills, high enough to escape the fog and smoke that hung over Christchurch in winter, when low-grade coal from the West Coast was the main source of domestic heating. Although by 1953 a diagnosis of TB was no longer the death sentence it had been not many years earlier, it was still a nasty disease requiring painful treatment and a long slow recovery. The powerful antibiotic streptomycin, usually in combination with para-aminosalicylic—PAS—was effective but had unpleasant side-effects such as loss of balance and hearing problems. Hospitals didn't like the expense of it: each excruciatingly painful jab in the backside cost one pound. And PAS, which was taken orally in large doses, caused nausea, vomiting, diarrhoea and drug rash. The inexpensive new drug isoniazid, available only since 1952, was a considerable advance.

In light of Juliet's serious illness and hospitalisation, Hilda and Henry decided there was only one thing to do: carry on regardless. Although they arranged for Nancy Sutherland to visit Juliet when she could and take care of her laundry, it was another heartless abandonment at a time of need and must have awoken in Juliet bitter memories of her early childhood.

On the eve of his departure from New Zealand, Henry Hulme was approached by a deputation of council members, who told him that while he was in the United Kingdom he should look for another job. He told them he had a fixed appointment and would do no such thing, but the rejection was a blow for the man who only a few years earlier had been touted as "really too good" for New Zealand. It has been suggested that the real purpose of Henry's return to Britain was to be interviewed for an appointment at Cambridge, and for that reason it was necessary for Hilda to accompany him. It was not so. Hilda went because—notwithstanding her daughter's tuberculosis—she would not deny herself the pleasure of a trip home.

Juliet was fourteen and a half when she went into the sanatorium. She remained there for one hundred and twelve days and did not see her parents again until August 30. For long days she "lay in bed not allowed to talk, not even allowed to read … a long needle in your behind every third morning. They'd catch you while you were still asleep."

Hilda, quite unable to understand her daughter's sense of aggrievement, was tetchy about how little correspondence she had received from her. "Dr Hulme and I were absent for three months and during that time I received only two letters. Both were short and appeared to have been written without much care. … When I returned to New Zealand she seemed very much more withdrawn. I noticed the friendship with Pauline was the only thing that mattered to her."

Juliet's sense of abandonment by her parents had made her more and more dependent on Pauline. It was now absolutely proven that Paul Rieper was the only person in the world who loved her.

Visitors to the sanatorium were restricted. Nancy Sutherland went once a week. Jan and Diony visited a couple of times but were made to stay outside and could only call and wave to Juliet. At Henry Hulme's request, a psychiatrist, David Livingstone, dropped in regularly "just to see if she was all right". Pauline came with her mother three times—a visit per month. She was there one day when three or four Girls' High classmates came to visit Juliet, bringing her a potted cyclamen. Seeming pleased to see them, Juliet reclined in bed and chatted graciously. Pauline stationed herself behind the bedhead and glowered, willing them to leave.

The correspondence between the two girls during Juliet's time in the sanatorium was prolific. Pauline came up with the "brainwave" that they should write to each other as Charles and Lance. Charles was a Juliet character: Prince Charles, second son of the emperor of Borovnia. Lance was a Pauline character: Lancelot Trelawney, a soldier of fortune who had wheedled his way into the affections of the Empress of Volumnia.

In the story Lance and the empress have a vicious daughter, Marioli, who herself becomes empress at the age of thirteen. In Borovnia, Charles stages an insurrection and deposes his elder brother to make himself Emperor Charles II. Deborah, his mistress, by whom he has fathered an exceptionally evil bastard son, Diello, becomes empress.

A few days before Henry and Hilda Hulme set sail for England, Pauline launched the correspondence with a six-page letter in the person of Lance, and two pages from herself, signed "Paul". Juliet responded with a letter from Charles and one from herself, and this became the usual pattern of their correspondence: Juliet wrote dispatches from Borovnia as Charles, Deborah or Diello; Pauline wrote back from Volumnia, mainly as Lance or Marioli.

In Volumnia and Borovnia, vengeful murder, suicide, rape, seduction and betrayal were daily occurrences. Marioli, the teenage empress of Volumnia and obviously Pauline's alter-ego, was merciless in wreaking revenge on all those who crossed her. Pauline described her as having "a violent temper and when in a tantrum has killed all the people who have incurred her wrath". She is "very proud" and "refuses to interview anyone in the lower classes" but is loved, nevertheless, by her subjects.

Not to be outdone, Juliet's Diello kills without compunction or conscience, with insouciance reminiscent of Rupert of Hentzau. "Barton ... silly bounder ... tried to shoot me, and I have a terrible temper when roused and I am afraid I broke his back and put him in the mere ... (stupid blighter). And Linker ... poor fellow ... you know I really quite liked him ... indiscriminate in his choice of friends and is now ... alack! ... in the mere with Barton." The face and caramel voice of Juliet's evil persona was that of James Mason.

On May 29 a girl sharing a table with Pauline in a milkbar complimented her on how beautifully she spoke English: she "almost had an Oxford accent". Pauline delightedly recorded the remark in her diary: she had clearly succeeded in imitating the way Juliet and Hilda spoke. That same day a young New Zealander, Edmund Hillary, and a Nepalese Sherpa, Tenzing Norgay, became the first people to stand on top of Mount Everest. The news reached the world on June 2, the day of the coronation of Queen Elizabeth II at Westminster Abbey, and caused tremendous excitement in New Zealand, Britain and throughout the Commonwealth. It was seen as a brilliant portent of a happy and glorious reign to come.

The royal coronation was a source of inexhaustible fascination in New Zealand. Every schoolchild in the country was given a fold-out panorama of the coronation procession. Countless children and adults acquired models of the gilded coach, drawn by eight greys in gold and crimson harness and escorted by Yeomen of the Guard on foot, with the Household Cavalry riding fore and aft. Almost every man, woman and child had a commemorative coronation mug, thousands of which sit in china cabinets to this day.

For weeks it was impossible to open a newspaper or magazine without receiving riveting new snippets of information, such as the names of the aristocratic ingénues chosen as maids-of-honour to the queen. Many New Zealanders went by ship to England especially for the event. Those who were not so fortunate sat close to their wirelesses listening to every unctuous word of Richard Dimbleby's commentary.

On June 12 the pupils of Christchurch Girls' High were marched in formation to see the documentary *A Queen is Crowned*. "I thought the picture was rather boring as a picture," Pauline felt bound to record. But she was impressed by the pageantry, ritual, rigmarole and regalia, which far outshone even the MGM studio's enactment of the coronation of King Rudolf of Ruritania in *The Prisoner of Zenda*.

Pauline's detailed report would help Juliet create the forthcoming coronation of Emperor Charles II of Borovnia, and there was much to pass on: the girding with the sword; the clothing with the royal robe; the presentation of the orb with the cross, the ring and the sceptres of Justice and Mercy. Then came the anointing: holy oil was poured from the ampulla into the anointing spoon, from which the Archbishop of Canterbury lubricated two fingers before touching the new sovereign on her head, her breast, and the palms of both her hands while intoning, "And as Solomon was anointed king by Zadok the priest and Nathan the prophet, so be you anointed, blessed and consecrated queen over the peoples, whom the lord your god hath given you to rule and govern."

The queen's heels were touched by the Lord Great Chamberlain with St George's golden spurs, the symbol of knightly chivalry. Saint

Edward's crown was taken from the high altar and the archbishop held it aloft for a moment before lowering it on to the queen's head. At that instant the peers and peeresses in their ermine robes put on their coronets, the trumpets sounded, and the guns at the Tower of London boomed. It was wonderfully inspiring stuff.

An alarming passage appeared in the Borovnia-Volumnia correspondence. "I don't kill people," a female character said. "I thought you might like to know since you asked me some time ago. My father hasn't killed anyone for quite a while. I would like to kill someone some time because I think it is an experience that is necessary to life…."

Pauline Rieper was certainly avid to gain experience of life, but right then it was sexual experience she was looking for. In 1950 Commonwealth foreign ministers, meeting in Ceylon, had set up a new aid programme "designed to achieve security [through] economic assistance to and friendship with underdeveloped countries whose enmity would be dangerous should low living standards foster the growth of communism within them". New Zealand embraced the Colombo Scheme enthusiastically. By 1953 there were a dozen male students from Ceylon at Canterbury University College. When Pauline and Juliet met some of them at a reception given by Henry Hulme at Ilam, they were fascinated by the young men's exoticism and became friendly with three of them, Nada, Muthu and Jaya. Pauline eyed Jaya's lithe mahogany body with interest. On June 26, and again a week later, she visited his room at night. They talked about sex and she hopped into bed with him, but nothing happened.

Unlawful carnal knowledge—the law's majestic phrase—of a girl under the age of sixteen was a criminal offence, commonly drawing a prison sentence of six months or a year, although this was usually suspended if it were a first offence and the age difference between the parties not great. The crime was committed only by the male, the law's premise being that girls younger than sixteen needed protection from predatory men. Pauline was just over fifteen. Jaya seems sensibly to have decided to steer clear of such jail bait.

The same cannot be said about one of the boarders in the Rieper establishment. John Nicholas Bolton was a law student from Invercargill. "A pasty-faced fellow with long lank hair who always turned up late for lectures" was how one of his contemporaries would remember him. On Sunday, July 12, Pauline slipped into his bed, where she remained until three next morning. Despite their energetic efforts, Nicholas did not succeed in penetrating her. They had another try, again without success, the following Tuesday night, this time in her bed. In the early hours of July 15 they were caught by Bert Rieper and the young man was summarily expelled from 31 Gloucester Street.

Pauline wrote in her diary: "A terrible tragedy has occurred … I lay there mesmerised. It was just too frightful to believe … When I got up I found Father had told Mother. I had a nasty foreboding feeling at first. But now I realise my crime was too frightful for an ordinary lecture … I am terribly cut up. I miss Nicholas terribly."

Nicholas had been "quite consoling" about the trouble in which she found herself. "Mother thinks I will have nothing more to do with him … Little she knows…"

The return of Henry and Hilda Hulme to New Zealand on August 30 was a welcome distraction. Pauline was overjoyed to receive several gifts from Mrs Hulme, who also gave Nora a powder compact in gratitude for her kindness to Juliet. Nine days later Juliet, improved but not fully recovered, was released from Cashmere Sanatorium into the care of her parents. The medical staff were all too aware of the unhappy time she had been having with her mother and father overseas. Spring was in the air. Dr and Mrs Hulme could presumably be counted on to take good care of their daughter. Fresh air, bed rest and not too much excitement were prescribed.

Pauline accompanied the Hulmes when they went to collect her. "It was wonderful returning with Juliet," she wrote. "It was as if she had never been away. … I believe I could fall in love with Juliet." What in heaven's name did she mean? To most people's way of thinking she already loved Juliet as much as any friend could.

Things were not easy in the Hulme household. Juliet punished her parents for their neglect with tantrums, cold hostility and calculated insults. She was unrelenting in comparing the love and loyalty shown her by Pauline—even by Mrs Rieper—with their own dereliction. She pushed her parents further and further away and drew Pauline closer.

Pauline, however, had plans of her own that did not include Juliet. She continued to see Nicholas, visiting him late at night at the house where he now boarded. "I long for Nicholas very much," she wrote. But surrendering her virginity was proving difficult. In time medical experts would be asked why this was so. As far as Dr Reginald Medlicott was concerned she was "never erotically involved" with Nicholas, just "seeking experience". The episode was, he thought, "an attempt at hetero-sexual functioning".

Whether this was true or there was a physiological problem, Pauline's persistence was undeniable. When she visited Nicholas on September 14 she found him "very ardent". She wrote in her diary that she loved him. A week later she visited him at two in the morning. On September 29 there was another attempt at intercourse, but it was very painful. Three days later the same thing happened.

Then, on Sunday, October 4, "Nicholas was very pleased that I was so early. We sat around and talked for an hour and then went to bed. I declined the invitation at first but he became very masterful and I had no option. I discovered that I had not lost my virginity on Thursday night. However, there is no doubt whatsoever that I have now."

Four days later she and Nicholas had a tiff. This, she thought, was a good thing: she and Juliet could now continue their friendship "unmolested, with no outside interests". The two girls sat around thinking of all the people they would like to wipe out. On October 28, Juliet's fifteenth birthday, Pauline told Nicholas she was "no longer very much in love with him" and "it was better if they discontinued seeing one another". It was as if she felt her affair with Nicholas had been an act of disloyalty, to be put right on Juliet's birthday.

A month later Juliet decided she no longer wished to be called Juliet. Henceforth she would be Antoinette, after Antoinette de Mauban, mistress of the wicked Duke of Streslau in *The Prisoner of*

Zenda. A little later, probably inspired by Deborah Kerr, who had played Princess Flavia in *The Prisoner of Zenda*, she changed her name again, this time to Deborah, pronounced De-*bor*-ah. This was also the name she had given the mistress of Charles II of Borovnia, mother of Diello. Pauline became Gina. Most likely this was in honour of the buxom Italian film star Gina Lollobrigida, whose first American film, John Huston's *Beat the Devil*, had appeared that year.

Still convalescing, Juliet did not return to Girls' High in 1953, nor the following year, nor ever. For Miss Stewart, the girl's illness had solved the tricky problem of her overripe friendship with Pauline Rieper. Juliet, for her part, now had unlimited time to indulge her imagination. She had little need to engage at all with the mundane world.

By the end of November, with her fourth form year at an end, Pauline was busy assisting Juliet with her plans for an important event in Borovnia. Charles II, usurper of the throne, had at the age of thirty-five decided to relinquish the purple in favour of his bastard son Diello. The coronation, to be acted out as a pageant, would be held on Friday, December 10. Once enthroned, the youthful new emperor Diello would embark on a reign of terror that would not have disgraced Caligula.

Two days later, the coronation over, Pauline stole out of bed just after midnight and presented herself to Nicholas. Next day she was taken by her mother to visit Dr Francis Bennett at his rooms in Armagh Street, just off Cranmer Square. Since Hilda Hulme had returned from her travels, she had changed her mind about the relationship between her daughter and Pauline Rieper. Although the girls had seen each other only three times during Juliet's three-month stay in the sanatorium, Hilda was convinced the friendship had developed while they had been away. "It became apparent to my husband and myself that her real affection lay with Pauline. ... I had noticed Mrs Parker was concerned about that friendship—I knew her daughter had lost weight during my absence. ... She looked quite ill. She sought medical advice largely at my suggestion and my husband's."

Bert Rieper would later explain it was Dr Hulme's idea that Pauline see Dr Bennett; he had hinted Pauline might be lesbian. For their part, the Riepers were more concerned about their daughter's precocious sexual interest in boys and her weight loss. Around the time she lost her virginity to Nicholas Bolton, Pauline developed what would today be recognised as an eating disorder. It was almost certainly bulimia nervosa, a condition that involves binge-eating and self-induced vomiting. From her diary it seems Pauline did not have a period for six months from October 21. This kind of interruption of menstruation was a common side effect.

Nora was understandably worried. She threatened her daughter that if her health did not improve she would never see Juliet again. "The thought is too dreadful," Pauline wrote. "Life would be unbearable without Deborah. I rang Deborah and told her of the threat. I wish I could die. That is not an idle or temporary impulse. I have decided over the last two or three weeks that it would be the best thing that could happen altogether, and the thought of death is not fearsome." It did not come to that, but Pauline's weight loss remained a matter of concern in the Rieper family in the months to come.

Dr Bennett's recollection of events was that he was consulted by Dr Hulme on December 9; the appointment with Pauline was then arranged by Dr Hulme and Mrs Rieper. Although Hulme "was worried over what he regarded as an unhealthy association, and wanted me to see Pauline from a psychiatric point of view", Pauline's mother was "worried over her loss of weight and vomiting". He assured Nora there was no physical illness to account for Pauline's weight loss.

Bennett's psychiatric evaluation of Pauline at the request of Dr Hulme, a third party, was unorthodox to say the least. In the event, it was also unsatisfactory. Pauline refused to cooperate and mostly answered questions with only a simple yes or no. She did say she was unhappy and that her mother nagged her. She also told him her only friend was Juliet and she didn't in general like girls—she thought girls were silly. Bennett suggested she should enlarge her circle of friends but could see he was getting nowhere. Pauline Rieper was "strange", he wrote in his case notes.

The inadequacy of the interview did not deter Bennett from informing Mrs Rieper there was a homosexual attachment between her daughter and Juliet Hulme. He may well have been assisted in this diagnosis by a prior briefing from Hilda, his colleague on the Marriage Guidance Council. Under the circumstances, he told Nora, not much could be done about it. He thought the whole thing would eventually fizzle out. Pauline was unimpressed: "Mother carted me off to see a doctor after work, which was a half-witted imbecile thing to do, especially as I feel perfectly well. The doctor was a bloody fool..."

Afterwards, Nora mollified Pauline by taking her to see *Pandora and the Flying Dutchman*. In this peculiar fable, a man has to live forever unless he can persuade a woman to fall in love with him so the two can die together. The film starred James Mason and Ava Gardner. Pauline, who had been aflame with anticipation all day, was enraptured. "It is the most perfect story I have ever known, the best picture (easily) that I have ever seen. Pandora is the most beautiful female imaginable and Him is far too wonderful to attempt to describe. I feel depressed and will probably cry tonight." The two girls had recently decided to refer to James Mason as "Him"; this would evolve into a bizarre system of encryption only they could unravel.

The Hulmes now disappeared to Port Levy for Christmas and the long summer holidays without inviting Pauline, whose influence on Juliet, they had decided, was a matter of real concern. On Christmas Eve, Pauline noted that she did not feel very Christmassy. It was nothing like as exciting as the night before Diello's coronation.

CHAPTER 14

Angelic Behaviour

In 1954, "Rock Around the Clock"—the first worldwide rock 'n' roll hit—was recorded by Bill Halley and his Comets. Elvis Presley recorded his first songs "That's All Right, Mama" and "Blue Moon over Kentucky" for Sun records. It would be another year, though, before this new music gained popularity. Meanwhile, sentimental ballads, lugubrious harmonies, and Italian-flavoured novelty songs, from "Secret Love" by Doris Day to "Three Coins in the Fountain" by The Four Acres and "Papa Loves Mambo" by Perry Como, held sway.

Juliet Hulme preferred the soaring arias of Puccini, Mascagni, Verdi, Donizetti and Bellini, and Pauline soon joined her. The girls spent hours listening to the Hulmes' collection of the great artists—Jussi Björling, Tito Schipa, Benjamino Gigli, Maria Callas, Nellie Melba, and especially Enrico Caruso—and Pauline trawled second-hand shops to buy records of her own. She and Juliet became infatuated with Mario Lanza, the American-born tenor who had played Caruso with extraordinary success in the 1951 film *The Great Caruso*.

Now, however, with Juliet away at Port Levy, life for Pauline was dreary as a month of Sundays. In her new *Whitcombe's Handy* Diary, inscribed "To Yvonne, Love from Daddy", she wrote an unsettling New Year's Resolution: "Eat, drink and be merry, for tomorrow you may be dead." An attempt was made to patch together a truce with her sister Wendy, who delighted her by reporting that Mr Tredrea, a family friend, had said Pauline was the finest-looking girl he had ever set eyes on. Wendy also offered to lend her money any time she needed it.

On January 3 Pauline attended church, played with her sister Rosemary, who was home for Christmas, and did some baking. In the evening she wrote to Nicholas and "Deborah, or rather Diello". She wrote to Nicholas again on January 7, feeling well disposed towards him but unable to think of anything to say. She was under close watch by her parents and no longer free to slip in and out of the house in the early hours of the morning.

A few days later, with her mother in an unexpectedly good mood, she broached the subject of being allowed to see Nicholas. "I think there is hope but I shall not expect it as I don't want to be disappointed," she wrote in her diary. Evenings were spent working on Plasticine models of wild horses. She wanted "to get into Mother's good books". For a brief moment Juliet raised her hopes that she would be invited to stay at Port Levy—"Joy of Joys!"—but nothing came of it.

A day or so later Pauline again raised the topic of Nicholas. Nora was unhappy about his "bohemian ways"; she would have to consult Pauline's father. That was not hopeful, Pauline thought. Her father was maddeningly cautious in such matters. "I was rather annoyed by Mother's attitude as I have been positively angelic for over a week, which is incredibly hard and she ought to show her appreciation more."

Her spirits rose after a family picnic at Coe's Ford on the Selwyn River. "It started to rain a little and we piled into the car and started off. I had the car window open and a warm breeze blew which was heavenly. I felt more light-hearted and glad than I have for months. I made wonderful plans for the future. When we arrived home (6.30) I had a bath and came straight to bed feeling clean, sweet and happy."

The angelic phase did not stop her making a surreptitious purchase. She had been having riding lessons for years with a Miss Rich in Hackthorne Road and was keen to have a horse of her own. Using money saved from a holiday job and payments from her mother for helping with the boarders, she secretly bought a gelding, whom she named Omar Khayyám, and arranged grazing with a Mr and Mrs Purvis two miles out of town. "I was very frank, and all that I did not tell them was that my parents knew nothing of my horse. All they asked for was 5/- weekly so I was very relieved and everything was settled."

On January 16, a Saturday, she recruited Nicholas to help catch Omar Khayyám and take him to his new paddock. They were unsuccessful, but Nicholas took the chance to tell her he loved her and to report that her mother had phoned and said he was not to see her. Pauline was furious. She had been led to believe that if she continued to be good she could see Nicholas again; she had been "perfect for a fortnight" and "amazingly good". Her mother was "dreadfully mean"; she felt "very much double-crossed". Seeing the biblical epic *The Robe* at the Savoy that night put her in a better frame of mind. "Caligula was exactly like the Devil," she noted, referring to the evilly smirking Roman emperor played by Jay Robinson.

In the next few weeks Pauline talked to Juliet on the telephone almost daily and the two exchanged numerous letters. Nicholas, though, was continually out when she rang. When she finally reached him, he revealed that her mother had now written to him. "Apparently my angelic behaviour during his absence has convinced her he is a bad influence on me." The thought that her mother had let her down— even betrayed her— weighed heavily on her mind. She would never forgive her.

From January 18 to 22, 1954, Christchurch was in a ferment of excitement over the visit of the newly crowned Elizabeth II— Queen of Britain, New Zealand and numerous other countries of the old Empire—and her handsome consort the Duke of Edinburgh. Buildings were painted, bunting was hung, flags fluttered, and flowers, the gaudier the better, were everywhere in profusion. At night, Cathedral Square and the river banks were lit up. After the young couple arrived by train from Greymouth, crowds massed in Oxford Terrace outside the Clarendon Hotel, where the royal party was staying. The Royal Christchurch Musical Society, women in long white ball dresses and men in dinner jackets, launched into a medley of songs it was hoped might please the royal ears. After wave after wave of deafening cheering, their highnesses appeared on the balcony to shouts of "Long live the Queen!"

Next day the royal couple was driven eight miles through the city, cheered en route by 150,000 well-wishers. The elaborately planned route took them along Ilam Road to the new site of Canterbury University College. Henry and Hilda Hulme had invited a few people to watch the procession from the lawn of their house. Among them was a retired surgeon and former member of parliament Sir Hugh Acland and his wife. As the queen passed, Lady Acland caught sight of Juliet out of the corner of her eye. She was writing furiously in a notebook, ostentatiously ignoring the proceedings. She was, Lady Acland thought, a very peculiar girl.

That evening there was a ball at the Christchurch Club, which Henry and Hilda Hulme would certainly have attended. "Magnificent jewels and gowns were on display," *The Press* reported next day. "Many of the older women guests wore handsome tiaras." A marquee draped with vines, grapes and ivy boasted a special dance floor. Roses, frozen in large blocks of ice, were placed in alcoves, "electric fans throwing the cool air from the ice into the ballroom". The guests were disappointed when the queen sent a message saying she was too tired to attend: the presence of the prime minister, Sidney Holland, and his wife was small consolation.

Like Juliet, Pauline was treating the royal visit as beneath her notice. If in the recesses of your mind you are Emperor of Borovnia or Empress of Volumnia, people line the streets cheering *you*. The night after the ball she happily watched James Mason in *Secret Mission* but the main thing on her mind was what to do about Omar Khayyám. At breakfast next day her mother dropped a bombshell: Mrs Purvis had phoned—something about the grazing—and so her mother now knew all about the horse. Pauline, she said, should tell her father, confess all, as if of her own accord. Initially his reaction was "mediocre" but that evening she talked it over with both parents, who were "really jolly decent". Bert and Nora had decided the horse was to be encouraged: it might take their daughter's mind off Juliet Hulme.

It was a vain hope. For the first time since her visit to Dr Bennett in December, Pauline biked off to Ilam. It was now January 23. Hilda may have had a change of heart, or perhaps just agreed to the visit to gain respite from Juliet's incessant pestering. In any case, something else was occupying her mind by then.

The girls played all their favourite records, and while Juliet rested Pauline read her nearly completed novel *The Beautiful Lady in Blue*. It was very good indeed, she thought, and would make a superb picture if ever filmed. The pair then spent a happy afternoon strolling around the grounds talking about James Mason. "It is really extraordinary that two people could be so very much in love with the same person and yet never quarrel over him and obtain infinite pleasure from discussing the possibility of one of them's future with him," Pauline noted in her diary.

Next day, with the help of Mr and Mrs Purvis, she managed to catch Omar Khayyám and bring him on a leading rein from Bexley to their paddock. The Purvises gave her a bridle and said they knew someone who would lend her a saddle. Nora, Bert, Nana Parker and one of the boarders, Darren, came out to see the horse, and that evening the Rieper family drank a toast to him. Pauline was allowed to spend time with Juliet again. Her life was looking up wonderfully.

CHAPTER 15

The Temple in the Garden

No one is exactly sure when Walter Andrew Bowman Perry arrived in New Zealand, nor how Hilda Hulme came to meet him. A Canadian engineer, Bill Perry, as he was known to everyone, had had a good war. In the rearguard at Dunkirk and one of the last of the fighting men evacuated from the beach, he had been awarded the Military Cross and attained the rank of major. A close acquaintance recalled that he was "very handsome ... a clever fellow, very tall... athletic looking ... striking looking". Mrs Grinlaubs, the Hulmes' housekeeper, thought him "very good-looking, tall ... charming".

Perry was employed by Associated Industrial Consultants, a London consulting firm that had been retained to advise a Christchurch company, Booth and MacDonald, manufacturers of agricultural implements, on restructuring their business. The company being in urgent need of his services, he had flown out to New Zealand while his wife followed by ship. On the way she had fallen in love with the ship's purser and disembarked in Australia, spelling the end of Perry's marriage.

One account has him arriving in Christchurch on July 2, 1953, but it may have been earlier. Renée Stockwell believed he had known Hilda Hulme before he arrived in New Zealand, may even have had an affair with her in England, and traced her through the Marriage Guidance Council. Helen Garrett, whose husband Professor John Garrett was also a Canadian, remembered it differently. Perry, she thought, had come to see Hilda about his divorce when the Hulmes were living in the Port Hills. She claimed Hilda had interviewed Bill

Perry in the matrimonial bedroom on the grounds that it was a "neutral place". This would date their meeting—or reunion—before October 1950, which is unlikely.

The commonly accepted version is that Perry first met Hilda Hulme when he went to the Marriage Guidance Council for counselling, which made their subsequent relationship a grave embarrassment to the organisation, especially as Hilda was its vice chairman: sexual relations between counsellors and those they counselled were strictly forbidden. Hilda's close friend Nancy Sutherland, who described Perry as "one of Hilda's lovers", thought they were both counsellors on the Marriage Guidance Council. That is another possibility. What is certain is that towards the end of 1953 Hilda was becoming increasingly involved with Perry. What had started as a fling was turning into a serious love affair.

Around Christmas, Hilda asked Mr and Mrs Grinlaubs and their two children to move out of Ilam: the flat was required for Mr Perry. Mrs Grinlaubs was not surprised: she had seen the relationship developing. Once, when cleaning an upstairs room and shaking her duster out the window, she had seen Perry and Mrs Hulme kissing in the garden below. "I drew back my duster and didn't say anything," she said.

Nancy Sutherland and friends of Perry tried to talk him out of moving into the flat. Sooner or later, they were sure, Juliet and Jonathan were bound to notice what was going on. Nancy thought it wrong of Hilda to flaunt her affair so recklessly, without regard for her children's or Henry's feelings. Jan Sutherland, Nancy's daughter, remembers her mother talking to Hilda on the phone, tears streaming down her cheeks, saying she could not be her friend any longer.

In the Rieper household, the lull brought about by Omar Khayyám did not last. Relations between Pauline and her mother were again volatile. "This morning Mother gave me the most fearful lecture because I started to wash the kitchen floor in my housecoat," Pauline wrote in her diary. "She nagged on and on bringing up all my past misdemeanours and of course I was insolent. (I can never manage to be contrite.) Anyway, she ended up saying I could not go to Ilam today as I had planned. I was very upset when I rang Deborah as Mother's lectures always make me hysterical and the strain of pretending not to care is great. Deborah was very worried by some of Mother's threats, and all the Hulmes were, which is pleasant. ... I rang Nicholas but he was out and that caused me to fly into a rage. ... This evening I fixed my old jodhs [jodphurs] for wearing tomorrow. I am reading a murder at the moment."

Pauline phoned Nicholas whenever her mother was out of the house and met him at every possible opportunity. On Sunday, January 31, she saw him when she was on the way to Miss Rich's for a riding lesson. He seemed rather depressed. The following Sunday she hoped to visit him on her way to church but Wendy was with her. She was "annoyed desperately" on February 20 when she tried to phone him and he was out. He was still out when she phoned again that evening.

The affair limped on until February 25. That evening she rang Juliet and they talked about Him—James Mason—for a long time, after which she felt "much cheered" and wrote a letter to Nicholas saying she wished to discontinue their relationship. She took the letter, together with a parcel of books he had lent her, to the boarding house where he lived and left it there.

The teenage romance had ended. In her diary, Pauline had made no mention of having sex with Nicholas other than the night she lost her virginity, and presumably on December 12, a couple of nights after Diello's coronation but, given Nicholas's profession of love and her dogged persistence in contacting him and arranging to meet, it is likely they had taken whatever opportunities presented themselves. Later everyone would seek to make light of the relationship, including Pauline herself, who told Dr Bennett she gave Nicholas up because he was "weak-kneed and unpleasant" and "just a trophy", and informed Dr Medlicott: "It wasn't for me. I wasn't interested." But anyone charting the course of the relationship through Pauline's diary would come to the conclusion that, while it lasted, it was at least as intense as any other schoolgirl's first love.

After she came home from the sanatorium Juliet had lost interest in her horse, but Pauline remained passionately interested in Omar Khayyám.

Throughout January and February in the scorching summer of 1954, she had ridden miles on her bicycle almost every day to visit and ride him. She even went to groom him on February 2, the hottest day in Canterbury for forty-three years. But by the time she severed relations with Nicholas her interest was petering out, and by March 11 she was trying to sell him.

Pauline's dumping of Nicholas and her decision to part with Omar Khayyám coincided with renewed contact with Juliet—allowed by both sets of parents despite their being well aware Dr Francis Bennett considered the girls' relationship to be essentially homosexual. Pauline and Juliet had moved on from the empires of Borovnia and Volumnia. Pauline was finishing her new novel *The Donkey's Serenade* and Juliet putting the final touches to *The Beautiful Lady in Blue*. Sexual matters increasingly occupied their thoughts, and a certain luxurious physicality entered their friendship.

On January 26 Juliet telephoned Pauline to say that her Alsatian dog "Rommel" had arrived, a wonderful thrill as she had thought she would not be getting "a Rommel dog" until her birthday. It turned out to be a tease. Next day she admitted it was Bill Perry's dog and was to be called Carlo. (In the end the dog was called Retzi.)

Pauline stayed two nights at Ilam. The dog, she noted, was a "lovely animal with the loveliest ears". The girls played records and walked around the garden eating grapes filched from the hothouse. In the afternoon they lay on Hilda's bed discussing what the charges would be for their services if they were prostitutes.

Next day they celebrated "He's Day" in honour of Mario Lanza, eating birthday cake, drinking a toast, playing Lanza's records, and building him a shrine. They decided "His"—Guy Rolfe—should be shifted to the Gods. Rolfe, a tall, lean, good-looking Hollywood actor, specialised in treacherous villains such as Prince John in *Ivanhoe* and a Parisian safecracker in *The Spider and the Fly*. An actress who worked with him called him "strange, very saturnine": there was a whiff of sulphur about him. Later, the girls worked out how much prostitutes earned and decided they would definitely take up the profession.

School resumed on the second day of February. Pauline was now in her fifth form year. Preparing to visit Ilam on the weekend, she found a glittering black dress in which to celebrate "Him's Day". On the Saturday, Hilda and Henry Hulme went out and the girls had the house to themselves. They wore black, changed into Hilda's most elaborate evening dresses, and made themselves "look really beautiful". They talked about the Saints, mainly Him, and their books and laughed so much they ached.

The following Friday, Nora was in a dreadful temper. "Mother gave me a fearful lecture along the usual strain and declared I could not go out to Ilam tomorrow," Pauline wrote. She immediately rang Juliet. "I had to tell someone sympathetic how I loathed Mother. The past tense is not necessary."

Next day Nora was unrelenting. "Mother told me I could not go out to Ilam again until I was eight stone and more cheerful. … one cannot help recalling that she was the same over Nicholas. She said I could not see him again until my behaviour improved and when I did she concluded it was not having his influence that caused it. She is most unreasonable. I also overheard her making insulting remarks about Mrs Hulme while I was ringing this afternoon. I was livid. I am very glad because the Hulmes sympathise with me and it is nice to feel that adults realise what Mother is. Dr Hulme is going to do something about it I think. Why could Mother not die? Dozens of people are dying all the time, thousands, so why not Mother, and Father too."

The day after she so fervently wished her parents dead, Pauline's behaviour was exemplary and her mood unusually sweet. The turbulence had passed, even if the cause was not forgotten. She went to church and with her parents visited Rosemary at Templeton Farm. Later she cycled to Omar Khayyám's paddock and spent an hour or two giving rides to Mrs Purvis's sister's three young sons. "Omar was beautiful," she wrote. "With the children he was positively marvellous. … I enjoyed myself more than I have for years."

Although Nora had told Pauline she could not go to Ilam again until she weighed eight stone, by the following Thursday she had yielded: she could now go the weekend after next. Pauline was mystified by her mother's change of heart. "Curiouser and curiouser," she wrote in her diary. By way of further atonement, Nora bought her a nightgown and took her to see *Julius Caesar*, starring James Mason as Brutus and Marlon Brando as Mark Antony. Pauline recorded that "Him was almost too wonderful to be true. The picture did not depress me greatly as a good many Him ones do. Although I wept over it when I came to bed. However I was much pleased to see how young Him looks. That fact cheered me greatly and Him's superb physique..." She finished *The Donkey's Serenade* and began a new book called *Leander or Léandre*. There was a moment of delight when a girl asked her how long she had been out from England. "Five years," she answered.

By the end of January 1954, the Hulmes, whatever their concern about the homosexual nature of the girls' friendship, had again extended Pauline an open invitation to stay at Ilam. That Saturday, feeling they were making up for lost time, she and Juliet spent a "heavenly day" wandering around the garden, playing their records, reading each other's books, and talking about the "Saints", which gave them the giggles; they lay down on Bill Perry's bed and "simply roared".

The Saints were a private pantheon of film actors, opera singers and fictional characters they worshipped and adored—and about whom, to one degree or another, they harboured lustful thoughts. At first it was relatively simple. Strictly speaking, James Mason—Him—and Guy Rolfe—His—were Gods above the Saints.

In schematic form it looked like this:

GODS
James Mason = Him
Guy Rolfe = His

SAINTS
Mario Lanza = He, Mario or Poor Mario
Orson Welles = It or Harry Lime
Mel Ferrer = This or The Angry Man
Jussi Björling = That
Rupert of Hentzau = Who
(Charles) Boinard =?

*

Neither Juliet's novel *The Beautiful Lady in Blue*, which she wrote in school exercise books, nor Pauline's *The Donkey's Serenade* have survived. Neither seems to have been as extravagantly violent as the Borovnia-Volumnia correspondence. The title of Pauline's book came from a famous song by Hollywood singing star Allan Jones: more importantly, Mario Lanza had recorded a cover version. Bill Perry considered *The Beautiful Lady in Blue* "an innocent adventure ... the sort of thing you would expect a teenager to write". It reminded him of *The Prisoner of Zenda*. Pauline thought it "amazingly amusing and Himish". Henry Hulme also thought it marvellous. One day he stopped Len Hensley, a university colleague, in Hereford Street, fished the exercise books out of his briefcase, and made Hensley skim through them so he could share the admiration he felt for his brilliant daughter. Hilda did not share his enthusiasm, pronouncing the work "ordinary".

On Sunday, February 28, the girls made a momentous decision: they would "hurry up terrifically" the quest for Him. To go to Hollywood and introduce themselves they would need to get money and book passages. After school next day Pauline traipsed around shipping companies asking about fares and schedules. The news was not encouraging: "It looks as though we will have to make the journey in spasms. Probably going to Honolulu for some time at first."

On Wednesday the pair had another long feverish talk "mainly of ... boats and our plans for the future". The following Saturday Pauline, in a frenzy of activity, got up at six in the morning, iced a cake, peeled potatoes and shelled peas for lunch, took Wendy breakfast in bed, and then biked to Ilam. Once there she and Juliet spent hours in the garden, clearing a small grotto where they had established a graveyard of mice, birds and other small creatures. They were building a temple which they planned to sacrifice when they left on their travels, along with a record of the Donizetti aria "Una furtiva lagrima".

The first time Pauline mentioned the temple in her diary it was to be dedicated to Minerva but it became the Temple of Rafael Pan. The Archangel Raphael, protector of pilgrims and other travellers, was

Juliet's favourite angel. Artists such as Verrocchio and Perugino had depicted him as a beautiful young man with elegant wings. If Raphael were an emissary from spiritual realms, Pan was the opposite, a lascivious, rutting nature-god with the horns and hairy legs of a goat, ravisher of goddesses, nymphs and maenads, the wildly uninhibited acolytes of Bacchus. The temple symbolised the duality of the wonderful new life they dreamt about.

That evening the girls worked on *The Saints Book*, a collection of photographs and articles from magazines about their objects of adoration. With Hilda and Henry out of the house, they had an "absolutely wonderful" time together, becoming "weak with laughter".

On Tuesday night Pauline read *Rubáiyát of Omar Khayyám*, and went with Wendy and two of the boarders to *The Wicked Lady*, starring Margaret Lockwood and James Mason. Juliet was also there and they ended up sitting together.

"Him," Pauline noted approvingly, "was terrifically lustful and swore a lot" and "spent a lot of time in bed seducing and raping odd bods". She would have to develop this side of Meredith Lanyon, her leading man in *Léander or Léandre*, who was based heavily on James Mason. That night she found herself passionately making love to the side of her mattress.

To raise money for her passage to America, or at least Hawai'i, she put an advertisement in a newspaper offering Omar Khayyám for sale. On Saturday she and Juliet spent most of the day arranging the Temple of Rafael Pan, having "a positively wonderful time". She would, she wrote, "quite willingly forego having heaven in [the] afterlife if I could always have such heaven in this one".

Sunday was very different. At home with her family, Pauline polished the furniture in the lounge, then went to church. After dinner she provoked Wendy over some trifling incident. Nora flew into a rage. Pauline, she said, was not going back to school. "I don't see why I should keep a horrid child like you," she snapped. She had no wish to continue supporting her.

Pauline was delighted. School was of no interest without Juliet there; she had wanted to leave but hadn't dared ask. She would do everything she could to keep annoying her mother in case she changed her mind. Next day, to her joy, she was still not allowed to go to school. At dinner her father said she could return if she wanted but Pauline declined. She had already proposed getting a job as a governess in the country and Nora had agreed. That evening Nora's mood changed: she was, in Pauline's words, "nicer than she has been for weeks".

Two days later, on March 16, the girls went to see *Scaramouche*, a swashbuckler with Stewart Granger, Eleanor Parker, Janet Leigh and "This"—Mel Ferrer. "Absolutely superb... thoroughly divine," Pauline thought. She stayed over at Ilam. "It is a heavenly night and I feel wonderfully happy," she wrote in her diary. Next morning there was trouble at the Temple of Rafael Pan: "Some bloody son of a bachelor pulled up all our crosses. Curse the bastard." Nevertheless the girls made good progress building a four-poster bed that was an adjunct to the temple. Thoroughly exhausted, they lay down on the rustic bed in the grotto and talked and talked.

Next day Pauline finished *Leander or Léandre* and the family plus boarders at 31 Gloucester Street had a glass of wine to celebrate. On Friday she returned to Ilam to discover that Miss Stewart had telephoned Hilda Hulme, concerned to hear her daughter's friend was leaving school. Hilda tried to talk her into staying on, which Pauline found "all very flattering ... but nevertheless a bloody nuisance". When Henry and Hilda went out, the girls strolled around in Hilda's evening dresses.

On Monday there was another angry scene between Pauline and her mother: "Mother and I had a long, loud disagreement and I got absolute hell from her. ... She went into the usual ... and brought up a new series of threats. One day she will carry out all her dire threatening and she will be left without a leg to stand on." Next day Nora's rage had passed. "I decided to use the sweet and loving tactics to help her get over it," Pauline wrote in her diary. "She really is a bloody fool."

By now, Pauline and Juliet were rarely out of each other's company and were seizing every chance to go to bed together. On Thursday Pauline was allowed to go to Ilam and stay until Sunday. She delightedly recorded that Mrs Hulme was pleased to see her. On

Friday she and Juliet played recordings of *Pagliacci*, *Cavalleria Rusticana* and *Tosca* and, when Hilda, Henry and Bill Perry left to go to a film, shared a long bath. Afterwards they lay in Juliet's bed in the dark, becoming "very skittish", until the Hulmes' car came up the drive and Pauline scuttled off to her own bed.

Next day as the girls were having lunch "a rather extraordinary thing happened". "Mrs Hulme," Pauline recorded, "was standing near the door and suddenly Mr Perry half walked in and put his arm around her. She immediately said, 'Not now, the children are here' and he went bright pink and looked nervous. Deborah and I were amazed. We came to the conclusion that Mr Perry and Mrs Hulme were having an affair. All the facts tied up beautifully and his behaviour later was extremely guilty.

"Under the circumstances we may be able to catch them red-handed some time and blackmail them. This idea appeals to both of us greatly, and we spent the rest of the day discussing it. If everything goes as we hope, it should solve all our troubles."

CHAPTER 16

Serious Trouble

It seemed to Juliet and Pauline they had hit on the perfect plan to raise the money, or a good bit of it, needed for the great quest. It remained only to catch Hilda *doing it* with Bill Perry and the rest would fall into place. On Thursday Pauline went with her mother to the Civic Theatre for the Christchurch Harmonic Society's performance of Mendelssohn's *Elijah*, in which Nana Parker was singing. Next day at Ilam she and Juliet excitedly revisited their travel plans. Loath to return home, Pauline let the air out of one of her bike tyres and phoned her mother, claiming to have a puncture that would keep her there overnight. She and Juliet then went to bed together and lay talking in the dark until they heard everyone turn in; they had taken the precaution of putting a dummy in Pauline's usual bed in case anyone checked.

At one-thirty in the morning they went down to the kitchen and took a tin of spaghetti, which they ate cold in bed. They talked until five then slept for two hours, dreaming of Him. "No one suspected our midnight happenings," Pauline gloated. On Saturday she was back home when Juliet phoned to say Bill Perry had given her £50 for her horse, and could sell Omar for Pauline for £20 and get her a position for £5 a week. "We should have money coming in from all directions," Pauline wrote excitedly. She was working hard, aiming to complete her third book, *The Queen of Hearts*, before Easter.

Next day Nana Parker brought her the words of Tosti's *Good-Bye!* "They are really beautiful," Pauline wrote, "and I intend to use them in my book as much as possible." Francesco Paolo Tosti was an Italian-born composer who moved to England, was appointed singing teacher to the royal family by Queen Victoria, and knighted in 1908. His famous ballad, with febrile lyrics by George Whyte-Melville, was once a favourite drawing-room piece:

"What are we waiting for? Oh, my heart!
Kiss me straight on the brows! And part!
Again! Again! My heart! My heart!
What are we waiting for, you and I?
A pleading look—a stifled cry.
Goodbye, forever! Goodbye, forever!
Goodbye! Goodbye! Goodbye!"

Four days later Pauline went back to Ilam. She and Juliet had the house to themselves apart from Bill Perry's housekeeper. They wandered around talking about sex, the Saints, and "the matter in hand"—the quest for Him—listened to some new records of Juliet's, read Rupert Brooke poems, and after a long bath went to bed. "I pretended to go to my own room," Pauline wrote, "but of course did not. We spent most of our time in the dark making up dirty little jingles … talking most of the night, mainly about the old subject."

In the morning they took each other's photographs. For some they wore Hilda Hulme's evening dresses; for others they posed naked. Pauline had an inspiration: they would send the photographs to Hollywood and try to get into films that way! That night, after another long bath together, they went to bed early, again putting a dummy in Pauline's bed. Next day they spent hours together in Henry Hulme's bed.

They had somehow learned that the housekeeper was known to be light-fingered. "This pleased us enormously … we now shall be able to take various articles and people will naturally conclude that she is responsible. In fact she is going to be an extremely useful scapegoat." Nothing came of this as the woman was ordered to leave a few days later, although the suspicion against her was probably groundless.

On Sunday evening, back at Gloucester Street, Pauline was in a cheerful mood. *The Queen of Hearts* was going well and Juliet's and her plans for the future were progressing wonderfully. "I feel very pleased with myself on the whole ... and also [about] the future. We are so brilliantly clever!"

The ebullient mood continued. Pauline spent Easter at Ilam and on Good Friday she and Juliet practised singing. They had decided that, of the arts in which they were interested, singing was the only one they had not mastered. "We were both astoundingly good," Pauline wrote.

Juliet would go further. "Caruso ... goes from bass to second highest tenor ... We neither of us aspire to that range but Pauline to his lowest, being a contralto, and I to his highest, being a coloratura soprano. Amazing to state, we reached them! We spent at least two hours a day practising for power to hold his longest notes and keep in tune without breaks, cracks or undue sound of effort—which believe me was hard. ... For a long time I could not go through O Paradiso, which soars around for an age on top C and one or two lower. But after many failures I succeeded. ...

"My favourites, needless to say the ones I found easiest, were Caruso—anything—Gigli, "O Soave Fanciulla" and "Celeste Aida" ... Tito Schipa—anything—Gigli—anything ... Richard Tauber—anything —Schipa—a bit—Björling—rather too high usually. He is incredibly high you know. We both tried Lanza but he's awfully hard without a lot of practice. It's ridiculous I know but I can't hit a note lower than soprano or high mezzo. I just don't sound it all or go off key. Oh we try Melba, Callas or Gladys Moncrieff too but we don't like their songs so much."

On Easter Saturday Juliet had an altercation with her mother after Hilda found she had taken one of her records from Bill Perry's flat. Furious at the telling-off, the girls sat on a log in a nearby field shouting nasty remarks at passers-by on horseback. Returning home, they wrote out the Ten Commandments so they could make a point of breaking them. For the next three nights, Pauline slept in her assigned bed in the verandah room. The following Tuesday the girls went to nearby Fendalton to collect the photographs they had put in for developing. Jonty tagged along and the girls were "thoroughly rude to him ... called him all sorts of horrid things ... made an utter fool of him", Pauline boasted in her diary.

*

Pauline's plans to become, Charlotte Brontë-like, a governess in the country had come to nothing. Instead, at Nora's instigation she enrolled at Mrs Hilda Digby's Commercial School to learn shorthand typing. Nana Parker may have wished something better for her intelligent granddaughter but Nora merely wanted a child able to earn her bread and butter. Pauline herself was not averse to the idea: typing would be a useful skill for the literary career that—along with Hollywood stardom and marriage to James Mason—lay before her.

On April 23, there was a dramatic new development. After returning home from Digby's and playing her record of *Tosca*, she phoned Juliet to learn some stupendous news. The previous night Juliet had woken at two in the morning. She had gone into her mother's bedroom, and finding it empty gone downstairs to look for her. When she couldn't find her, she had crept as stealthily as she could into Bill Perry's flat. She had heard voices coming from his bedroom, crept up the stairs and waited for a little while. Then she had flung open the door and switched on the light.

Perry and her mother were in bed together drinking tea. Juliet had suppressed an hysterical urge to giggle: even though she had known what she would find, she was shaking with emotion and shock. "I suppose you want an explanation," her mother said. "Well, you see, we are in love. Your father knows all about it." They intended to live together as a threesome.

If Pauline's account of the incident is correct, Juliet had the presence of mind to remember that blackmail was the primary objective. She told her mother and Perry that she and Pauline were planning to go to America in six months. She would later say that Perry gave her £100 for entry permits. He flatly denied this but did acknowledge that Juliet "discussed the fact that she was going to blackmail me on the night she found Mrs Hulme giving me tea".

Hilda knew the situation was bad. Nancy Sutherland remembered her arriving at her house looking unusually serious. "I was busy in the kitchen but offered her a cup of tea. She leaned against the fridge and said, 'Last night Juliet walked in on Bill and me in bed, Nancy … There's going to be serious trouble.'"

Pauline rode out to Ilam. It was bucketing with rain. Henry Hulme went up to Juliet's bedroom and asked the two girls to come down for a chat. They must, he said, tell him everything about their plans for going to America. He was, Pauline wrote, both hope-giving and depressing. "We talked for a long time and Deborah and I were near tears by the time it was over. The outcome was somewhat vague. What is to be the future now? We may all be going to South Africa and Italy and dozens of other places or not at all. We none of us know where we are and a good deal depends on chance.

"Dr and Mrs Hulme are going to divorce! The shock is too great to have penetrated in my mind yet. It is so incredible. Poor Father. Mrs Hulme was sweet and Dr Hulme was absolutely kind and understanding. Poor Jonty is ill. Deborah and I spent the day soaring between hell and heaven. ... Such a huge amount has happened that we do not know where we are. Dr Hulme is the noblest and most wonderful person I have ever known of. But one thing—Deborah and I are sticking to[gether] through everything. (We sink or swim together.)"

CHAPTER 17

A Lovely Remark

H enry Hulme was having a rough time. As well as his marriage being on the rocks, he was in strife at Canterbury College. Although the previous June he had resisted efforts by some members of the college council to force him to resign, dissatisfaction with his rectorship had not abated. The school of engineering debacle was to his opponents a prime example of what was wrong with him. The school was the pride of the college, respected the world over for its excellence. Hulme's support for a rival engineering school to be developed at Auckland University was seen as an egregious betrayal of his own college. It was all too reminiscent of his treachery over the school of forestry. He had learnt nothing!

From a broader perspective, Henry had right on his side. As a member of the senate of the University of New Zealand, he considered his primary duty was to do whatever he believed would best serve the national interest and not allow himself to be subverted by parochialism. But this stance won him no friends at Canterbury.

In *A History of the University of Canterbury, 1873–1973*, an unnamed source describes Dr Hulme as "a charming conversationalist, a man with profound appreciation of music, a person of intense outflowing sympathy, a man none could really dislike". The truth was that many people disliked him greatly. He was frequently accused of running with the hare and hunting with the hounds. Neville Phillips, a young history professor, thought him unreliable and dishonest. Others commented that he was "mad as a maggot" and "round the twist". He was widely held to be a disaster as rector.

On March 3, 1954 the professorial board passed a resolution that the rector no longer had its confidence. The reason given amounted to a technical impropriety: he had disclosed a board report to some members of the college council. It was not a hanging offence but enough of a pretext. Next day Hulme wrote to the council giving his resignation with effect from January 31, 1955; this was accepted by letter on March 15. When the drama ignited by Juliet's discovery of Hilda and Bill in bed rattled the Hulme household, it had already been decided that Henry would leave New Zealand.

According to Hilda, the initial arrangement with Henry was that he would return to England in January 1955 to secure another post, while she and the children remained in New Zealand during the summer to give Juliet time to fully recover her health. That decision, she would say, changed when they learned of the girls' plan to run away together to America, where they hoped to have their books published and films made of their stories. She and her husband discussed the situation and came up with a plan. Juliet would go to South Africa to stay with Henry's sister, Ina Buyse, who ran a girls' boarding school in Johannesburg. The climate there would be beneficial. She could go on to England in early spring.

Hilda was almost certainly fudging the truth: as long as she had Juliet's passport Juliet could not run away to America or anywhere else. It is more likely she did not want her devious daughter sabotaging her romance with Bill Perry. Hilda considered Juliet inconsiderate and highly egotistical. Things would be better with her out of the way.

Pauline's moods fluctuated. She continued her studies at Digby's and in the last week of April went to *King Of The Khyber Rifles* with "absolutely joyous anticipation"; Guy Rolfe and Michael Rennie were "utterly divine" even if the heroine was "ghastly ... no saving graces". But soon afterwards, when she and Juliet had a bath together at the Riepers' house, she was depressed and "quite seriously" considered committing suicide. Life seemed not worth living and death an easy way out. On April 28 she wrote: "Anger against mother boiled up inside me, as it is she who is one of the main obstacles in my path. Suddenly a means of ridding myself of this obstacle occurred to me. If she were to die..."

The following day she and Juliet went to see *Dangerous Crossing*—advertised as "A World of Terror and Evil"—starring Jeanne Crain and the adored Michael Rennie. "I did not tell Deborah of my plan for removing Mother," Pauline wrote. "I have made no definite plans yet as the last fate I wish to meet is one in Borstal. I am trying to think of some way. I do not [want] to go to too much trouble but I want it to appear either a natural or accidental death."

Next day she talked with Juliet on the telephone for two hours and told her of her intention to murder her mother. "She is rather worried," Pauline wrote, "but does not disagree violently."

When she went to spend the weekend at Ilam more fuel was added to the fire. "Mrs Hulme came in and showed us a lovely ring Mr Perry had given her," she noted in her diary. "She made a lovely remark. She said, 'Won't it be wonderful when we are all back in England? Do you think you will like England, Gina?' I was delighted. … Deborah and I had a bath and came to bed quite early. … We did not sleep together as we were afraid Dr Hulme might come in."

On Sunday the girls had a heart-to-heart about whom they would allow to live if they could wipe out the rest of the world, made a list of their names, and added four new characters to the Saints, who were now multiplying like bacteria. In addition to He, Him, It, This (Mel Ferrer), That, His, Who and Boinard, there were now Her (Ava Gardner), Rico (Cornell Wilde), Yours (Michael Rennie), Mine, Which, Either, One, Neither, Other, Hollander, Else, Mora, Leso, He's, Julius, Christopher Robin, Wain, Hugo Did, Geanne, Hildegard, Antoinette and Julian.

A week later, on May 7, Pauline and Juliet's ardour for James Mason was further fanned by *The Man Between*. Sporting a German accent, Mason played a shady ex-Nazi scratching a living trafficking people and other profitable cargo between the east and west sectors of post-war Berlin; Hildegard Knef, a statuesque blonde to whom the ex-Nazi turned out to be married, was also one of the Saints.

Pauline raved. The film was "wonderful, beautiful, heavenly and Mine. Claire Bloom [Mason's lover in the film and in real life] was horrid but Hildegard lovely. … Him was rather bitter but hard to describe. He was different to what he had ever been before but I love him more than ever now. (Oh Him! Him! Him!) Him means so much to us I could gladly watch him forever. I could do almost anything for him." Over the next two weeks she and Juliet would go to the film four more times.

On May 8 there was a mysterious entry in Pauline's diary: "We are going to wangle it so that we can go to the Island soon. There I shall attempt to make Julian fall in love with me and persuade him to marry me. Of course his mind will have to be improved but that should not be too hard. Everything shall be wonderful." There were no clues as to the identity of Julian.

That night Juliet went to a dance given by Dr and Mrs Bennett in the Knox Church hall to celebrate the sixteenth birthday of their son, Colin. While Juliet was fox-trotting unenthusiastically with Colin Bennett and his friends, Pauline occupied herself writing letters to 20th Century Fox, James Mason, Guy Rolfe and Michael Rennie. Next day, though, in a surprising moment of realism, the girls decided their plans involving 20th Century Fox and Hollywood were too far-fetched. From that moment their main focus became to go to South Africa together, before moving to England and living with Juliet's father as soon as he found a job. After all, James Mason and Guy Rolfe were English. They surely visited England from time to time. And England was far closer to Hollywood than New Zealand was.

On Sunday Pauline went to church and then with her family and Nana Parker visited Rosemary at Templeton. Rosemary was "very happy and amusing"; Nana gave Pauline her old typewriter.

The girls' behaviour was becoming increasingly strange. Pauline dreamt that she and Juliet were imprisoned for committing a murder. After watching *Hans Christian Andersen* with Danny Kaye and Farley Granger, she said to Juliet in a very English voice, "Absolutely smashing show wasn't it?" to which Juliet replied, "Simply spiffing old girl." The effect on the people around them was "most amusing". On the way home on the bus the girls talked with thick German accents.

The following week they went to see *Mogambo*, a heady romantic drama set in Kenya. Although they loathed the hero, Clark Gable, they greatly admired his love interest, Ava Gardner. They decided they needed both Ava Gardner and Marilyn Monroe as close friends to keep them looking their best: they had been "slipping on appearances" and needed to smarten up. Inspired by Monroe, Juliet bought a bottle of hair colouring called Golden Rinse. This was quite outré: in conservative Christchurch nice girls didn't dye their hair.

On Friday, May 21, they found a new amusement. After sleeping the night together, they got out of bed on the wrong side—presumably for luck—then set out for the centre of town, where, after buying ribbons for the Saints and fawn velvet for Juliet, they began stealing from Woolworths and other shops. "It was great fun," Pauline enthused, "and we were really expert by the time we had finished." They had managed to shoplift £11 worth of goods, most of it cheap jewellery. They had nearly been caught once but had bluffed their way out of it.

On Sunday Pauline handed her mother some socks and slippers she had stolen for Rosemary. She concluded she had no conscience whatsoever. "Mother kept saying how pleased Rosemary was with the slippers and how good it was of me to buy them for her ... each time I glowed with pride and resolved to do some more shoplifting in the near future."

The following Sunday Juliet rang to say Mr Perry had suddenly taken ill. "I do hope he does not die," Pauline wrote calmly in her diary. "It would spoil everything."

Meanwhile Henry Hulme was having second thoughts about his future plans. On May 24 he wrote to the Canterbury University College council asking that his resignation be brought forward to July 31. With leave entitlements he would be free to leave New Zealand in early July.

Juliet's fate was now settled: she would be staying with her Aunt Ina in Johannesburg. What was the price of an airfare from New Zealand to South Africa, she asked Bill Perry. He thought about £150. "Good," she said. "We have only £50 or so to get. We already have nearly £100."

Pauline was determined to get her hands on the £50. On May 26, her sixteenth birthday, her parents went to *Folies Bergère*, a revue attracting full houses to the Theatre Royal, but she stayed home typing *The Donkey's Serenade* and drinking a large glass of apple wine to give herself courage: she was going to commit a burglary and felt "rather queer and jumpy".

Before going to bed she helped herself to her father's shop keys. At twelve-thirty she got up and headed towards Colombo Street, intent on opening Dennis Brothers' safe. Unfortunately a policeman was watching; there had been a spate of burglaries in central Christchurch and the police were being particularly vigilant. "At first I thought I had met a fellow criminal and that he was also intending to break in. ... I was about to go up to him ... when I realised that I hadn't and he wasn't so I didn't. I [waited] around for a while but he did not shift so I came home and spent a very restless night."

Next day she learned that "something ghastly" had happened to Juliet. Her father had been going through his mail. When she had asked him if there was anything interesting he had said, "Yes, this" and handed her an anonymous letter. The writer had seen Juliet shoplifting. Luckily Juliet had managed to convince her father it was a spiteful lie.

Despite Juliet's narrow squeak, both girls were feeling very happy about prospects for the future. Clearly Henry Hulme had assured them he would do everything he could to ensure they were not separated. "Dr Hulme really is to be relied upon," Pauline wrote in her diary. A few days later a photograph of Rudi Gopas's portrait of Hulme appeared in *The Press*. Pauline cut it out and pinned it to the wall of her bedroom.

Henry Hulme's request to bring forward the date of his resignation was accepted. He was to be given a retiring allowance of £1,126.4.0, plus a grant of £900 to meet the homeward fares of himself and his family and £150 reimbursement for money he had spent on maintenance of the rectory. Having forced him to resign, the professorial board passed a resolution expressing its appreciation of the friendly and tolerant way in which Dr Hulme had presided over it for the past five and a half years, and for his advocacy of "many forward-looking proposals, in particular those concerned with the welfare of students".

On June 3 lectures were cancelled between 10.45 and twelve noon to enable students and staff to attend an official farewell in the Great Hall. The air was ripe with hypocrisy. It was announced that Dr Hulme had accepted another appointment in England, although this was not true: he had only renewed his fellowship at Gonville and Caius. Bill Cartwright, chair of the council, spoke of Hulme's "inestimable contribution" not only to Canterbury College but to the University of New Zealand. Mrs Hulme, too, had provided excellent support with "assistance and sympathy with the individual in trouble or difficulty, in the reception of visitors to the college, in her leadership in college social activities, and in her participation in many forms

of social and community life outside the college". Dr Parton, the professorial board's deputy chairman, observed that the burden on the rector was heavy, "perhaps too heavy", and that the university would remember him as a man of friendly informality. The subtext was not lost on those in the know.

In reply, Dr Hulme said Christchurch was one of the friendliest cities he knew, and he could truly say he and his wife had more friends in Canterbury than in England. Quite likely that was true.

On June 4 Pauline and Juliet saw James Mason's new film *Prince Valiant*, a rollicking fantasy in which a young Viking prince tries to become a knight in King Arthur's Court so he can restore his exiled father to his throne. The picture was dreadful, Pauline thought, but "Him was wonderful". They were thrilled to see him wearing a beard. Pauline became even more excited with the thought that the Saints were all "greasy" and This (Mel Ferrer) "the most repulsive-looking man alive … even worse than It [Orson Welles] in revoltingness". She had discovered a new erotic stimulus.

By now the girls had become convinced they were telepathic. When Juliet phoned to tell Pauline about the anonymous letter, Pauline said she already knew. Two days later they made another momentous discovery. "We realised why … Deborah and I have such extraordinary telepathy and why people look at us the way they do and why we behave as we do," Pauline wrote in her diary. It is because we are MAD. We are both stark raving MAD. There is no doubt about it and we are thrilled by the thought."

And they were in good company. "All the cast of the Saints except Nino are mad too. This is not strange as it is probably why we love them. We have discussed it fully. Dr Hulme is MAD as MAD as a March hare."

CHAPTER 18

Hectic Nights

For Pauline and Juliet, life had taken an exciting new turn. "We felt very strange knowing how mad we are," Pauline wrote. "We realise now that we cannot be revolted. We can discuss the most unsavoury subjects (such as whether the Saints' sanitary habits are prevented by sex) during a meal." It was a licence to behave any way they liked. "I was feeling particularly mad today," Pauline boasted. "I raved quite a lot at Digby's and terrified the girl next to me."

On June 9 she and her mother had another barney. "I wished to see *Trent's Last Case* and the bloody bitch would not let me." Next day the girls had an engrossing conversation about sex. "Mrs Hulme has told Deborah a great deal about the old subject," Pauline reported. "We have discussed it fully. We know a great deal more now ... I am feeling particularly close to Deborah."

While the girls were revelling in their new-found madness and sexual knowledge and Hilda was enjoying stolen hours in the arms of Bill Perry, Henry Hulme had in mind a romance of his own. Vivien Dixon was a beautiful young English violinist with the New Zealand National Orchestra who had given violin lessons to Nancy Sutherland's daughter Jan. Whenever Vivien was in Christchurch she stayed with Nancy at Ashgrove Terrace. One evening Henry met her there and was immediately smitten. When he learnt the orchestra was playing next day in Timaru, a town ninety miles to the south, he offered to drive her. It was quite unnecessary, Vivien told him: the orchestra had a bus arranged. However, he persisted and eventually she accepted. Next day, to her embarrassment, he sent her a large bunch of flowers. She thought him a strange, colourless, rather buttoned-up man and had no romantic interest in him whatsoever.

At Henry Hulme's invitation Vivien Dixon gave several lunchtime recitals at Canterbury College. After each one he invited her back to the house at Ilam. She wondered what he had in mind and thought he might pounce; to her relief he never did. On each occasion Hilda was absent. Henry told her he and his wife were going to divorce. It was Hilda who wanted the divorce, he said, but he seemed quite happy about it, and relaxed about Hilda's affair with Perry, perhaps grateful to Perry for taking his wife off his hands. He asked Vivien to go back to England with him. She refused. It was a ridiculous proposition.

On Friday Pauline completed her shorthand-typing course at Digby's and immediately headed to Ilam. That evening, their heads full of Hilda's stimulating sex talk, she and Juliet went to see *Trent's Last Case*. In the film a journalist suspects the death of a tycoon is a murder; Orson Welles plays the tycoon in a series of flashbacks. Although the actor had long been an anointed Saint, Pauline had never before seen him on the screen.

Welles' appearance ignited in the girls a craving different from their passion for such personifications of evil as Count Rupert of Hentzau, Field Marshal Rommel and the traitorous valet in *5 Fingers*. "Deborah had always told me how hideous he was and I had believed her, though from his photos he did not look too bad. It [Welles] is appalling. He is dreadful. I have never in my life seen anything in the same category of hideousness but I adore him …. We returned home and talked for some time about It, getting ourselves more and more excited. Eventually we enacted how each Saint would make love in bed, only doing the first seven as it was 7.30 a.m. by then. We felt exhausted and very satisfied then slept for about an hour."

In the morning Juliet rose to sit for Rudi Gopas, who was painting her portrait. That evening she and Pauline went to bed early and spent the night "very hectically", almost "getting through" all the Saints. "We definitely are mad," Pauline wrote happily, "but very pleasingly so."

On Sunday morning two new Saints of unknown origin, "Onward Heel" and "Buster", entered the canon and the girls enjoyed "an amusing discussion about God, Christ and the Holy Ghost". Pauline phoned her mother, falsely claiming she had found a job and would be starting the following week. Delighted to hear this, Nora agreed to let her stay at Ilam until the following Sunday. The girls were ecstatic. That night, by Pauline's account, they went to bed very excited and spent a hectic night going through the Saints. "It was Wonderful! Heavenly! Beautiful! and Ours! We felt very satisfied indeed. We have now learned the peace of the thing called Bliss, the joy of the thing called Sin."

On Monday they woke at ten, exhausted. There was more discussion of Saints; Robert Wagner, the hero of *Prince Valiant*, and Johnny Weissmuller, better known as Tarzan, were added to the list. And there was some good news. To indulge Juliet, Dr Hulme was taking Omar Khayyám off Pauline's hands for £15. He had proved himself a better man by far than Mr bloody Perry, who had promised to find a buyer at £20 and then reneged.

That night they slept like tops and next day, after helping Hilda, went to see *All The Brothers Were Valiant* ("The Turmoil of the South Seas!") with Robert Taylor, Stewart Granger and Ann Blythe at the Majestic in Manchester Street. In the evening they attended a recital at the Civic Theatre by Jan Smeterlin, a Polish-born maestro considered the greatest living interpreter of Chopin.

Tuesday was another hectic night. "We only did ten Saints altogether but we did them thoroughly ... I prefer doing longer ones ... We enjoyed ourselves greatly and intend to do so again. We did not get to sleep until 5.30 a.m."

The girls were becoming increasingly manic. On Wednesday they threw out eight Saints and had "several brilliant ideas". They would each write an opera—these could easily be staged at Covent Garden when they were living in England—and then produce their own films. They discussed how they would "moider all the odd wives who get in our way".

This seems to have been in jest: "We planned our various moiders," Pauline wrote in her diary, "and talked seriously as well." But by Saturday the talk was deadly serious. "Our main idea for the day was to moider Mother," Pauline recorded. "This notion is not a new one but this time it is a definite plan which we intend to carry out. We have worked it out carefully and are both thrilled by the idea. Naturally we feel a trifle nervous but the pleasure of anticipation is great. I shall not write this plan down as I shall write it up when we carry it out (I hope)."

That night they burnt most of their film books. Next morning, after Juliet had again sat for Rudi Gopas, they discussed the plan further. "Peculiarly enough," Pauline wrote, "I have no conscience (or is it peculiar, we are so mad)."

On Sunday afternoon, after Pauline had been at Ilam for over a week, Bert, Nora and Wendy collected her and the family drove to Templeton to visit Rosemary. Later that evening, Bert Rieper would recall, Pauline sat in front of the fire writing a novel; actually it was the libretto of her new opera. "She seemed much brighter in the house than she had been before she left for Ilam," he said. "She was much nicer to us than she had been for a long time."

CHAPTER 19

To Be Together Forever

Pauline wished her mother dead. She had wanted to kill the bloody bitch for ages. Her mother had it coming to her for her ill humour, her nagging, her stupidity, her small-mindedness. Pauline would never forget the unhappiness of her childhood, everything that had happened to her. The way she had been double-crossed over Nicholas was unforgivable: her mother had promised she could see him again if she were good, but when she was good she had backtracked. And there was the way she repeatedly threatened her with not being able to see Deborah again if she didn't put on weight, or didn't do this or didn't do that. She had not forgotten, either, the time in February, the insulting remarks she had made about Deborah's mother.

From the start of the girls' friendship Juliet had been the source of almost all their peculiar ideas and Pauline her handmaiden, but after Juliet came home from the sanatorium and the relationship became more sexualised this had changed: Juliet had come to need Pauline every bit as much as Pauline needed her, perhaps more. Hilda Hulme would say Pauline was one of the few people Juliet ever treated as an equal. Bill Perry noticed that whenever Pauline left Ilam to return home Juliet would become ill and stay in bed for a day or two. When she recovered she would demand Hilda's constant attention. This was why Pauline's presence at Ilam was so willingly tolerated: it was a welcome diversion.

Now it was Pauline who had come up with the plan to kill Nora Rieper. When she revealed it, Juliet had had some reservations but soon agreed. If Gina were prepared to commit murder, how could she,

Deborah, be so ignoble and weak-kneed as to stand aside and not take part? What was it anyway to extinguish the life of an unhappy woman whose existence was displeasing to Gina? By what right did such a woman continue to live? Diello wouldn't hesitate to do what was necessary. Nor would Field Marshal Rommel, Rupert of Hentzau, Prince John, or anyone else of true worth. Their deed would prove they were alive—not, like the rest of humanity, ruled by a cowardly voice that always put caution first.

Juliet's acquiescence with the murder plan came at the time Hilda Hulme made her "lovely remark", encouraging Pauline to think she might accompany Juliet to South Africa and afterwards to England ("Do you think you will like England, Gina?"). Next day Henry Hulme went a step further. As he told Vivien Dixon, he offered to pay Pauline's fare to South Africa.

Dr Bennett would attest that on May 8 Hulme again consulted him about the girls' relationship. May 8 was a Saturday, the day of Colin Bennett's birthday dance. Hulme, who attended the dance, had clearly seized the opportunity to chat with the doctor, seeking reassurance that the girls would grow out of the homosexual phase. Next day he told Pauline he would write to her mother and ask permission for her to go overseas with them.

It is highly unlikely Henry did write to Nora Rieper. His game was to mollify Juliet by appearing to do everything possible to keep the two together while knowing it was not going to happen. Playing both ends against the middle, stringing people along with false promises and hopes—that was Hulme's style, as his colleagues at Canterbury University College would attest. He knew Nora would never agree to her daughter leaving the country. He had already told her he and Juliet were leaving New Zealand in three weeks. He knew how delighted she was that the friendship would soon be coming to an end. She and Bert were counting the days until he and Juliet sailed for South Africa.

Hilda was also stringing the girls along. In her initial statement to the crown solicitor after the murder, she said it was apparent the two girls were determined not to be separated—"They tried to induce us to allow Pauline to go to South Africa with Juliet." Later she claimed she and Henry were in no way encouraging. "Juliet asked if it would be possible for Pauline to go with her and we said it would be right out of the question. Both girls were made to realise that Pauline would not accompany Juliet. That is what we understood—we made it plain to them."

Clearly they had done nothing of the sort. If they *had* made it plain that Pauline could not, under any circumstances, go to South Africa, Nora Rieper would not have been put in the position of appearing to be the chief, if not the sole, obstacle to the girls being together. Juliet herself would years later confirm that her father had offered to take Pauline with them.

Time was running out. Juliet and Henry were to leave Christchurch on July 3 for Wellington, where they would begin the first leg of the journey on the *Wanganella*, bound for Australia. It is unlikely Pauline directly asked her mother if she could leave New Zealand with them: she knew there was no chance she would agree. She also knew that, although Dr Hulme had declared himself willing to pay for her passage, he would take her only with her mother's consent— and as a practical matter she would need her parents' consent to get a passport. She must have believed, or hoped, she had a good chance of getting her way with her father—if he were her only surviving parent. By June 19, murdering Pauline's mother had become "a definite plan".

Seven weeks earlier, when Pauline had first mooted the idea, she had not wanted to go to too much trouble: the death should appear natural or an accident. The girls now decided it would be an "accident". They would persuade Pauline's mother to go for an outing with them to Victoria Park, a safe distance from the city. They would take the Cashmere Hills bus to the Sign of the Takahe and from there walk up to the park. They would then suggest a walk down a quiet track that Pauline remembered from a visit six months earlier. Pauline would have a sandbag in her shoulder bag. Juliet would go on ahead, drop a pink stone on the track, and point this out to Pauline's mother. While Mrs Rieper was bending down looking at the stone, Pauline would whack her over the back of the head with the sandbag and she would collapse, dead. They would push her off the track so it would look as if she had fallen, banged her head and died. They would rush up the track and call for help, acting shocked and distressed.

It was a fairly simple plan. They thought they had an even chance of getting away with it. If it didn't work it wouldn't be the end of the world. As minors, they wouldn't hang. Probably they would get only six or seven years in jail, maybe less time in the loony bin if they could convince people they were insane, but they would still be together. That was the important thing. Pauline would have the great satisfaction of having avenged all her mother's miserable misdeeds and unpleasantness, but more than that the world would know of her wonderful, beautiful friendship with Juliet Hulme, who had been prepared to commit murder with her, for her, so they could be together. Forever.

The murder was to take place on Tuesday—June 22. It was vital Pauline did not have a row with her mother in the meantime or she might refuse to go with them. As Bert reported, on Sunday night the Rieper household was a model of harmony and tranquillity. On Monday Pauline, again employing the sweet and loving tactics, energetically helped her mother with housework and chatted to her cheerfully. When the moment seemed right, she suggested they go with Juliet the following afternoon for a picnic in Victoria Park. It was a lovely idea, Nora thought, but she would first have to give Father and Wendy their midday dinner. The three of them could go to the park after that.

When Juliet phoned, Pauline was able to report that everything was going according to plan. Going over the details again, they decided to use a brick in a stocking instead of a sandbag: a blow with a hard object would make it seem more as though Pauline's mother had fallen down a bank and banged her head on a rock. Juliet would bring a half-brick from home, and also the pink stone, removed from an old brooch: this artistic touch and attention to detail was typical of Juliet. Pauline, meantime, would find one of her old school stockings. Juliet told her mother that Mrs Rieper had invited her to lunch the next day, and afterwards was going to take Pauline and her for a walk in Victoria Park. Hilda was pleased to give her permission.

Bert noticed that when he arrived home for lunch his wife was feeling very happy about her daughter: "She had been working so well and had talked such a lot to her. ... my daughter seemed much happier about the house." Pauline had been discussing the Saints with her mother, thinking it would be interesting to have her opinion of them.

In the afternoon she washed her hair and she and Juliet went to a two o'clock film at the Regent in Cathedral Square. One of their former classmates from Girls' High saw them outside the Avon Theatre in Worcester Street, just around the corner from the Regent, at about four-fifteen and chatted to them. They were waiting for a bus or tram to take Juliet home to Ilam. The discussion was brief but friendly. The classmate remembered their manner as "quite normal", not hyped up or giving any indication they were sharing a tremendous secret.

Pauline went to bed that night at eight forty-five. As usual she wrote up her diary. "I feel very keyed up as though I were planning a surprise party. Mother has fallen in with everything beautifully and the happy event is to take place tomorrow afternoon. So next time I write in this diary Mother will be dead. How odd yet how pleasing..."

The next morning, Tuesday, June 22, she wrote her diary while still in bed, carefully heading the page in fancy writing "The Day of the Happy Event". "I am writing a little of this up on the morning before the death. I felt very excited and 'The night before Christmas-ish' last night. I did not have pleasant dreams though. I am about to rise!"

That morning Juliet Hulme picked up a half-brick from a pile of old bricks beside the garage at Ilam, wrapped it neatly in newspaper and put it in her shoulder bag. To Bill Perry she seemed "very gay" as she left the house. Her mother noticed she was radiantly happy and very calm—"if anything more affectionate than usual".

At the Riepers' house, while Bert was pottering in his vegetable garden and Nora was getting ready to serve dinner, the two girls went to Pauline's bedroom, removed the half-brick from Juliet's bag, slipped it into the foot of one of Pauline's old school-regulation lisle stockings, and tied a knot at the ankle to hold it in place. They then put the weapon into Pauline's bag.

At the lunch table Juliet and Pauline were in sparkling form. The day was pleasant; by one o'clock the temperature was 63.6 degrees Fahrenheit. The warm and balmy weather was so unusual for the year's shortest day that the *Christchurch Star-Sun* would say it was suggestive of late spring or summer "although trees were bare and lawns were damp".

All had gone well. In the tea kiosk, the girls quietly and pensively ate buns and cakes and sipped soft drink as Mrs Rieper chatted to the woman in charge. Just before three o'clock, the three of them set off from the kiosk. As they descended the zigzagging bush track, Pauline took the lead, with Nora in the middle and Juliet walking behind.

As the foliage grew denser, the path became muddy underfoot. A quarter of a mile down the track they crossed a small rickety wooden bridge. Nora decided she had had enough and would go no further. The girls walked on a short way, perhaps for a last-minute conference, before turning back and rejoining her.

The time had come. The three of them seemed to be miles from any other sign of human existence. Juliet announced she was going on ahead a bit. Pauline walked behind Nora, intently fumbling at the buckle of her shoulder bag. When Juliet got far enough ahead to let Pauline get ready, she dropped the pink stone on the track and called for Pauline and Mrs Rieper to come and see what she had found. As Nora squatted down to look at the stone, Pauline, coming from behind, swung the brick as hard as she could at her mother's skull. Nora yelled and instinctively covered her head with her hands. She was now fighting for her life.

Pauline bashed away mercilessly but her mother was slow to go down. She and Juliet forced her to the ground. Juliet grabbed the loaded stocking from Pauline and landed further furious blows on Nora's head. Blood was spraying everywhere. Her resistance was weakening.

The stocking broke. Nora was now lying face upwards, making a terrible noise. Juliet kneeled, gripped her around the throat and held her head against the ground while Pauline, grasping the half-brick in her hand, hammered her again and again and again—on the forehead, the temples, wherever she could land a blow. Nora writhed and twisted, then twitched convulsively. They tried to drag her to a place where they could roll her down a bank but she was already a dead weight. It was all they could do to shift her a few feet. She was still gurgling blood as they left and raced back up to the kiosk.

The killing had been far messier than they had imagined: in films one good whack on the head and a person was dead as a dodo. But they kept their wits about them. Juliet later boasted that her hysteria and Pauline's appearance of shock were part of the plan, drawing on their great acting skills. Perhaps it was true. When Pauline groaned theatrically in Agnes Ritchie's presence "Mummy! She's dead!" it was unlikely she was bemoaning her mother's loss. It is perfectly believable that after Agnes Ritchie had brought them towels and left them alone to clean themselves up, Juliet said, "Oh dear, isn't she *nice*?" and the girls collapsed in a fit of giggles. It was *so funny*!

Colin Pearson, the pathologist, made a count. There were forty-five external injuries to the deceased. Some of the twenty-four lacerated wounds to the face and scalp had penetrated to the bone. There were extensive fractures to the front part of the skull. The majority of the head wounds were serious. "It would not take many of them, only a few, to produce unconsciousness," Pearson reported. That was a morsel of comfort to those who hated to think of Nora Rieper suffering. With the woman's convulsive spasms and gurgling noises it would have been impossible for the girls to know exactly when death occurred. They had bashed her a good twenty or thirty times.

CHAPTER 20

No Ordinary Crime

The arrest of Juliet Hulme and Pauline Parker for murder caused enormous excitement. The shock waves radiated from Christchurch to the extremities of New Zealand, across the Tasman to Australia and on to England, where people who knew the Hulmes heard the news in disbelief. New Zealand was a law-abiding country and murder of any kind was a major event. In the early 1950s there were only two or three a year, and convicted murderers became household names. Women who killed were rarities. As for teenage girls, matricide—it was unheard of. That they were educated girls, Girls' High girls, schoolgirls until just a few months before, and one of them a very attractive girl from a well-known family, added to the furore. At Christchurch Girls' High a stunned Miss Stewart convened an assembly and announced a new rule: no girl at any time was to speak to any newspaper reporter about "a certain matter". Serious consequences would, she said, befall anyone who as much as gave the newspapers a class photograph showing the two girls.

The international press quickly realised this was a crime well out of the ordinary. On June 24 *The Times* and *Daily Mail* of London and *The Sydney Morning Herald* ran reports from Reuters, noting that the father of one of the accused had been Britain's director of naval operational research during the war. Next day the *Manchester Guardian* reported that Juliet Marion Hulme had been charged with murdering the mother of one of her school friends and that her father, Dr Henry Rainsford Hulme, who had recently resigned as rector of Canterbury University College, was a former lecturer at Liverpool University and had held the posts of chief assistant at the

Royal Observatory, Greenwich, and scientific adviser to the Air Ministry in London.

On June 25 Henry Hulme telephoned Vivien Dixon in Wellington. "You've probably already heard but Juliet and Pauline killed Pauline's mother with a brick," he told her. The way he said it Vivien thought it was some kind of strange joke. When he insisted it was true she still didn't believe him. He didn't sound shocked or upset, she remembered, just spoke in a matter-of-fact voice. "Look at the paper," he said. "It's in the paper."

When she spoke to him again a couple of days later he told her Bill Perry had been marvellous, taken charge of everything. Henry was sure Juliet would be convicted, although there was going to be a plea of insanity. He was going back to England with Jonty to get the boy out of it. He was being shunned by everyone in Christchurch. He had just been to the post office and no one spoke to him. They all turned away and ignored him. He asked her if she would visit Juliet in prison. She agreed, although she had never met her.

On July 1, the day Pauline and Juliet were to be brought before Rex Abernethy S.M. at the Christchurch Magistrate's Court, some three hundred people—mostly women—queued up outside the court to get a look at them. They were at the wrong entrance. The No. 1 courtroom normally used for remand hearings was under renovation and the prisoners were delivered by police patrol car to a smaller courtroom entered from Armagh Street. Rex Abernethy had worked closely with Hilda Hulme on the Marriage Guidance Council: it is likely the occasion was stage-managed to minimise her embarrassment. When the girls were driven away a minute or two later, further remanded in custody, the crowd was still hanging around the wrong door.

Bert Rieper, despite being in as miserable a situation as a man could ever be, did not hesitate to organise legal representation for Pauline. He contacted the only lawyer he knew, Eric Cleland of G.W.C. Smithson, Cleland and Wicks: Nora had once been Cleland's secretary. Cleland passed him on to the firm's court man, Jimmy Wicks. Wicks, knowing murder was beyond his expertise, engaged Alec Haslam, an irascible but erudite barrister who practised on his own and often acted as leading counsel.

Haslam was a square-jawed, fit, energetic man. He had been a Rhodes Scholar at Oriel College, Oxford, where he had rowed in the college eight and distinguished himself as a distance runner while gaining a doctorate of philosophy. A widely respected lawyer, he had lectured part-time at Canterbury's law faculty and been president of the Canterbury District Law Society. It was rumoured he would not decline an appointment to the Supreme Court if it were offered.

Haslam moved swiftly. On June 24—less than thirty-six hours after the murder—he had his close friend Dr Francis Bennett, also a friend of the Hulmes, interview Pauline and Juliet at the Central Police Station.

The Hulmes, meanwhile, engaged their friend Terence Arbuthnot Gresson. A partner in the firm Wynn Williams, Gresson, Reid and McClelland, Gresson had a legal pedigree second to none. His great-grandfather, Henry Barnes Gresson, had been Christchurch's first resident judge. His father, Maurice Gresson, had been a leader of the profession in the city, and his uncle, Sir Kenneth Gresson, was a judge of the Supreme Court.

Gresson was a product of two private schools, Medbury and Christ's College. At Christ's he had excelled at tennis and squash racquets and become a member of the First XV and captain of athletics. He had gone on to Gonville and Caius College at Cambridge, where he was a contemporary of Henry Hulme. While a member of both the Cambridge and British Universities' athletics teams—a photograph of him standing with Jack Lovelock at the 1934 Oxford-Cambridge athletics meeting was always on display in his office—he had found time to take an honours degree in the Law Tripos. He had been called to the bar at Inner Temple in 1935 and returned to New Zealand the following year.

Now, at the age of forty, Gresson was, in the words of one of his former clerks, the complete aristocrat, urbane and somewhat arrogant but a delightful companion. He spoke with a BBC accent and on the streets of Christchurch seemed dandified, with hair longer than was usual and a large signet ring on the little finger of his left hand. He often sported the old-fashioned rig of striped trousers, black worsted coat and waistcoat favoured by English barristers. A racehorse owner and breeder of dogs, he was on the committee of the Canterbury Jockey Club, the holy of holies.

Although by this stage of his career Gresson rarely did more than half a dozen trials a year, he was known for his polite but highly effective cross-examinations. If he seemed indolent at times, he was capable of bouts of intense industry, turning out screeds of notes in tiny neat handwriting. He took the brief to defend Juliet Hume for the not insubstantial fee of £500.

Gresson, not a great one for visiting criminal clients in police stations or urine-scented prison cells, was fortunate to have an outstandingly capable junior partner to do the legwork. Educated at Christ's College on a scholarship, Brian McClelland, known to his friends as "Clicks", would become one of the most persuasive jury advocates ever to practise in New Zealand, due in large measure to his rare ability to empathise with ordinary working men and win them to his cause with humour that was often caustic. His slender, almost frail appearance belied hard years in the North Atlantic with the Royal Navy. His rather prominent liquid brown eyes would inspire Juliet to nickname him Bambi.

When Gresson and McClelland read Juliet's written confession they realised they couldn't move a yard on the facts. Cursing the unfathomable stupidity of the Hulmes in allowing their daughter to make a statement to the police without first seeking legal advice, they resigned themselves to presenting, if it were possible, a defence of insanity under section 43 of the Crimes Act, 1908.

In New Zealand anyone found not guilty of murder (or any other crime) by reason of insanity was, and still is, detained indefinitely in a mental institution. Accused persons facing the death penalty not unnaturally regarded this as an attractive alternative. But this was not the case here. As Juliet Hulme and Pauline Parker were under the age of eighteen, if found guilty of murder they would be sentenced to imprisonment pending Her Majesty's pleasure—in other words, until the authorities decided to release them. Most people, given a choice, would have preferred this to indefinite detention in a mental institution, outside the parole system and in conditions often greatly worse than those in prison.

Henry and Hilda Hulme were, however, anxious that the lawyers strive for a verdict of insanity. For Hilda it was a matter of face. If it could be established that her daughter had helped kill Nora Rieper only because she was suffering from a mental illness, that would be preferable to people thinking she and Henry had raised an evil brat. Gresson advised Hilda and Henry to retain Reginald Medlicott, a brilliant psychiatrist who was medical superintendent of Ashburn Hall, a private institution in Dunedin. After winning a Rockefeller Fellowship in 1949, Medlicott had pursued advanced studies at Case Western Reserve University in Cleveland and got to know many of the leaders of American psychiatry. He would come to be recognised as the father of modern psychiatry in New Zealand. Tall and stylish, with a slight stammer and a penchant for bow ties, he loved classical music, sports cars and fine brandy. If there was a weakness in his curriculum vitae, it was his limited experience appearing as an expert witness in court.

Medlicott's wife Nan, according to everyone who knew her, was a darling, as adorable as she was beautiful. She had been on stage with the J.C. Williamson theatre company, and at the superintendent's house at Ashburn Hall she and Medlicott presided over a salon that attracted Dunedin's leading artists, intellectuals and visiting theatrical personalities. When Rudi Gopas and his first wife Natasha lived in the city they had been among the regulars.

Accompanied by Nan, Medlicott spent the weekend of June 27 to 28 in Christchurch, interviewing Juliet and Pauline separately on both Saturday and Sunday. He and Nan also visited the Hulmes at Ilam. Medlicott found Henry Hulme two-dimensional and felt he didn't grasp anything. Nan, for her part, was appalled by his stiff-upper-lip demeanour. Playing the perfect host, Hulme invited her to sit by the fire as if nothing had happened. His manners even extended to Bill Perry: Medlicott was surprised when he excused himself and went to get a glass of bicarbonate of soda for his wife's lover.

Henry Hulme left for Wellington on July 3, accompanied by his son, Jonty. Although the murder had been the talk of Christchurch for a week, ten-year-old Jonty had not the faintest idea his sister had been arrested. It had been possible to keep him in this state of ignorance only because he had been in isolation in the sickbay at Medbury School, suffering from chickenpox. He had spent the long days teaching his only fellow sufferer, a boy named Forbes Mackenzie, to play chess.

In Wellington Henry Hulme was looked after by Clarence Beeby, the country's director of education. While Beeby's nineteen-year-old son Christopher took Jonty to the zoo and for a ride up the city's cable car, Hulme conferred with Sam Barnett, the secretary for justice. He was, he told Barnett, quite sure the girls would be convicted. Barnett promised to help all he could and Hulme said he would return to New Zealand immediately if it might assist. He thought he had a friend and ally in Barnett. He could not have been more wrong.

On the *Wanganella* bound for Australia, Henry and Jonty occupied themselves playing deck games. When they reached Sydney, Henry bought the latest available works on nuclear physics to get himself up to speed: he was already thinking about job prospects in England. At their next stop, Adelaide, where the pair were to board the P&O liner *Himalaya*, the *Wanganella* was besieged by reporters and Hulme, unable to delay doing so any longer, finally told Jonty about Juliet.

The Australian journalists demanded to know how any decent father could leave New Zealand while his daughter was facing a murder charge. "The world must just consider me an unnatural father," Hulme was reported as saying. A photograph of him, with a sickly grin on his face, was widely published.

Brian McClelland condemned Hulme as "a weak, gutless sod" for leaving New Zealand, and refused even to give him credit for his war work. "All he did was make sure the wine was served at the right temperature," he would remark. But the decision was not Henry's alone: Hilda wanted him out of the way. The most unwished-for publicity would soon be filling the newspapers. Henry needed to find a job in England as soon as possible and Jonty needed to be settled in a decent little prep school.

*

Even before Henry Hulme's departure, all sorts of rumours that could only have seeped out of Central Police Station were circulating in Christchurch and further afield. The two girls were lesbians. They had written bloodthirsty novels and made plans to become prostitutes. They had acted out perverted sexual fantasies under the rector's roof in the big house at Ilam. The conspicuous house, with its park-like gardens, became the object of intense curiosity.

Not only was Pauline—"the one from the fish shop" as she was often unkindly described—a lesbian, it was said, but before she was sixteen she was being done over by at least one of her parents' boarders and students from Ceylon, black as your hat. Furthermore, her parents were not married. They had been living in sin for over twenty years! And plenty were willing to believe what was being said about Henry and Hilda Hulme and Bill Perry. They lived together in a *ménage à trois*, three of them sharing a bed. Even the vicar's wife Mrs Norris believed that. It would be hard to imagine a gamier hotpot of fact and fiction.

CHAPTER 21

The Only Possible Defence

In all Dr Reg Medlicott's considerable experience he had never come across a pair like Juliet Hulme and Pauline Rieper. Neither showed the slightest remorse for the death of Honorah Rieper. On the contrary, their mood was jubilant: they had set about the murder with joyous abandon and now exalted in what they saw as their brilliant success.

Their arrogance and conceit were "quite out of normal proportions". They did not accept Medlicott as their intellectual equal and their contempt was never far from the surface. At times they were openly hostile and abusive, and even if the abuse was puerile their hostility could be venomous. When he raised with Pauline the likelihood that she would be separated from Juliet, whether in prison or a mental institution, she glared at him menacingly and seemed about to throw an inkwell at him. When the object was taken away by a guard, she jeered unpleasantly, "You're not worth it!"

Another time she called him "an irritating fool... displeasing to look at". He had, she said, "an irritating way of speaking". She hoped a bomb would land on New Zealand with him right under it. Once, after he completed a physical examination, she shouted, "I hope you break your flaming neck!" He had to struggle to check himself from reacting.

Medlicott found Juliet a little more sophisticated and less vituperative, but just as challenging to his professional detachment. Once she admonished him for failing to speak clearly. On another occasion, when he refused to be drawn into an argument about religion, she sneered schoolmarmishly, "You do *think*, don't you?"

Dr Francis Bennett, too, was shocked that neither girl showed any contrition for Nora Rieper's death. "There's nothing in death," Juliet said loftily. "After all, she wasn't a very happy woman. The day we killed her I think she knew beforehand what was going to happen and didn't seem to bear any grudge." Asked if she had any regrets she replied, "None whatever. ... Of course we did not want my family to get involved in this but we have both been terribly happy since it happened, so it has all been a blessing in disguise."

Pauline, likewise, was sorry for the trouble she had brought the Hulme household but had no regrets about her mother. She would willingly kill her again if she were a threat to her relationship with Juliet. Juliet went even further: not only was Mrs Rieper's murder justified, but so would be the murder of anybody else who threatened their friendship.

Bennett was inclined to accept Juliet's assertion that her hysteria and Pauline's appearance of shock at the tearooms and later at Ilam had been an act. If two young girls had really suffered a sudden horrifying emotional experience there would usually be some blunting of memory, even merciful amnesia, but there was none of this. When he told Juliet he had worked out how they probably did the murder, she interposed quite brightly, "Well, would you like me to tell you how we did it?" Out came every detail. She remembered everything and was more than happy to tell him.

Reg Medlicott, for his part, was not sure whether the girls had displayed a normal emotional response after the murder, but he certainly doubted that normal girls would have asked for and eaten a meal so soon after such a brutal and bloody incident.

After interviewing Juliet and Pauline, Medlicott questioned the Hulmes and Bert Rieper and conferred with Francis Bennett. He took Pauline's 1953 diary and a copy of *The Donkey's Serenade* back to Dunedin to read, as well as a large quantity of Juliet's writing, including her poetry, some of the Borovnia-Volumnia correspondence, and part of her second book.

The following weekend he returned to Christchurch, where he studied the transcript of Pauline Parker's 1954 diary prepared by the police, and talked again to Hilda Hulme and Bert Rieper, and for the first time to Bill Perry, Pauline's sister Wendy, her grandmother Amy Parker, and a teacher at Christchurch Girls' High. Again he twice interviewed Juliet and Pauline separately. After the second prison visit Medlicott called on his friend David Livingstone, a Christchurch psychiatrist. Ashen-faced, he asked for a large whisky. He had, he told Livingstone, never encountered such pure evil as he had in those two girls.

Medlicott was now ready with a diagnosis that might support a defence of insanity. It was launched at a meeting in Terence and Eleanor Gresson's Fendalton house, down a long drive opposite the fashionable St Barnabas Anglican Church. Terence Gresson, Brian McClelland, Alec Haslam and Jimmy Wicks sat around the Georgian dining table with Medlicott and Bennett.

It was decided at the outset that the only possible chance of a successful defence would be for the lawyers and psychiatric experts acting for Juliet to collaborate with Pauline's team. As Pauline had forecast in her diary on April 25, "We sink or swim together." It was on this understanding that Bennett and Medlicott had each interviewed both girls and swapped notes freely.

Because of the written confessions the girls had made, insanity was the only possible defence. To put the psychiatric diagnosis into context, Gresson summarised section 43(2) of the Crimes Act. No person would be convicted of an offence, he reminded them, by reason of an act done when labouring under natural imbecility—which did not apply here—or a disease of the mind to such extent that the person was incapable of understanding the nature and quality of the act or knowing the act was wrong. Under section 43(1) every person tried for a crime was presumed to be sane, so the onus of proving insanity rested with the accused. Proof was judged according to the civil standard: not "beyond reasonable doubt" but "more probable than not".

The gate was a narrow one. The lawyers could not possibly call Juliet or Pauline as witnesses. There was no legal obstacle to either girl giving evidence, but their rudeness, their arrogance and conceit, their abusiveness—which Medlicott and Bennett had recently experienced—

would alienate the jury. The fact they crowed about having killed Mrs Rieper would appall anyone who had to listen to them.

It was a difficult problem. Juliet loved the limelight and was so convinced of her own brilliance she believed she could not fail to be a wonderful witness. Brian McClelland couldn't tell her she would be dreadful. He would have to persuade her gently that it was far better to let her mother and Bill Perry do the talking on her behalf.

CHAPTER 22

A Crime in a Million

O n July 16 Juliet Hulme and Pauline Parker were committed
for trial by jury in the Supreme Court of New Zealand. It
had been conclusively established that Herbert and Honorah
Rieper had never legally married, so from now on both mother and
daughter would suffer the indignity of being officially known by
Nora's unmarried name.

Evidence taken from Agnes and Kenneth Ritchie, Harold Keys, Dr
Donald Walker, Sergeant Robert Hope, Constable Audrey Griffiths,
Herbert Rieper, Hilda Hulme and Walter Andrew Bowman Perry had
been presented in deposition form. Statements taken from the girls
had been presented by Senior Detective Brown and Detective
Sergeant Tate.

Juliet had painted a dramatic picture. "On the way back I was
walking in front and was expecting Mrs Rieper to be attacked. I
heard noises behind me. It was loud conversation in anger. I saw Mrs
Rieper in a sort of squatting position. They were quarrelling. I went
back. I saw Pauline hit Mrs Rieper with the brick in the stocking. I
took the stocking and hit her too. I was terrified. I thought that one
of them had to die. I wanted to help Pauline. It was terrible. Mrs
Rieper moved convulsively. We both held her. She was still when we
left her. The brick had come out of the stocking with the force of the
blows…"

At last the press had some facts to get their teeth into. The
committal hearing was fully reported in *The Times*, *The Manchester
Guardian* and *The Sydney Morning Herald*. Even *Time* ran a short
piece, although the writer had a shaky grasp of the *mise en scène*: "One

day, three weeks ago, Pauline and Juliet, like many other fashionable New Zealanders, sat taking tea with Pauline's mother at a restaurant in lofty Victoria Park..."

The Manchester Guardian reported that gasps had arisen in the crowded court when Senior Detective Macdonald Brown read out a few extracts from a diary found in Pauline's bedroom. "Why could mother not die?" Pauline had written. "Dozens of people are dying all the time, thousands ... Anger against mother boiled up inside me as it is she who is one of the main obstacles in my path ... I want it to appear either a natural or accidental death ... The pleasure of anticipation is great."

The London *Daily Mail* reported that during the seven and a half hours the girls were in court they "giggled, whispered, yawned and scribbled notes". *The Sydney Morning Herald* noticed that they smiled and whispered together unconcernedly, and twice had to be rebuked by a police matron. The matron told a reporter from Sydney's *Sun-Herald* that they found it "all very boring".

Christchurch Prison was in the countryside at Paparua, about ten miles from Christchurch, and close to Templeton Farm where Rosemary Rieper lived. While Pauline and Juliet awaited their trial they lived in the women's section, a modern bungalow-style facility housing seven or eight prisoners. Kept apart from the other prisoners, they were reported by the *Sun-Herald* to spend much of their time on the verandah. Free to write, they wrote voluminously, and were allowed to listen to classical music for an hour each morning and afternoon. "They are very happy together and seem completely unconcerned at the seriousness of their position," the newspaper told its readers.

Such titbits of information whetted the public appetite, not only in New Zealand but around the world. The noses of seasoned news editors told them this was a crime in a million. Many saw a similarity to the famous 1924 Chicago case in which two wealthy college students, Nathan Leopold and Richard Loeb, believing themselves superior beings, had decided to commit the perfect murder. Leopold had been nineteen and Loeb eighteen.

To many the evil act of Parker and Hulme was a prime example of the moral rot afflicting adolescents. Even a year before rock 'n' roll was unleashed on the world and teddy boys appeared in zoot suits and rebellious youths in leather jackets and jeans, the older generation was despairing of youth. On April 21, 1954—a week before Pauline fixed seriously upon "removing Mother"—in New York City a sub-committee of the Senate Judiciary Committee investigating juvenile delinquency had launched an inquiry into the comic book industry. Horror comics aimed at young readers were believed to be an important contributor to juvenile delinquency. The subcommittee's star witness, Fredric Wertham, was a psychiatrist with expertise in criminal behaviour, and author of an alarming book called *Seduction of the Innocent*. Wertham believed "normal" children were particularly at risk from horror comics. "Morbid" children, he said, were less affected, being "wrapped up in their own fantasies". The description fitted Pauline Parker and Juliet Hulme perfectly.

New Zealand was not immune from the general moral panic. Hilda Ross, the straight-shooting government minister in charge of the welfare of women and children, blamed youthful immorality on "lustful images flowing from trashy magazines and unclean reading matter", and in July 1954, as the trial of Pauline Parker and Juliet Hulme was about to begin, the government convened a special committee to investigate. It reported that both comics and working mothers were to blame. The government quickly passed legislation banning the sale of contraceptives to anyone under sixteen.

To sober citizens, the fetid secret lives of Pauline Parker and Juliet Hulme were clear evidence of a sickness infecting youth. During the trial, parents throughout New Zealand would do their best to prevent their children reading about it in the papers. Who knew what effect reading such sordid muck might have on immature minds?

In August 1954, while Terence Gresson and Alec Haslam were laying plans for a defence of insanity, the prosecution was being driven forward at full speed by the crown solicitor, Alan Brown. Brown had been only recently appointed to his position on the death of Sir Arthur Donnelly, who had held it since 1921. For more than twenty years as his deputy, Brown had done a large part of the prosecution work while Donnelly, an able, affable and immensely popular man, was otherwise engaged with horse-racing and business interests. The prosecution of Pauline Parker and Juliet Hulme for murder, a case that had captured the attention of most of the English-speaking world, was the perfect opportunity for Brown to make his mark now the coveted office was finally his.

Aged forty-three, Brown was a stocky man who dressed in the style of a Chicago gangster. From the 1920s, while studying part-time at Canterbury College and working in the offices of Raymond, Stringer, Hamilton and Donnelly, he had distinguished himself as the director, song writer and star of such graduation revues as *You're Hit*, *Crash*, *Gosh* and *Jubilations*. According to the college's official history, "Brown produced in the Ziegfeld tradition, a cast of forty girls was not uncommon, and the songs were sung and whistled about the college for the rest of the year."

Later, as a leading light in the Christchurch Operatic Society, he had become one of the best known amateur actors in the city, with a particular talent for comedy. During the Depression he had risen to national fame as the frontman and clown for a series of "community sings" that started in Christchurch as a means of lifting people's spirits and raising money for the families of men out of work. Brown had a wonderful line in jokes, patter and repartee and led a fast-paced show with more than thirty songs to the hour. His catchphrase was "Let's all sing like the birdies sing", whereupon the audience would start raucously tweeting, clucking and quacking. The singalongs ran on radio for more than three years and Brown got fan mail from all over the country. Community sings were started in Auckland and Wellington but no one else did it like Alan Brown.

In court Brown was a different person. Where his predecessor had believed the crown prosecutor's duty was not to strive for a conviction by aggressive advocacy but to calmly present the evidence so justice could take its course, Brown was driven. He was unquestionably a very capable lawyer, with a memory envied by his opponents, but his style was too forced and intense for some tastes. Being of a theatrical temperament he could not resist grandstanding with a colourful turn of phrase, and was never lost for an apt quotation or literary allusion. And he loved to win. Perhaps he loved to win a little more than was desirable in a crown solicitor.

The influx of journalists from newspapers around the world put pressure on Brown to make a good showing. It was even a little unsettling for the urbane Terence Gresson. And Dr Francis Bennett, preparing to give evidence for the defence, clearly felt edgy. He wrote to his wife Pearl, who was overseas at the time, "I believe there are a number of foreign correspondents coming. The publicity glare will be fierce. The local glare doesn't matter, it's the historical one I fear."

CHAPTER 23

Dirty-Minded Girls

T he foreign correspondents who flocked to Christchurch were at once struck by the incongruity of a murder of the foulest kind occurring in what the Sydney *Sun-Herald* called "New Zealand's quietest, staidest, most Victorian-English city—a city of bicycles, lace and old ivy". The Supreme Court stood beside the Avon River in the heart of the city. The building's grey stone, neo-Gothic walls and sombre interior might have been designed to intimidate all who had business there. The cheerless place had not seen such a large and excited audience since the trial of Thomas Hall and Margaret Graham Houston for attempted murder in 1886. On that occasion admission had been restricted to ticket holders only. It was a "society crime" so most of those attending had been from the city's well-off, whose hansom cabs had battled through the milling masses surrounding the court.

On Monday, August 23, 1954 when Pauline Yvonne Parker and Juliet Marion Hulme stood before judge and jury charged with the murder of Honora Mary Parker it was more of a free-for-all. By eight in the morning the first would-be spectators were trying the doors of the court. By nine there were several dozen standing outside. When the doors opened, the hundred or so public seats at the back of the court were quickly filled, mainly with women, who were, one newspaper reported, fashionably dressed. No standing was allowed downstairs. Next, the gallery was opened and sixty people stampeded into the first three rows.

Juliet had rebuffed her mother's attempt to have a few words with her in the holding cell upstairs before the trial began. Now, far from being daunted by their surroundings, Juliet and Pauline gave every appearance of enjoying themselves, standing at an upstairs window smiling, waving and posing for the ruck of press photographers below, until court staff taped sheets of newsprint over the windows.

At least a dozen correspondents, most representing overseas newspapers or press agencies, took their assigned places on the press bench, pencils poised, notebooks at the ready. In the front row of a small box reserved for witnesses, Hilda, accompanied by Bill Perry, sat grim-faced. A whisper went around the crowd: the rector's sex-mad wife was publicly flaunting the lover she had installed in a flat at the back of the family home. Most members of the public who had succeeded in securing seats were savouring her comeuppance. They didn't like the snooty English upper-class look of her one jot. It was obviously her adultery with Perry that had broken up the home and caused the whole thing. And she called herself a marriage guidance counsellor!

Bert Rieper had not been able to bring himself to attend—he would turn up only when he was needed to give evidence—but Hilda, in her beautifully cut brown tweed suit, would sit in the court for the whole dreadful five days. During lunch adjournments and other breaks she and Perry would retire to the barristers' robing room with Terence Gresson and Brian McClelland to drink coffee delivered in thermos flasks by Gresson's clerk.

After being loudly announced, the trial judge, Mr Justice Adams, entered the court and took his seat while the crowd scrambled respectfully to their feet. Francis Boyd Adams was a sixty-six-year-old widower. Before his elevation to the bench four years earlier he had been for nearly thirty years Dunedin's crown solicitor, a position he had inherited from his father, when his father became a judge of the Supreme Court. Adams lived for the law. His book *Adams on Criminal Law*, of which he was editor and principal contributor, would be published ten years later and become the bible on criminal law for generations of lawyers. An austere man, he lived alone in the Gainsborough, a private hotel in the centre of the city, but there must have been some stirrings in the undergrowth. An associate—as the judges' female secretary-typists were called—once complained he had chased her around a room. Young women who might be called on to dance with him at Law Society balls were warned to beware of wandering hands.

Adams had a reputation as a hanging judge. Partiality toward the prosecution was a hard charge to escape for a judge who had been a crown prosecutor for most of his professional life and the son of a crown prosecutor, but Brian McClelland went further. In his opinion Adams was an "awful, mean bastard ... a miserable, narrow-minded, teetotal, Scottish Baptist shit". It was certainly true that he was a teetotaller and for many years an office-bearer of the Hanover Street Baptist Church in Dunedin.

Juliet and Pauline entered the courtroom and sat side by side in the portable dock that was wheeled into place whenever the room was used for criminal trials. Between them sat the police matron, Mrs Felton. Pauline was wearing a brown dress and a small brown hat, and Juliet a green coat and a pale green headscarf. After the charge was read to them both girls quietly murmured, "Not guilty".

Looking a little flushed, Alan Brown rose to his feet, adjusted his wig and launched into his opening address. He had the cocky air of a man holding all the aces. The evidence to follow would, he promised, make it clear that the two young accused had conspired together to kill the mother of one of them and horribly carried out their plan.

"It was arranged," Brown went on, "that the accused Hulme should go with her father as far as South Africa. The accused Parker wanted to go with her ... Both girls were determined not to be parted and both girls knew that Mrs Parker would be the one who would most strenuously object to their going away together. They both decided the best way to end Mrs Parker's objection was to kill her in such a manner that it would appear she had been accidentally killed. ... Their plan miscarried, and as a result repeated blows had to be struck at the head of the unfortunate Mrs Parker, causing the terrible injuries she received.

"The behaviour of the two accused may have been shockingly unusual and their deed a most dreadful one, but both the accused knew what they were doing when they battered Mrs Parker to death, that what they were doing was wrong, and they were by all medical and legal standards perfectly sane."

There were one or two more things about which he would have to remind the jury. The case had received much publicity but it was their duty to forget all they had read or heard about it and decide the case on the evidence that they would hear in court and nothing else. And there was no room for personal feelings. "You may pity the dead woman and be incensed against the young persons in the dock, or you may feel pity for the two accused in the dreadful situation they find themselves in today. These things have nothing to do with this trial at all. Sentiment and emotionalism have no part in British justice. Your duty, as you have sworn to perform it, is to deal with the case on the facts and not allow your judgement to be swayed by feeling either for the dead woman or for the two accused in the dock."

Brown was right that prejudice against an accused person should have no part in a criminal trial, but the defence lawyers were certainly hoping for sympathy. If the jurors could be persuaded that Juliet and Pauline were suffering from a serious mental illness they might deal with them generously, without pedantic regard for the exact letter of section 43(2) of the Crimes Act. Wasn't the beauty of the jury system the fact that justice could be tempered with mercy, that the common sense and humanity of the ordinary man in the street could prevail, if need be, over the strict letter of the law?

Having paid lip service to the doctrine that sentiment and emotionalism should be put aside, Alan Brown felt free to attack the accused with all the vehemence at his command. "The contention of the prosecution is that this plainly was a coldly, callously planned and premeditated murder committed by two highly intelligent but precocious and dirty-minded little girls." The phrase "dirty-minded little girls" tripped off his tongue; he would use it again before the trial was over.

At the end of his opening address, Brown sought to introduce in evidence the gruesome photographs of the battered face of Honora Parker that had been taken at the morgue. Terence Gresson objected strenuously. The photos proved nothing, he said, and could only shock and disgust the jury. Mr Justice Adams agreed. Brown had to be content with less graphic images that showed her body lying on the track, with the stocking and half-brick clearly visible.

A succession of witnesses now gave their accounts of the events of the afternoon of June 22. Agnes Ritchie described the two girls returning, blood-splattered, to the tea kiosk. Kenneth Ritchie said Juliet Hulme was "excited ... but not hysterical". The Ritchies were followed by Eric McIlroy, the ambulance driver Harold Keys, Dr Walker, Sergeant Hope and Constables Donald Molyneaux and Griffiths, but it was Bert Rieper who made the greatest impact on the hushed gallery. It was almost impossible to imagine the heartache this mild harmless little man had endured. His description of his middle daughter treating him "with disdain" was tragic. So was his account of the last time he saw his wife alive. "We all had the meal together, my wife, the two accused and other members of the family. The lunch hour was very bright indeed. The two accused seemed very happy ... laughing and joking."

Nothing, though, was more chilling than to hear the pathologist, Dr Colin Pearson, describe Honora Parker's horrific injuries—the extensive fractures in the front of the skull, the multiple small contusions of the brain itself. The injury to the skull suggested a crushing type of injury, with force applied while the head was immobile against the ground. The bruising in the neighbourhood of the thyroid bone suggested that at one stage the deceased had been held forcibly by the throat. There was also a lacerated wound to the little finger of one hand, which could have been caused by the deceased attempting to defend herself. It was all too easy to visualise Pauline's mother's last terrible struggle.

Brown next called Hilda Hulme to the stand. Her evidence, while of immense interest to the jury, the press bench and the public, would be of no real use to the prosecution case. He went easy, not even asking her what had happened to Juliet's diary, although it was obvious she had kept one.

In response to his questions, Hilda sketched a faint outline of Juliet's unhappy childhood: the bomb shock she had suffered as a two year old in London during the war; her excitable nature, "very demanding ... even in early childhood"; how, when she was six, she had been separated from her after Jonathan's birth; how she had subsequently suffered a severe breakdown in health with pneumonia and bronchitis, and how this had led to her being sent away to live with strangers in the Bahamas; how, after a year, these people had taken her to New Zealand, where she had finally been reunited with the rest of the family; how she had then been sent to board at Queenswood, a Rudolf Steiner school in Hastings, and later, after contracting tuberculosis, been left in the Cashmere Sanatorium while she and Henry went to Britain and the United States.

Her daughter was incapable of being disciplined easily, tended to want to be the centre of attention, and was always critical of other people, Hilda Hulme told the court. At one time she and Dr Hulme had wondered whether it might be wise to have her psychoanalysed, but medical friends who knew Juliet advised that psychoanalysis was unwise at such an early age. Hilda preferred not to name these friends but one was a doctor of psychology. She was probably referring to David Livingstone, the psychiatrist who had visited Juliet in the sanatorium.

As they would throughout most of the trial, Juliet and Pauline looked nonchalant, calm and apparently unconcerned. One of the newspapermen described their demeanour as "contemptuous amusement". One of the few times Juliet reacted visibly was when her mother told the court she had never accepted her young brother, never played with him much, and "definitely resented him". She half stood up in the dock as if about to say something but quickly sat down again.

Alec Haslam now took over, inviting Hilda to explain the episode, described in Pauline's diary, which had taken place at three in the morning in Mr Perry's bedroom. Mr Perry, Hilda said, had been seriously ill for about a fortnight, suffering severe pain. Hearing a disturbance in the house, she got up, put on her dressing gown, went through the door that led to his flat, and called out to him. As he was in obvious pain she went down to the kitchen, made a pot of tea and took it upstairs to his room. She gave him a cup of tea and had one herself. She sat on a chair at the side of his bed. He, too, was wearing a dressing gown. The light was on.

While they were having tea they heard the door to the flat open quietly and close again. Thinking it might be one of the children, she called out, "Does somebody want me?" When her daughter appeared in the open doorway she said, "Do you want me, darling?" Juliet replied, "Oh, so you are here." She asked her to come in and have a cup of tea. Mr Perry, who was by then feeling a little better, went down to the kitchen to get a cup and saucer for Juliet.

Juliet, Hilda continued, seemed to be amused at a secret joke of her own. When Hilda asked her why she was laughing, she said something like, "Oh, the balloon has gone up. I was hoping to catch you out."

"I had no idea to what she was referring," Hilda said. She could not remember every detail of the conversation but recalled Juliet saying to Mr Perry, "Pauline and I had hoped to get £100." She had no idea of the remark's significance until recently reading Pauline's diary.

Haslam then fed her a leading question: as he was, strictly speaking, cross-examining it was allowable. "You did your best," he suggested, "just to stop her from being silly about a very routine incident?"

"Yes," she replied. The account of the incident in Pauline's diary was "totally inaccurate … entirely untrue".

It is doubtful anyone believed her. The notion she would enter Perry's bedroom only in a medical emergency was widely seen as an outrageous lie. The future of her marriage was more than just, as she described it, "uncertain": years later the family gardener would disclose that when he was called to investigate a blocked drain outside Perry's flat he found it choked with condoms.

Bill Perry attempted to support Hilda's story. What Mrs Hulme had said about the night she came to his room and made him tea was quite correct, he told the court. Juliet did discuss the fact she was going to blackmail him but nothing improper whatever had taken place. There had never been any deception of Henry Hulme, he added. Before the bedroom incident he had told Hulme that he and Mrs Hulme found themselves falling in love.

All that was left was for Senior Detective McDonald Brown and Detective Sergeant Tate to describe interviewing the two accused and to produce the girls' signed statements. By mid afternoon on August 24, the prosecution case was concluded and Terence Gresson stood to open his defence of Juliet Hulme.

CHAPTER 24

A Rare Form of Insanity

Terence Gresson had little leeway. That the accused girls killed Mrs Rieper was not in dispute, he told the jury. The sole question was whether they were of sound mind. After reading out section 43 of the Crimes Act, he informed them that whether the accused were sane or insane was a medical question. As Dr Medlicott and Dr Bennett would explain, the girls were suffering from paranoia associated with *folie à deux*, or "communicated insanity". This made them not legally responsible for their crime. They knew what they were doing when they killed Mrs Rieper, but because of their paranoiac constitutions they were unable to form any rational view of the rightness of what they were doing. They were not ordinary "dirty-minded little girls"; they were mentally sick. Their preoccupation with sexual matters was a symptom of their mental disease. Their homosexual relationship was fatal to both of them, accelerating their inevitable downfall.

Reg Medlicott stepped into the witness box. Although called by the defence as an expert witness, he was sworn to tell "the whole truth and nothing but the truth". As a psychiatrist he may have wondered whether the whole truth was ever within human understanding, but his professional obligation and overriding duty to the court was to give his honest opinion of the case to the best of his knowledge and ability.

Medlicott's opinion was that the girls were suffering from paranoia of the exalted type in the setting of *folie à deux*. Paranoia, he explained, was a relatively rare form of insanity. It was difficult to diagnose because paranoiacs appeared lucid while harbouring weird delusions, often for years, without their closest relatives realising. The delusions were usually unfounded feelings of persecution, but in this case they were fantastically inflated opinions of genius, uniqueness, literary talent and great beauty, accompanied by an exultation of mood and sense of grandeur. *Folie à deux* referred to delusions shared by two, or sometimes more, people. In most cases the communicated insanity was *folie imposée*, the result of the influence of a stronger character on a weaker one. The present case, in his view, was an even rarer form, *folie simultanée*, with each girl developing psychoses simultaneously and "resonating" the delusions of the other back and forth. There was no evidence, he thought, that either girl imposed her ideas on the other. Conscious, perhaps, of the eyes of Hilda on him, Medlicott would not admit Juliet may have been the dominant one.

Each girl, he observed, had suffered a good deal of ill health in early childhood. At the age of five or six, Pauline had had osteomyelitis. Long confinement in hospital had removed her from home at an important time in her development. She had heard her parents say it was touch-and-go whether she would live. Some children who went through such a near-death experience developed a sense of being special. Pauline had also experienced a period of religious mania during her illness.

Mr and Mrs Rieper, Medlicott contended, had produced only one normal child out of four. Their first was a blue baby who died within twenty-four hours. Rosemary was a "Mongolian imbecile" institutionalised at Templeton. Pauline had a rare form of insanity. Wendy was the only normal one. In his opinion, all this raised a question as to the stock from which Pauline came.

He moved on to Juliet. Her chest trouble at the age of five or six had disrupted her schooling and resulted in separation from her family. This could have had a deleterious effect, tending to break normal developments between parents and child and move her away from normal associations and interests. Her time in the Cashmere Sanatorium had also removed her from school, giving her more time to live a fantasy life and write. It was a remarkably bland account of Juliet's terribly neglected childhood.

Adolescence, Medlicott suggested, was "a significant part of the picture". At such a time, increased self-love and preoccupation with oneself were not uncommon: this had been called "the arrogant megalomania of childhood". And then there was the sexual aspect. Before developing a mature capacity to love a person of the opposite sex, the adolescent frequently went through a stage of forming passions for members of his or her own sex. The association was tragic for the two accused in that their relationship rapidly became homosexual, although there was no proof it was physical.

At that Mr Justice Adams sat up. "What is homosexuality but a physical relationship?" he wanted to know. Medlicott replied that homosexuality did not have to involve a physical relationship, although there was a lot of "very suggestive" evidence from the diaries that there had been one between Pauline and Juliet. Pauline's 1954 diary contained frequent references to the girls bathing together, spending a great deal of time and late hours in each other's beds, and frequent sexual talk between them. This was not, from a medical point of view, healthy. Most importantly, it prevented development of normal adult relationships with the opposite sex. And homosexuality and paranoia, Dr Medlicott stated, were frequently related.

Before the doctor expanded on his consultations with the girls, there was a problem to be dealt with. When Medlicott had first seen the two accused, they were claiming to be insane. Even accepting his point that paranoiacs were lucid and could plan and reason, it was a more serious problem for the defence than Medlicott seemed to recognise. Surely it would be difficult to persuade the jury that two girls who were mad might *pretend* to be mad? It was well known that mental hospitals were full of lunatics insisting they were sane, but insane people pretending to be insane?—this was something members of the jury were bound to have trouble accepting.

Medlicott was vague about when exactly the girls had stopped pretending they were insane. He had seen each of them twice on the weekends of June 27 to 28 and July 11 to 12. "Within a very short time in both interviews they had given me what they considered proof of their insanity." One of them said she occasionally had a compulsion—which she had never acted upon—to thrust her hand into the fire. Both claimed they had telepathic powers and received "unusual communications" from each other. They also claimed to suffer mood swings between ecstasy and depression, with thoughts of suicide. He did not accept any of these statements as evidence of insanity.

By the third round of interviews—it was not clear when exactly these had taken place— both girls were quite definite they were not insane, he said. A doctor had told them they would be better off in jail than in a mental hospital. On August 23—the day before he gave evidence—Pauline had told him, "We are both sane. Everybody else is off the mark. Our views are much more logical and sensible..."

The most striking abnormality that convinced Medlicott both Juliet and Pauline were insane was their mood during his interviews. "There was persistent exaltation and ... they would suddenly swing into fury," he told the court. "Their mood was grossly incongruous. They exalted over their crime ... with this exaltation there was quite gross excitement. Each girl would have sudden spells of intenseness. They would, you might say, click into gear, talk so rapidly for a time as to be almost incoherent.

"They showed a conceit that was quite out of the world of normality. Their ideas about their looks are not based on any reality. Their ideas about their genius were not based on any sound ground, except one of them had a high IQ. ... They were prepared to accept their books as world-shattering without deferring to any outside authority whatsoever."

The girls, he said, had suffered "a very gross reversal of morals or of moral sex ... they admired those things which were evil and condemned everything the community considered good. It was obvious that the normal personality's defences against evil had almost completely gone." Their super-egos—in Freudian terms the voices of conscience and self-restraint—had been all but silenced.

The girls' delusional—paranoiac—thinking, Medlicott declared, was clearly demonstrated in Pauline's diary entry for Good Friday, April 3, 1953: "Today Juliet and I found the key to the 4th World. We realise now that we have had it in our possession for about six months but we only realised it on the day of the death of Christ. ...We now know we are not genii as we thought. We have an extra part of our brain which can appreciate the 4th World. Only about ten people have it. When we die we will go to the 4th World, but meanwhile on two days every year we may use the key and look into that beautiful world which we have been lucky enough to be allowed to know of."

During his July visit both girls had, he said, given him consistent accounts of the 4th World, which by then they were calling "Paradise" or "Paradisa", and of the extra part of their brains. He was convinced that, because of their belief in their own special paradise, the thought of death did not disturb them in any way. This delusion was quite different from the ordinary fantasies they spun.

Medlicott had also been struck by the "quite fantastic conceit" revealed in Pauline's poem *The Ones That I Worship*:

"… two beautiful daughters
The most glorious beings in creation;
They'd be the pride and joy of any nation.
… The outstanding genius of this pair
Is understood by few, they are so rare.
Compared with these two, every man is a fool.
The world is most honoured that they should deign to rule,
And above us these Goddesses reign on high …"

When he had questioned Pauline about this jejune nonsense, she had allowed that she was "a bit more than usually conceited" the day she wrote it, but insisted it was essentially true. When he had asked Juliet about religion, she had become so excited and ecstatic he often found it almost impossible to follow what she said. They had their own religion, she told him. In it all people were not equal: there were only twenty-five people on their own level who would go to Paradise, "a world of music, art and pure enjoyment". Their god was not a Christian one but a more powerful version of the human. "He has the same powers, only greatly magnified." The extra part of their brain "attached to the usual part … makes the whole thing different. … You can appreciate the whole nature of everything."

"I don't wish to place myself above the law," she said. "I am apart from it."

Pauline had given Medlicott more details of the 4th World. She and Juliet had known about it, she said, six months before their experience at Port Levy. When Medlicott asked her about the two days each year when they could look into it, she had replied, "We see it now whenever we wish to."

The day after what Medlicott called "the Port Levy revelation", there had been a particularly bloodthirsty episode in Pauline's writing. Roland, in a blazing fury, had shot Roderick, and the horse Vendetta had killed Gianina on the eve of her marriage to Nicholas, then trampled Nicholas to death before galloping into a blood-red sunset. This writing had come so soon after the delusions at Port Levy that Medlicott believed the delusions had released murderous impulses. Had he read the passage a year earlier, he would have been fearful that some day the girls would break through into action.

Entries in Pauline's diaries, including about making love with the Saints, also supported his diagnosis that both girls were suffering from paranoiac delusions, Medlicott told the jury. They showed that as time went on "evil becomes more and more important ... they ultimately become helplessly under its sway".

Juliet and Pauline's irregular hours and activities at night were, he said, symptomatic of their growing exaltation. He was convinced that by June 1954 both girls were grossly insane. Even before they started to play with evil, as shown by their shoplifting and attempts at blackmail, there were warning signs that their normal defences were being overwhelmed. Their conceit had to be fed continually by their making fun of other people, proving everyone else wrong. The paranoiac had an inability to appreciate the rights of others — "even [the right] to live".

But, he said, although Parker and Hulme were insane when they attacked Mrs Rieper, they were aware of the physical nature and quality of their act: they knew they were killing a human being. They were "aware at times of the rightness and wrongness of acts. This awareness is so temporary they will switch between what they know about the law and back into their own fantastic ideas at a moment's notice. Paranoia affects the judgement very definitely... always the delusional theme drives them." Neither girl, Medlicott said, had ever acknowledged to him that what they did was morally wrong.

Alan Brown was eyeing the psychiatrist impatiently, eager to get started on his cross-examination.

CHAPTER 25

The Thing Called Bliss

Alan Brown was determined to show that Pauline Parker and Juliet Hulme were legally sane when they killed Nora Rieper. He began by getting Reg Medlicott to admit that all three doctors who would be called by the Crown to rebut insanity—James Hunter and James Saville of Sunnyside Mental Hospital and Kenneth Stallworthy, senior medical officer at Avondale Mental Hospital—had considerably more experience in medico-legal matters than he did.

He then homed in on a clear weakness of the defence case: the fact the girls had *pretended* to be insane. Medlicott was not sure why they had done this, he said. It was possible they thought being insane might lessen their time in detention. Brown put it to him that they thought they would be better off in a mental hospital than in jail having to work.

Brown turned to the fact that during Medlicott's first interview with Pauline she had told him she knew murder was considered wrong, against the law. The Hulme girl, too, had admitted knowing that in killing Pauline's mother she and Pauline had done something wrong in law. She had added, "There is no right and wrong. ... If I ran a country I would make laws for others to stick to and I would punish them if they didn't. As king, of course, the laws would not apply to me." But she had understood that the law of New Zealand applied to her. If she had been old enough to be hanged, she had told Medlicott, she would not have cared. "It is a nice thing to go to Paradise."

Although the girls knew the killing was wrong in law, he had never been able to get them to admit it was morally wrong, Medlicott rejoindered. He was forced to conclude they did not know their action was morally wrong. They understood the generally accepted community standards of right and wrong, but did not recognise them as applying to themselves.

"Do you think these girls were convinced that battering Mrs Parker over the head was morally right?" Alan Brown said.

"I think they were," Medlicott could only reply.

Wasn't there, Brown went on, an apparent contradiction between the girls considering themselves beyond the pale of the law yet knowing they would be punished if they were caught breaking it?

Paranoiacs did that, Medlicott answered. They considered the moral standards of the community did not apply to them.

"They were permitted to do that [commit murder] but no one else was?"

"Yes."

Why, then, had the girls been anxious not to be caught and lied to the police, Brown asked.

Their plan would be frustrated if they were caught, Medlicott said. Until Juliet finally confessed, they thought Pauline would be found insane and the Hulmes would be able to take responsibility for her and take her out of the country. "It is a fantastic belief," he acknowledged.

Brown pressed on. "When was the first point in time either of them became grossly insane?" he asked.

The onset of paranoia was insidious, Medlicott replied. It was difficult to pick the exact point, but he felt the Port Levy incident in April 1953 was when they went over from their constitutional paranoid personality into actual paranoia.

"Was their belief that they were highly intelligent a delusion?"

"No."

"Their thoughts that [Mrs Rieper] was in their way was not a delusion?"

"No."

"It was a very great reality?"

"Yes."

"And was not their reason for killing Mrs Parker to put her out of their way?"

"Yes."

"It was not the result of a delusion at all, was it?"

"Not directly."

"Was not their main plan in life to remain together?"

"It was."

"Was not Mrs Rieper's interference doing something to interfere with their plan?"

"It was."

"And their doing away with Mrs Parker would remove the interference to their plans?"

"That is what they thought."

It was a good point. Even if the two accused were suffering from paranoiac delusions, it did not follow that the killing of Honorah Rieper was due to a delusion—a false belief in a state of affairs that did not exist.

Alan Brown was on a roll. What emotional state were the girls in when they ran up to Mrs Ritchie at the tea kiosk, he wanted to know. Did they not display the emotions you would expect from two sane girls who had committed a dreadful deed?

"I think there was some definite emotional response to the deed. I think the blood shocked them," Medlicott replied.

Brown pressed his point. "Do you agree that they behaved immediately after killing Mrs Parker as you would expect two people who had done such a deed to behave?"

"Yes. They showed signs of shock."

"Did they behave as people who had committed such a deed could be expected to behave: yes or no?"

"I don't know," was all Medlicott could say.

Brown continued to pummel the witness. "You say [Pauline] said she had a period during primary school of religious mania … Were they her words?"

"I am not clear. I went over my notes. I may be getting confused by what was told to me by her sister Wendy."

The judge intervened. "You say you can't assure us that either of the girls used the phrase about religious mania?"

"No. I went back on my notes and could not find it. I did find it in my notes about the interview with Wendy and regret it very much that at the time I became confused…"

Alan Brown had Medlicott on the ropes. "You realise it is very important that evidence be accurate."

It was a small thing but it had damaged Medlicott's credibility. If, as soon as discovering a mistake had been made, he had offered the court a correction no harm would have been done.

Brown was not finished yet. He wanted to know why Medlicott had said in evidence that problems with the Riepers' other children raised a query as to the stock from which Pauline came.

"Do you not think you are being unjust to Mrs Rieper in saying that?"

"I said no more than it raises a query."

"Do you not think it was being unjust to say even that?"

"I don't think so."

"What do you mean by it?"

"It's simply what I said—it suggests the possibility of defective stock."

"That is, hereditary insanity from father to son or mother to daughter?" Brown asked.

"There is no evidence of hereditary insanity that I could find."

"Your suggestion is that there might be?"

"That is not the intention of my suggestion."

"What do you mean by it?" Brown continued. "Simply that they are a family of four, the first child died within twenty-four hours, the second one normal, the third one I consider suffers from paranoia, and the fourth one is in Templeton?" Brown was enjoying Medlicott's increasing discomfort. "Do not your words imply that the insanity which you allege exists in Parker was hereditary?"

"No."

"What did you mean?"

"It suggests defective stock."

"Defective stock means what?"

"A generation can be defective."

"It means hereditary insanity?"

"I don't consider it means that."

"What does it mean?"

"I can't elaborate further."

"It is meaningless?"

"It means what I said."

"What does it mean other than as a suggestion of hereditary insanity?"

"I can't answer any more," Medlicott said.

Mr Justice Adams popped in a question of his own. "Do I understand from you now, doctor, that the fact there was a child that died and another child a Mongolian imbecile has no bearing whatever on the accused Parker's sanity or insanity?"

"I think they did, but not because of any heredity because we know of no heredity," Medlicott replied. "I may be wrong, but I think that a family in which there is only one normal member—that has some significance."

"In what way?" Brown interrupted.

"Just defective stock. I can't elaborate any more."

Brown was browbeating the witness, having a go at him over something that was essentially unimportant. Now he suddenly did a u-turn. "Would you agree," he asked Medlicott, "there is no suggestion from the fact of the blue baby and the imbecile that there was any hereditary insanity?"

Some of the spectators exchanged looks. Hadn't Medlicott made this clear all along? It was Brown who had been insisting "defective stock" meant hereditary insanity.

The peculiar twists and turns of Brown's cross-examination were by now noticeable to the other counsel, and had not escaped the judge's attention. The crown prosecutor seemed not quite in control. Brown's junior, Peter Mahon, stiffened with embarrassment. By then he and Brown were barely on speaking terms and he knew Brown was drinking heavily. During the trial "Brown filled up with grog the whole time" he would tell Brian McClelland.

As Brown's next line of questioning began, the crowd leaned forward and the reporters sharpened their pencils. This was really what they had come to hear.

The prosecutor did not mince words. Medlicott had said that the relationship between Juliet and Pauline was homosexual but that there was no proof it was physical. "To ordinary people like myself and the jury," Brown thundered, "homosexuality is thought to mean physical contact between two persons of the same sex."

"That is a completely erroneous view," Medlicott countered.

"Your reading of the diaries shows plainly that these young people played about with each other sexually and physically."

"I have tried to get evidence of that but can't get absolute evidence."

"It is very strong," Brown insisted, "so strong that anyone with any intelligence must know that is what they did."

Medlicott was not ready to concede. "There is also very plain evidence that, as far as Parker is concerned, she was heterosexual as well, that she had sexual intercourse with boys—with a boy, at any rate."

"Homosexuals can have sexual intercourse with persons of the opposite sex," Brown boomed. Pauline had done so "over and over again". She had had intercourse with a boy.

"That is reported in the diary," Medlicott allowed.

"Over and over again!"

"That is denied. She said only once."

Brown took Medlicott through all the entries in Pauline's diary that dealt with her attempts to have sexual intercourse with Nicholas. He seemed to have no obvious purpose, unless to create prejudice against the accused girl.

"She had a good deal of sexual knowledge of the other sex," he put to Medlicott.

At that point, the *Sun-Herald* reported, "Juliet Hulme's expression was savage. She leaned forward, grinding her teeth and spitting silent words through her rage-distorted lips" while Pauline "bowed her head down to her knees". Pauline had told Medlicott she had described all these events to Juliet. It seemed Juliet did not know quite as much as Pauline had led him to believe.

Alan Brown now set about challenging every aspect of Medlicott's diagnosis in a shambling fusillade of questions. "Have not various people seen visions? ... People who are perfectly sane have markedly different ideas about god and the afterlife? There are Buddhists, Moslems, Confucians, all have markedly different ideas? ... The native in the African jungle has peculiar ideas to us about religion? ... Are all these people mad? All the prophets had visions? These girls have one vision which they say they can conjure up at any time. Why does that make them mad? ... She rather liked intercourse? ... She tried it over and over again? ... She was under the age of consent!"

He was back on to sex. "Isn't it a fact that they acted sex matters with their Saints, or as their Saints?"

"Juliet maintained it was not actual sexual behaviour," Medlicott replied. "It certainly sounds like it from the diary but she denied it to me."

"Did you believe her?"

"I was very doubtful."

"You suspected she was not telling the truth?"

"On that occasion."

"Harry Lime?" Brown asked. "Heard of him?"

"Yes, he is a film star," answered Medlicott erroneously. "The girls ... told me they used their faces for their characters."

"Wasn't it a fact they used other portions of their anatomy?"

"At times they may have," Medlicott conceded.

"Even as far as private parts go?"

"I don't know about that."

"Didn't you ask?"

"No."

Brown charged on. Could Dr Medlicott imagine a girl who was fond of fornication?

He could.

"She might like to have intercourse with different types of men?" She might.

"Wasn't that what they were meaning in respect of these Saints?"

"I understand you thought they were homosexual," Medlicott retorted. The fact they described somebody as being long, bony or roly poly did not, he contended, have any great bearing on their intense preoccupation with these fictional characters.

"You think they play like innocent children?" Brown demanded, trembling with rage.

"There is no suggestion they play like innocent children," Medlicott replied in the quiet voice he might use to calm a dangerous madman.

Brown had the bit between his teeth. "Take one of them as an example. He—Mario Lanza—is roly poly?"

"In that entry," Medlicott answered.

"Therefore it is nice to pretend, when they roll around in bed together, that one of them is Mario Lanza?"

"It could be," Medlicott conceded.

Brown read out Pauline's diary entry for Sunday, June 13. "'We spent a hectic night going through the Saints … We have now learnt the peace of the thing called Bliss, the joy of the thing called Sin'. What did they mean by that?" he demanded.

"I would think there had been lovemaking between them."

"Physical?"

"I would think there has been," Medlicott replied "I know they are grossly homosexual. I have not the slightest doubt about that." But when he had asked Juliet about Pauline's diary entry for June 11—"We enacted how each Saint would make love in bed, only doing the first of seven as it was 7.30 a.m. by then"—Juliet had replied that the acting of love scenes did not amount to any physical relationship between them.

"You believed that?" Brown asked.

"I have already said I was extremely doubtful."

At that point Mr Justice Adams cut in. "Was the same question put to Hulme?"

"That was to Hulme," Medlicott said.

"Was the same question put to Parker?"

"That was Parker. I am sorry."

"Did you put it to Hulme?"

Medlicott was floundering, losing the imperturbable authority of a good expert witness. "I am confused as the notes are not labelled for different interviews," he said. "The interview is from Juliet Hulme. I was wrong. It *was* Juliet Hulme."

The judge was not satisfied. "You told us of one girl denying it was physical. Was the same point put to the other girl?"

"I have no specific reference. I don't think it was."

Brown pressed the point. "You don't think you asked Pauline Parker if there was a physical relationship between them?"

"I questioned her closely on her relationship with Juliet. She said, 'Juliet is not a close friend. She is much closer.' I suggested, 'Isn't that love?' She said, 'I don't know … I care for her more than anyone else in the world.'"

"Did you not ask her whether that love developed into sexual passion or orgies?" asked Brown leeringly.

"I did not. … Physicality, I am not concerned—I have no doubt of gross homosexuality."

Brown was reluctant to abandon the subject of sex. What, he asked Medlicott, was the meaning of Pauline's diary entry for Friday, 11 June: "It is appalling. He is dreadful. I have never in my life seen anything in the same category of hideousness… We returned home and talked for some time about It, getting ourselves more and more excited."

"'It' or Harry Lime represented evil to them, Medlicott said. "The adoring of hideousness is generally considered evil."

"I suppose you will agree that… some [men] have rather hideous features?" Brown asked. "You do find that some women fall properly in love with ugly men?"

"That is so," Medlicott agreed.

"Because a person is ugly, that cannot be evil?"

"Hideousness is different from ugliness."

After a few more exchanges, Brown turned to the matter of Juliet's diary. Had the girl ever written a diary?

"Not that I know of," Medlicott replied.

"Did you inquire?"

"I did."

"From whom?"

He could not remember specifically. From Mr Gresson, he thought.

"Did you not ask Juliet?"

"No. I was quite certain if she had written a diary it would be brought to my notice because it would have been evidence."

Brown pressed on. "Is there not a reference—or more than one— in Parker's diary: 'We went home and wrote in our diaries'?"

"There may be."

"Would that not make you enquire from Juliet and Pauline if Juliet had written a diary?"

"I made inquiries … Mrs Hulme gave me, I thought, a very straightforward story about the girl and made no reference to any diary. I was given a whole suitbox of what they could find of Juliet's writings to take away with me. I concluded it was self-evident there was no diary."

Brown was not finished. "Do you agree that, if there had been a diary or diaries, they could have been hidden?"

"They could have been," Medlicott replied.

Brown had made his point: Medlicott's answers were not convincing. Any discomfort Hilda Hulme may have been feeling during this exchange would have been nothing compared to her relief that she had arranged the destruction of a terribly embarrassing document.

Finally Brown returned to the main point of Medlicott's evidence, his diagnosis that the girls were insane in a setting of *folie à deux*. "Have you ever," he asked the doctor, "had under your personal experience any instance of two [insane] persons combining to commit a crime?"

"I have not," Medlicott replied, "but it is not out of keeping."

"Have you ever read in any text book of two insane persons combining to commit crimes and both committing them?"

"I have not read a lot of literature on *folie à deux*."

"The answer is no?" Brown persisted.

"I have not read it."

There was, Medlicott pointed out, the famous Leopold and Loeb case, but that was not quite the same as the accused "did not have the clear-cut insanity with gross emotional disturbance one sees here". Although insane people, he agreed, generally did not contrive, Parker's and Hulme's was a different type of insanity.

Brown had two last questions.

"They knew it [murder] was wrong in the eyes of the law?"

"They did."

"And they also knew that what they did was wrong in the eyes of the community?"

"In the eyes of the community, yes."

They were the answers he wanted. Reg Medlicott had been in the witness box for nine hours.

The defence was in tatters. As Brian McClelland put it, the crown prosecutor had given their principal witness a rough passage, made a mess of him.

Medlicott, meanwhile, was convinced Brown was showing psychiatric symptoms of his own. "Make no mistake," he told McClelland, "Alan Brown is certifiable. He will be in Ashburn Hall within two years."

He was even more outspoken to his fellow psychiatrist David Livingstone. Brown, he told him, was as mad as the two girls.

CHAPTER 26

Sleeping with Saints

Alec Haslam got to his feet to defend Pauline Parker. His opening to the jury was economical. They would not challenge the evidence provided by the prosecution. The only question was whether the accused girls were insane or not. The first and only witness for Pauline Parker's defence would be Dr Bennett.

Francis Bennett walked towards the witness box filled with a sense that the eyes of history were on him. Despite having no specialist qualification in psychiatry—he was a general practitioner, best known for his obstetric practice—he was bursting with confidence. Brian McClelland thought him "self-opinionated … not as clever as he thought". Reg Medlicott, too, saw him as self-important, a frustrated actor who loved the drama of it all and relished his close connection with the Hulmes.

If less cerebral than Medlicott, Bennett was certainly more pugnacious. In the war he had risen to lieutenant-colonel in the Medical Corps. He was used to being deferred to. He was determined not to be pushed about by Alan Brown the way Medlicott had allowed himself to be.

He got straight to the point. The actions of Pauline Parker and Juliet Hulme could, he said, be explained only on the basis of mutual insanity. Like Dr Medlicott he believed the girls were suffering from the major psychosis known as paranoia, from delusions, even though *apparently*—he stressed the word—capable of clear and logical reasoning. Once such delusions took hold, he continued, they became the paramount obsession in the patient's life, a relentless compulsion.

"Forced to choose between the moral values of the community or pursuing the delusion, the patient rejects the moral values. Paranoiacs have to, they must, follow the delusion wherever it leads. Such persons become amoral, anti-social and, in any community, dangerous."

The girls' delusion was that they were especially gifted, mentally brilliant, and immeasurably superior to the general run of mankind. The truth was, while the girls were certainly not dull and one was known to have a high IQ, they were not towering intellectuals. Their writings, he believed, were not of outstanding literary merit.

He considered the "mental disturbance" of both girls to be similar; it was an extraordinary coincidence that two such girls should meet in the same class at the same school. If they had never met, the full symptoms of paranoia would have developed at a much later date, he believed. "The lone paranoiac makes slow progress in his conflict with society."

The two girls had "delusions of grandeur ... whipped themselves up to a state of elation ... formed a society of their own ... dwelt ecstatically in their new society ... filled it out with the Saints and their families and their fictional characters." Thus far, it seemed, Bennett was making a better fist of describing the girls' delusional state than Medlicott had.

"They can persist in this delightful new society," he continued, "only if they are together. If separated [each has] to revert back to her lone, unhappy conflict with her contemporary fellow beings. Their attachment is a homosexual one and to them it is vital. Only in that do they feel secure. Had it never been threatened, they might have continued their morbid infatuation without any gross trespass against society. But it *was* threatened. The threat against it was a threat against the delusion of their superiority and, as is the nature of the paranoiac, they acted out to resist the threat."

Haslam was pleased with how well his witness was doing. Bennett now drew the jury's attention to numerous entries in Pauline's diary that illustrated the girls' delusions of grandeur, and then, with a flourish, summed up their oddities. The girls "spent all the time they possibly could at Ilam endlessly discussing the Saints and the plots of their books; bathing and bedding together; photographing each other in fancy borrowed dresses and in the nude; talking all night; dressing up; getting up at night, going out on the lawn and acting; ignoring other people; making a little cemetery in the grounds that they later extended into … the Temple of Rafael Pan, where they buried a dead mouse and put up a cross over it, and later put up a number of other crosses to represent the burial of dead ideas which they had once had and had since discarded. They had no friends of their own age; they never went to dances, with one exception; … they never read the newspapers; Pauline records how she hated school; she hated Digby's College; she said the girls … were fools. She went to the [school] swimming sports and wrote a novel all through the events. During the queen's visit they made no attempt to see the queen or the decorations. They preferred the company of the Saints."

The story progressed to its mad climax. The girls had "left this world behind them", were "mounting higher and higher in their ecstasy of infatuation". They were convinced there was survival after death. Everyone would go either to Heaven or Paradise. Heaven was for happiness; Paradise was for bliss. The vast majority went to Heaven. As for Hell, Juliet had assured him there was no such thing. The whole idea was too primitive, too *inartistic*.

He had put it to her that, on the basis of her own beliefs, she would probably meet Pauline's mother in Heaven or Paradise. "I suppose so," she had conceded.

"With blood on her face?"

"Well, she wouldn't arrive in that state. In any case she will be in Heaven and we'll be in Paradise. Even if we did meet her, we would not worry. There's nothing in death. After all, she wasn't a very happy woman."

Did Juliet know any people other than themselves who would go to Paradise?

"There probably are some, but we have not met any yet."

"Who are the best people?"

"The best people are those who fight against all obstacles in pursuit of happiness."

"Even to murder?"

"Oh yes, if necessary."

Juliet had insisted the bible was bunkum. They were going to write a new one. She was going to write it on parchment vellum and Pauline would illustrate it. Pauline boasted she had broken all ten of the Ten Commandments and Juliet nine.

Juliet had remembered and been prepared to cheerfully recite every detail of their attack on Mrs Rieper. In Bennett's view this was further proof of insanity. And having decided to murder Pauline's mother, neither girl had showed the emotional turmoil—fears, doubts, waverings, indecision, sleeplessness—to be expected of the sane. Pauline pretending to show affection towards her mother, making a play of industriously helping with housework to inveigle her to accompany them on the fatal outing, the "bestial and treacherous and filthy" murder itself—these, he insisted, were "a thousand miles away from sanity".

"If you want it better than I can express it, read *Macbeth*," he told the court.

At Bennett's last interview with Pauline, on August 14, she had just returned from Mt Eden prison, where she had been sent at his request as an experiment to see what effect, if any, a period of separation from Juliet would have on her. She had, he said, spoken freely and intelligently, admitting that some of their previous ideas about the Saints or going to America now looked a little foolish. His conversation with her had been "bright, easy, cooperative" until he got on to the murder. Pauline was adamant the murder was justified, as was anything else that would prevent her being separated from Juliet.

Towards the end of the interview she had suddenly grown impatient and become reluctant to answer any more questions. She had apparently had been told by a prison officer that as soon as he went she could rejoin Juliet. When he told her he had been informed she would have to wait until evening to see Juliet, she had become highly agitated. "She jumped up off her seat, began to stammer expostulations and... was obviously profoundly distressed. ... Her reaction revealed most convincingly the profound impulsive force of delusion."

In summary, he believed both the accused were *folie à deux* homosexual paranoiacs of the elated type, and definitely certifiable under the Mental Defectives Act. He was familiar with section 43 of the

Crimes Act. In his opinion, when both girls attacked Mrs Rieper they knew they were killing a woman and who she was, but did not appreciate the moral quality of the act. "They did not think it was wrong. They knew it was against the law of the country but they had another loyalty which was much more persuasive to them. It was the loyalty to a delusion. … They thought by killing her they would achieve two things. First, they would transfer an unhappy woman to heaven, and second, they would preserve the integrity of their association, which was so vital to their central, paranoiac delusions of grandeur."

Bennett's evidence-in-chief had gone well, but standing at the prosecutor's bench, champing at the bit, was Alan Brown. The prosecutor got straight to the heart of the matter. Did the witness, he asked, agree that the girls knew when they killed Mrs Parker they were committing a criminal act?

"They knew it was contrary to the law," Dr Bennett answered.

"If they knew it was against the law, they would know it was wrong in the eyes of society at large?"

"They probably did," Bennett allowed, although he very much doubted they gave any consideration to society at large.

Brown next got Bennett to agree that when he examined Pauline on December 14, 1953, although he thought she was "unusual" he had not considered her insane. Bennett further conceded that Mrs Parker's standing in the path of the girls' desire was a very real fact, not a delusion, but insisted her killing was "an effect that grew out of the delusion, as most paranoiac acts are".

"Would it be correct to say the only true delusion was the wrong belief as to their own qualities and importance?" Mr Justice Adams inquired.

"That is exactly it," the doctor said.

Brown turned to the Saints. Did Dr Bennett agree the Saints were film actors the girls liked to think slept with them, film actors whom they chose, one by one, to sleep with because of their physical qualities?

"No, I don't think so."

"That is very plain, I suggest, from the diary."

"No, I don't think it is."

"Do you think any man of average common sense would come to that conclusion?" Brown insolently inquired.

"There is more information about that than in the diaries," Bennett insisted. "There is my interrogation of them."

"But you know they are liars," Brown insisted.

"Sometimes, but not altogether."

"They will lie whenever it suits them?"

"Probably."

"Putting it baldly, they are liars?"

"Yes."

"Passages in their diary which refer to liking a 'large amount of man' and to visible characteristics of Him, Her and It, et cetera—that is suggestive of the film actors being persons they like to sleep with?"

"It is suggestive, yes. It is not proof."

"Strongly suggestive?"

"Yes, strongly suggestive."

Brown now homed in on the girls' sexuality. "Their attachment is a homosexual one?"

Bennett agreed.

"Physically?"

The doctor was inclined to think not. First, if Pauline was getting satisfaction out of heterosexual practices, as Brown was postulating, it was unlikely she would engage in homosexual acts at the same time.

Secondly, Bennett continued, the girls, "in a way that leads me to believe they are probably telling the truth", denied there was any physical homosexual relationship between them. He had questioned Juliet Hulme "with some delicacy" and "she seemed to have no idea what I was talking about". When he asked her directly about physical homosexual practices, she had looked very surprised. Her actual words had been, "But how could we? We are both women." Bennett found this "quite convincing".

Like Medlicott, Bennett was keen to stress that whether Pauline and Juliet's homosexual relationship was physical or not made no difference to his diagnosis.

Mr Justice Adams seemed unpersuaded. "Must there not be some sexual element, whether physical or not?" he insisted.

"Not necessarily," Bennett said. "The word comes from the Greek 'homus', meaning 'same'. Homosexual means same sex, without there being a physical aspect of sex."

"If the word be interpreted in this way," the judge shot back, "it would mean no more than that two persons are of the same sex."

"In the psychiatric world," Bennett explained, "it can be applied to this morbid association—love, if you like—between two people with an unhealthy exclusion of other people, and it very frequently and perhaps most often goes on to physical relations."

Here Brown interjected. Surely it was doubtful that the relationship between Pauline and Juliet was homosexual, given Pauline's plainly heterosexual interest in a Sinhalese boy, Jaya, and the fact she had had sex on at least one occasion with Nicholas.

Bennett was having none of it. Pauline Parker was, he said, "a silly, adolescent, amoral girl out for experience".

At four-thirty the court adjourned. The members of the public who had been fortunate enough to secure seats in the gallery left buzzing with excitement. They had got even more from the day than they hoped. Rarely had such disgusting goings-on in Christchurch been talked about so openly.

As the fifth day of the trial began, the dogged cross-examination of Dr Bennett continued. Rather surprisingly, Brown undertook to dispute that the girls ever displayed grandiosity in their thoughts. The witness had said that Parker's poem *The Ones That I Worship* exhibited this grandiosity, but did he know a line in English poetry: "Not marble nor the gilded monuments / Of princes, shall outlive this noble rhyme"? Wasn't that grandiose? Didn't it mean the poet considered his rhyme would outlive marble? Had he heard of the immortal Shakespeare? That was a line from Shakespeare. Had he read it? Did he not agree there was grandeur in it? Did he agree Shakespeare was a genius? Did he agree Shakespeare wrote about love and sexual love? Had he read *The Rape of Lucrece*? That poem was full of sex. The girls wrote a lot about sex.

In the public gallery they may not have noticed, but it had become clear to all the lawyers in court, and surely to the judge as well, that the crown prosecutor was behaving very oddly. He was like a runaway bus. What was the matter with the man?

He had now chosen to dispute with Bennett that there was anything delusional about the girls' religious ideas. Was it an insane belief that people went to heaven or paradise? Didn't millions of people believe this? Didn't some very famous churches think there were two or three places in the afterlife? Were *they* mad? Why were these girls mad for believing there were two places in the afterlife? Hadn't millions of people thought the bible was bunkum?

Still the torrent of questions kept flowing. When Bennett doubted a sane person could approach a crime such as murder with a completely calm mind, Brown retorted, "You heard of Judas Iscariot? Was not Judas Iscariot cool and calm when he took bread and wine with our Lord?"

Here Mr Justice Adams was moved to check him. "Mr Brown, whatever the temptation, I think it would be advisable not to continue that topic."

"I will not take it further, Your Honour."

"I am sorry we did not continue," Bennett announced. "It would lead us to where Judas hanged himself."

Undeterred, Brown moved his attention to Shakespeare. Did not Macbeth murder Duncan at the instigation of Lady Macbeth? Was she mad? Was not Lady Macbeth calm before the murder? Did she not behave before and after the murder of Duncan precisely the way these girls behaved?

The crown prosecutor no longer knew when enough was enough. "I must press this. Did not Lady Macbeth welcome Duncan to the castle on the evening of his death?" he demanded.

"Yes."

"Did she not find Macbeth was getting cold feet about the death?"

"Yes."

"Did she not spur him on to get it done?"

"Yes."

"Was she not calm and calculating throughout all that? ... Was she not a party to the killing beyond striking the actual blow?"

"She was out of the room. She kept away from it."

"She knew it was going to be done? She counselled it?"

"Yes."

Tears were now streaming down Alan Brown's cheeks. Seeing that the crown prosecutor was becoming overwrought, Mr Justice Adams stepped in with a question he hoped would sew the whole thing up. "May your view," he said, "be summarised in these words: that in your opinion [the accused] knew the act was contrary to law and knew it was contrary to the ordinary moral standards of the community but nevertheless it was not contrary to their own moral standards?"

"Yes," Bennett replied. "You have completely summarised it."

CHAPTER 27

"I See Nothing Insane..."

The three-man team from the government's Department of Mental Hygiene had a straightforward mission: to rebut the case that Juliet Hulme and Pauline Parker were insane. The leader, Dr Kenneth Stallworthy, had examined both girls over the course of several visits to Christchurch prison. He had also examined Pauline at Auckland's Mt Eden Prison when she was separated from Juliet. Although he had not seen either girl until more than a month after the murder, he felt able to say that at the time they killed Mrs Rieper neither girl had any disease of the mind. Both knew the nature and quality of their act in killing Mrs Rieper and both were sane medically and in the legal sense. He believed neither was certifiable under the Mental Defectives Act.

Further, both knew they were breaking the law. Pauline Parker had explicitly told him they knew they were doing wrong. "We knew we would be punished if we were caught and we did our best not to be caught." On another occasion Parker had told him she could hardly fail to know that murder was not encouraged, and Juliet Hulme had gone as far as to say, "You would have to be an absolute moron not to know murder was against the law."

As far as Stallworthy was concerned, insanity could, therefore, be ruled out. Both the accused had acted for an intelligible motive. Their crime was carefully premeditated and planned and they had weighed the prospects of getting away with it. They had given themselves a better than even chance. They were aware that because of their ages they would not be hanged if they were caught. Then there was the fact they wanted to be found insane if it would get them an earlier release.

Persons who were insane were always anxious to be considered sane.

Although paranoia was a relatively rare disease, Stallworthy informed the jury, he had seen dozens of paranoiacs in mental hospitals and they did not behave anything like these girls. In all cases paranoiacs' illnesses progressed to the stage where they no longer realised they were breaking the law. All were most insistent they were sane and indignant at being sent to a mental hospital.

Nor did he believe the girls were delusional. Delusions were beliefs that had no foundation in fact, and were staunchly maintained in spite of all logic and argument to the contrary. Undue conceit, even overwhelming conceit, did not constitute a delusion of grandeur. Adolescence was commonly a very conceited age, and the accused had much greater grounds for conceit than the defence had conceded. Hulme displayed the vocabulary, and the shrewdness in under-standing and answering difficult questions, of a highly intelligent and sophisticated person of a much greater age. Parker, too, was con-siderably above average in intelligence.

Stallworthy's argument that the girls were suffering from nothing more than the ordinary conceit to be expected in adolescents, especially intelligent ones with something to be conceited about, was thin and perhaps he realised it. "Suppose my views were wrong," he now allowed, "and the girls did have delusions of grandeur, I do not think it would explain their crime." There was no delusional basis in their motivation: Pauline's mother *was* standing in the way of their friendship. "These two girls were in love with each other…. The most important thing in the world for them was to be together."

Nor did Stallworthy think the girls' various fantasies indicated insanity. "I see nothing insane in having a vivid imagination and a fondness for using it at every opportunity." He had already stated that he saw nothing insane in two highly intelligent and imaginative adolescents being preoccupied with the hereafter, even toying with a private religion of their own.

Stallworthy also said that in interviews with the accused he had seen no evidence of inappropriate emotional reactions. Certainly they had not shown the remorse and regret one might imagine to be normal, but he had, he said, seen murderers about whom there was no suggestion of insanity show the same apparent coldness and callousness. Although there was evidence of the girls being quite unduly pleased with themselves, he did not consider this amounted to exaltation in the sense a psychiatrist would use the word. There was never the degree of elevation of mood that was, in itself, evidence of insanity.

In short, the chief medical office of Auckland Mental Hospital would not acknowledge the girls were suffering from mental abnormality of any kind.

Terence Gresson rose to cross-examine the witness. As was his style he stood languidly, one foot up on his chair. He quickly extracted a number of concessions. Yes, Stallworthy agreed, Dr Medlicott, whom he had known for many years, was a competent and capable psychiatrist and a man of professional integrity. Yes, whether a person was sane or insane was a matter upon which psychiatrists might disagree. Yes, there had been instances in the past when he had been proved wrong and his colleagues right. And yes, paranoia was one of the rarer forms of insanity and often hard to diagnose. Paranoia of the exalted type was, he agreed, a *very* rare form. He acknowledged that it was very common for paranoiacs to display gross conceit, and in the later stages to think they were gods or superior beings. Female paranoiacs, he had to admit, occasionally believed they were goddesses.

What, Gresson asked, would Stallworthy think about the mental condition of an adolescent who came into his consulting rooms solemnly telling him she had an extra part of the brain and persisting in that belief? He acknowledged that he would suspect she had a delusion and seek confirmatory evidence of mental disease. He further acknowledged that if the same person were to tell him she were destined for a paradise for which only ten persons qualified, she might have been described in earlier psychiatric terminology as a monomaniac.

He was also willing to confirm that *folie simultanée* was a rare but recognised mental condition in which, as Gresson put it, "the mental instability of one patient aggravates the mental instability of the other", causing "a kind of mutual acceleration of the mental illness". And he agreed that if a patient had paranoia, the disease would taint the whole of his reasoning and affect his judgement.

Gresson had made some useful points while avoiding a head-on collision that might alienate the judge and jury.

Next to take the stand was Dr James Saville, medical officer at Sunnyside Mental Hospital in Christchurch. Saville said he had examined thousands of mental patients, and never before had a case come to his notice of two insane persons combining to commit a crime. He, too, believed that the first two times the girls were examined by him they were trying to make themselves out to be insane. Juliet had told him she thought they might be released from a mental hospital in two or three years but were unlikely to get out of prison so quickly. In his considered opinion, at the time of the offence both the accused understood the nature and quality of their act in killing Mrs Rieper and that the act was against the law and wrong from the point of view of the general belief of the community morally. He had read the diaries of the girl Parker and skimmed through other writings. Nothing in them, or anything said to him in the course of the interviews, caused him to alter his opinion that the accused were sane at the time of the murder and sane today.

Dr James Hunter, the medical superintendent at Sunnyside Mental Hospital, was even more cursory. He seemed to be there to add weight of numbers, so that in the final count there would be three psychiatrists for the prosecution against two for the defence. He had never, he said, heard of two insane persons conspiring to commit a crime, except for one example mentioned in East's *Forensic Medicine*. He did not bother to explain what the example was. His opinion, surprising to no one, was that neither girl was suffering from any disease of the mind at the time of the killing and neither was certifiable.

Not one of the prosecution's three psychiatric experts, sworn to tell "the whole truth", had been prepared to acknowledge any mental abnormality whatsoever in either Juliet Hulme or Pauline Parker. There had been no concessions that might tempt the jury to take pity on the two girls.

ABOVE Greenwich, London, where the Hulme family lived during the Second World War, was hit time and again by German bombs. This photo was taken from the Town Hall on June 27, 1944, after a V1 rocket destroyed several houses. *Greenwich Heritage Centre*

BELOW Alcester Road in Moseley village near Birmingham at the turn of the century. When Honorah Parker was born in 1907, her parents lived in a substantial house in this street. Two years later her father was admitted to the City Asylum, the house was sold, and the family moved to a more modest dwelling. *History-in-Pictures*

Henry and Hilda Hulme and their children Juliet and Jonathan arrive in Christchurch in 1948; Hulme was taking up a position as the first full-time rector of Canterbury University College. The photo featured in the "Social Jottings" page of the *New Zealand Woman's Weekly*.

Canterbury University College, founded in 1873, stood in the centre of Christchurch. It had gone into decline during the war years, but from 1944 ex-servicemen began to swell the numbers. Henry Hulme's appointment was intended to boost the college's academic standing.

Christchurch City Libraries, CCL-KPCD16-IMG0074

ABOVE Queenswood School in Hastings, 450 miles from Christchurch, where Juliet was sent at the age of twelve. The school was run along lines advocated by the Austrian philosopher Rudolf Steiner. Juliet was unhappy at the school and lasted there less than a year. *Taikura Rudolf Steiner School*

ABOVE RIGHT The grand house at Ilam, where the Hulmes lived from 1950 to 1954. The house and its fifty-three acres of park-like grounds fuelled Juliet's and Pauline's imaginations and their fantasies about their future lives as beauties, geniuses, and even goddesses. *Stan McKay photograph, Canterbury Museum [1980.192.296]*

RIGHT 33 Gloucester Street, with the Riepers' house, number 31, on the right. In the early years the Riepers lived upstairs; to get there you had to walk along the dark, tree-lined path and climb an outside stairway. A young playmate of Pauline found the path so "creepy" she wouldn't brave it after dark. Number 33 was also a boarding house. *F. E. McGregor photograph, Canterbury Museum [12708]*

ABOVE Girls from Christchurch Girls' High School running in Cranmer Square in the late 1940s during physical education. When Pauline Parker and Juliet Hulme attended the school both were both exempted from games because of childhood illnesses. They became friendly during the hours they sat together while their classmates participated.
John Pascoe Collection, Alexander Turnbull Library, Wellington, N.Z., F-1567-1/4

LEFT Jean Isobel Stewart, the headmistress of Christchurch Girls' High from 1948 to 1954. She warned Hilda Hulme the girls' relationship might be going beyond normal healthy friendship. *Christchurch Girls' High School*

Detail from Pauline Parker's fourth-form class photo at Christchurch Girls'
High. Pauline, head bowed and scowling, is in the top row, second from right.
Christchurch Girls' High School

LEFT Henry Hulme with an unidentified man. Appointed with high hopes, after a glowing recommendation from scientist and novelist C.P. Snow, Hulme eventually fell out with many of his colleagues, who felt he was neither a good rector nor loyal to the college. *Christchurch Star-Sun*

BELOW LEFT Hilda Hulme found it easier to fit into Canterbury society. She became a prominent Marriage Guidance counsellor and radio personality, with a coterie of friends known for their candid views on sex and other matters.
Truth Weekender (N.Z. Truth)

BELOW Bill Perry, a Canadian engineer in New Zealand on a work assignment for a British firm, met Hilda Hulme when he sought help at the Marriage Guidance Council for his failed marriage. By the end of 1953 he and Hilda had embarked on a serious love affair.
Truth Weekender (N.Z. Truth)

Juliet Hulme photographed in the Ilam garden a year before the murder, aged fourteen. One of her contemporaries would remember her as tall and lovely-looking, but strange in some indefinable way, "rather a lonely child".
Christchurch Star-Sun

Rudi Gopas, painting *en plein air* circa 1950. Forced to paint portraits to make ends meet, Gopas would sometimes produce a second, private portrait of a subject, which he felt expressed their true nature. When the wife of one of Henry Hulme's colleagues saw Gopas's secret portrait of Hilda, she was amazed to see how successfully the artist had captured Hilda's "rather ruthless character".
Courtesy Chris Ronayne

TOP Port Levy, from the Māori cemetery on the east side of the bay. The cottage where the Hulmes stayed was near the wharf in the distance. On Good Friday 1953 the girls climbed the hill behind and "saw a gateway through the clouds. We sat on the edge of the path and looked down the hill out over the bay. The island looked beautiful. The sea was blue. Everything was full of peace and bliss. We then realised we had the key. … an extra part of our brain which can appreciate the 4th World." *Stacy Squires, The Press*

ABOVE The Port Levy bach, which Hilda Hulme dubbed "Christmas Cottage". By the end of 1953 Hilda and Henry had become so concerned about their daughter's friendship with Pauline they declined to invite Pauline to stay with them here for the summer holidays. *Truth Weekender (N.Z. Truth)*

ABOVE Cashmere Sanatorium, where Juliet spent over three months from April 1953. Although a diagnosis of TB was no longer a death sentence—by 1950 the death rate was only eleven percent of that in 1900—it was still a nasty disease requiring painful treatment and a long slow recovery. The rooms were designed to allow the patients plenty of fresh air. *Alexander Turnbull Library, Wellington, N.Z., G-17816-1/1*

ABOVE RIGHT Christchurch's Cathedral Square in the 1950s. The day before the murder Juliet and Pauline went to a film at the Regent Theatre (top, right). One of their former classmates saw them nearby at about four-fifteen and had a brief chat with them. Their manner seemed "quite normal". *The Press*

RIGHT MGM film *The Prisoner of Zenda* opened in Christchurch in April 1953. Juliet and Pauline became obsessed with James Mason, who played the evil, swashbuckling Count Rupert of Hentzau. They were fascinated by the ruthless, cold-blooded characters that were Mason's specialty, a line-up that included German Field Marshal Erwin Rommel. Juliet also adored Mason as the treacherous valet to the British ambassador to Turkey, busy selling military secrets to the Nazis, in *5 Fingers*, which screened around the same time.

JUNE 1954

22 TUESDAY

173—192

I am writing a little of this up on the morning before the death. I felt very excited and 'the night before Christmas-ish' last night. I did not have pleasant dreams though. I am about to rise!

ABOVE Pauline Parker's diary entry on the day of the murder, which reads: "I am writing a little of this up on the morning before the death. I felt very excited and 'the night before Christmas-ish' last night. I did not have pleasant dreams though. I am about to rise!"

BELOW The tea kiosk at Victoria Park, which enjoyed a spectacular view over the Canterbury Plains to the Southern Alps. The trio had tea, soft drinks, cakes and scones before setting off down the track. They were a quiet group, Agnes Ritchie remembered, "nothing out of the ordinary". *Truth Weekender (N.Z. Truth)*

RIGHT The murder scene. Honorah Parker's body lay with her head downhill, face up. Her eyes bulged. Her hair was matted with blood, which also smeared her face and was caked in her mouth and nostrils. Streams of clotted blood extended twelve feet down the track. *Truth Weekender (N.Z. Truth)*

BELOW, LEFT Agnes Ritchie, manager of the tea kiosk and first to hear of the "accident" when the girls raced into her kiosk covered in blood. *Truth Weekender (N.Z. Truth)* CENTRE Park caretaker Kenneth Ritchie, who found Honorah Parker's body. He realised immediately her death was not an accident, as the girls had claimed. *Christchurch Star-Sun* RIGHT Detective Sergeant Archie Tate, one of the first police officers to reach the scene of the murder. *Christchurch Star-Sun*

ABOVE LEFT Henry Hulme, photographed in Australia on his way back to England in 1954. Eleven days after the murder he fled Christchurch with his son Jonathan, leaving Hilda to attend the trial with her lover, Bill Perry. "The world must just consider me an unnatural father," Hulme was reported as saying. He would never return to New Zealand. *Truth Weekender (N.Z. Truth)*

ABOVE RIGHT Hilda Hulme was perceived by some in Christchurch as "sexy" and "steaming", and by others as "ruthless" and "hard as nails". She attended the trial every day even though Juliet refused to see her. *Truth Weekender (N.Z. Truth)*

Pauline Parker and Juliet Hulme leave the magistrate's court after being committed for trial. *Christchurch Star-Sun*

ABOVE LEFT The Supreme Court building, where the trial of Parker and Hulme took place. The building's grey stone, neo-Gothic walls and sombre interior seemed designed to intimidate all who had business there. *Stan McKay photograph, Canterbury Museum [1980.192.233]*

LEFT The interior of the Supreme Court, showing the judge's bench, witness box and press benches. *Alexander Turnbull Library, Wellington, N.Z., C-1998-1/2*

ABOVE The case was a cause célèbre. From the day the trial began crowds waited outside from early in the morning, trying to get a seat in the public gallery, while journalists from around the world crushed into the press benches. Newspapers reported that many of the female spectators were "fashionably dressed". *Christchurch Star-Sun*

TOP Alec Haslam, leading counsel for Pauline Parker. From the beginning both his and Juliet Hulme's defence teams realised that, as the girls had made signed confessions, the only possible defence was insanity. *Truth Weekender (N.Z. Truth)*

LEFT Christchurch doctor Francis Bennett. On June 24—less than thirty-six hours after the murder—the general practitioner interviewed Pauline and Juliet at the Central Police Station at the request of Pauline's defence team. He was shocked that the girls showed no contrition. *Christchurch Star-Sun*

RIGHT Terence Gresson (seated), leader of Juliet Hulme's defence team, with junior counsel Brian McClelland. The urbane Gresson was a Cambridge graduate and an old friend of Henry Hulme. After the trial McClelland felt Gresson had not made a strong enough pitch to the jury's emotions. *Nicholas Gresson*

ABOVE LEFT Psychiatrist Reginald Medlicott, the chief witness for the defence. After winning a Rockefeller Fellowship in 1949, Medlicott had pursued advanced studies at Case Western Reserve University and got to know many of the leaders of American psychiatry. However, he had limited experience appearing as an expert witness in court. *Christchurch Star-Sun*

ABOVE CENTRE Peter Mahon, junior to crown prosecutor Alan Brown. Mahon became increasingly concerned by Brown's heavy drinking and volatile behaviour during the trial. *Christchurch Star-Sun*

ABOVE RIGHT Kenneth Stallworthy, one of three psychiatrists called by the prosecution to argue that the girls were sane when they committed the murder. Stallworthy said he had seen many paranoiacs in mental hospitals and they did not behave anything like Juliet and Pauline. A weakness in the defence case was that the girls had claimed to be insane; people who were genuinely insane, Stallworthy contended, always insisted on saying they were sane. *Christchurch Star-Sun*

RIGHT Alan Brown, the prosecutor, arriving at the Supreme Court on August 24. After years as deputy, Brown had finally gained the top job as Christchurch crown solicitor and the high profile trial was a heaven-sent opportunity for him to prove himself. *Christchurch Star-Sun*

LEFT Francis Boyd Adams, the sixty-six-year-old Supreme Court judge who heard the case. Adams had a reputation as a hanging judge. The defence's Brian McClelland considered him an "awful, mean bastard ... a miserable, narrow-minded, teetotal, Scottish Baptist shit". *The Press*

BELOW The trial caused an international sensation. Here Brian McClelland, junior counsel for Juliet Hulme, walks towards the court with Hilda Hulme and her lover Bill Perry. The newspaper caption coyly referred to Perry as "the occupant of the flat in the Hulme home". *Truth Weekender (N.Z. Truth)*

fortuna CLOTH

The Sun-Herald

Incorporating "The Sunday Sun and Guardian" (No. 2679) and "The Sunday Herald" (No. 291)

PHONE: BO399 (23 Lines) — SYDNEY, SUNDAY, AUGUST 29, 1954 — Registered at the General Post Office, Sydney for transmission by post as a newspaper

JURY FINDS TWO N.Z. GIRLS SANE

Tense Murder Verdict Scenes

A.A.P And Special Representative

CHRISTCHURCH, Saturday.—In a dramatic, tense atmosphere, a jury to-day found that Pauline Yvonne Parker, 16, and Juliet Marion Hulme, 15, were sane when they murdered Pauline Parker's mother.

Mr. Justice Adams sentenced the girls to be detained in prison during her Majesty's pleasure.

Minimum Of Five Years' Gaol

Law authorities said to-night that this could mean a minimum of five years' gaol, or a maximum of at least 25 years.

'JULIET HULME

As sentence was passed a middle-aged man in the public gallery jumped to his feet and shouted, "I protest! I object!"

The Court crier called "silence," and police rushed into the gallery and hustled the man out of the court.

Honора Mary Parker (known as Mrs. Rieper), 45, was found battered to death on June 23 in a picnic reserve outside Christchurch.

The girls' trial lasted six days.

Neither showed any emotion as sentence was passed.

Air Of Calm

Throughout the trial they had maintained an air of calm, contemptuous detachment.

The two girls are likely to be placed in separate prisons. One of them will probably go to Paparua prison near Christchurch and the other to Mt. Eden prison, Auckland.

"During her Majesty's pleasure" means that the two girls will be kept in prison for an indefinite period and only released at the discretion of the Prisons Department and by order of the Executive Council.

New Zealand law provides that where a convicted murderer is under 18 years the sentence shall be detention during her Majesty's pleasure instead of the death sentence.

Juliet Hulme's mother sat with her eyes closed and hands tightly clenched as sentence was passed.

Earlier, while the jury was out, she had walked about near the courthouse smoking cigarettes and looking nervous and tense.

The jury was out for two hours 15 minutes.

Immediately it returned the accused girls were led into the courthouse by a police matron.

They smiled and laughed at each other as the jurywomen took their places.

The girls were standing when Mr. Justice Adams asked the jury foreman what verdict they had reached.

They showed no emotion whatever when he replied, "Guilty," thus rejecting the insanity plea.

Parker, however, glanced quickly upwards in surprise as the man in the public gallery jumped to his feet and cried out.

No Reply

The man was a stranger who had no connection with anyone concerned in the trial.

During discussion on the girls' ages, the Crown Prosecutor, Mr. A. W. Brown, appeared upset and several times had to stop as though he was finding it difficult to speak.

The girls were the only ones in the court who did not seem to be affected.

They looked straight ahead at the Judge as he asked each of them in turn whether there was anything they wished to say before sentence was passed.

Neither replied, but their counsel told the Court they had nothing to add to the evidence already given.

Mrs. Hulme sat only a few feet away from the girls, but neither looked at her.

After Mr. Justice Adams had passed sentence, he said: "The prisoners may now be removed."

The two girls walked out looking straight ahead and were taken through a side door to a prison van.

Immediately after the trial, Mrs. Hulme left the court accompanied by Mr. Walter Perry, an engineer, who lived in a flat at the Hulme home.

During the trial Perry told the Court he had fallen in love with Mrs. Hulme.

Mrs. Hulme is believed to be staying at a seaside resort about 35 miles from Christchurch.

Pauline Parker's father, Mr. Herbert Rieper, said:

"I have nothing to say about it," he said later at his home.

Tired, Pale

Juliet Hulme's father, Dr. Henry Hulme, left New Zealand with his 10-year-old son, Jonathan, soon after her arrest. He left the liner Himalaya at Marseilles and London newspapers since have been unable to trace him.

When the trial resumed this morning, Hulme and Parker looked a little tired and pale as they were led into court by a police matron.

They stared intently at the jury before sitting down to hear their defence counsel attempt to prove them insane.

At the outset to-day Dr. A. Haslam (for Parker) said there was no disputing the fact that Juliet Hulme and Pauline Parker had killed Mrs. Parker but they were insane to a degree that excused the jury.

The atmosphere was tense as Mr. Brown rose to address the jury.

Even the two girls, who had been whispering and unwilling to each other, were silent as he began to speak.

"The accused were depraved, but not insane," Mr. Brown said.

Bowed Head

"They were not incurably insane, but incurably bad."

At this stage Juliet Hulme bowed her head and blocked her ears with her fingers.

The girls sat pale-faced in silence as the Judge told the jury that if they accepted evidence that the girls had known the murder was against the law and moral code of the community they were bound to find them guilty.

In the morning, football fans wearing striped caps and team ribbons had queued with honey-eyes and teenagers for admission to the grey stone court building.

NEW MURDER LEAD

BRISBANE, Saturday. — Detectives are following a new lead in the Betty Shanks murder mystery. Inspector Frank Bischof, of Brisbane C.I.B., said to-night the lead was one of the strongest yet received in the two-year-old investigation.

He said a man had been admitted to the psychiatric ward of Brisbane Hospital muttering a garbled account of the murder. The man was under police observation. Betty Shanks, 22, was murdered near her home at Wilston on the night of September 19, 1952.

● Girls "incurably bad" says Crown.—P. 3

PAULINE PARKER

Mrs. Hulme, mother of Juliet Hulme.

Your Paper To-day

● News, pages 1-27.
● Features begin page 29.
● Leader page 28.
● Fact (including Macleans) begins page 49.
● Leon Gellert, page 58.
● Women's Section, pages 56-61.

Elsewhere you will find: Music, Theatre, Radio, Films, pages 54-55; Books and Crossword, page 56; Smart Homes Service, page 57; Finance, page 59; Garden, pages 60-61. PLUS: 8-page Comics Section.

WEATHER (CITY): Fine, mild day. Areas of morning fog. Frosty night. Easterly winds. Details P. 80.

Hilda Hulme and Bill Perry being driven away from the court. Both attended every day of the trial. Asked by Alan Brown, the prosecutor, whether there was anything to suggest her daughter "needed medical attention so far as her brain was concerned", Hilda replied, "No, she treated me with disdain but I did not notice anything like that." *Christchurch Star-Sun*

Bill Perry and Hilda Hulme, who had rapidly changed her surname by deed poll to Perry, depart Christchurch Airport on September 11, 1954, en route to England. Nancy Sutherland was shocked that her friend would leave the country while her daughter languished in jail. Hilda told the Australian press it was "not justice to send a young girl to jail when what she needed most was love, care, attention and affection". She firmly believed Juliet was insane. "She believed she was a god and able to break the law." *Nicholas Gresson*

Pauline Parker, who today goes under the name Hilary Nathan, captured in 1997 by a photographer for British newspaper *The Express*. Nathan lives far from the media glare in Scotland's remote Orkney islands, continuing her childhood passion for horses and riding. *Express Syndication*

Anne Perry, as Juliet Hulme is known today. In 1979, at the age of forty-one, Perry launched a successful writing career with the publication of *The Cater Street Hangman*, a grisly murder mystery set in Victorian London. At the time of writing she had over sixty books in print, with total sales of around twenty million copies; at least two books have made *The New York Times* bestseller list.

Express Syndication

Extracts from a large mural found on the wall of Hilary Nathan's former home in Hoo St Werburgh. Said to be painted by Nathan herself, the mural depicts two girls, one blonde and the other dark-haired, in imaginary situations, from caged despair to god-like exaltation. The work indicates that decades after the murder Nathan was still deeply troubled and had not been able to put Juliet Hulme and the horror of their parting out of her mind.

Andrew Ayres

Kate Winslet as Juliet Hulme and Melanie Lynskey as Pauline Parker in Peter Jackson's 1994 film *Heavenly Creatures*. *Time* magazine proclaimed the film one of the year's ten best. It launched Jackson's international career and made stars of Winslet and Lynskey, but resulted in public exposure for Parker and Hulme in their reinvented lives as Anne Perry and Hilary Nathan. *Miramax Films*

The Crown's case in rebuttal ended shortly before five in the evening on Friday, August 26. The time had come for closing speeches, followed by the judge's summing-up, after which the jury would retire. The judge asked the foreman to consult the jurors as to whether they would like to continue the next morning, Saturday. The foreman reported that they would.

There was general dismay. An event of utmost importance was taking place on Saturday afternoon: at two o'clock Canterbury was defending the Ranfurly Shield at Lancaster Park against a strong challenge by Waikato. Like almost all the city's rugby-lovers, Terence Gresson and Brian McClelland had plans to watch the game.

Surely the jurors, too, would hope to be there? Having them sit on a Saturday seemed to Brian McClelland a ploy by Mr Justice Adams to make the jury rush its decision. A quick verdict would be bad news for the defence, he thought glumly. An acquittal could come only after a long hard deliberation.

The court staff, too, were unhappy about having to work on Saturday, as was Alan Brown's junior Peter Mahon. What shape would his leader would be in next morning? Brown had already darted off in the direction of the Canterbury Club, where he did most of his drinking.

As the lawyers gathered up their papers, a message came from the judge. He wished to see counsel in his chambers at their earliest convenience. His Honour was told Mr Brown was indisposed; it was agreed that junior counsel could deal with whatever it was Mr Justice Adams wanted to discuss.

McClelland, Wicks and Mahon trooped into the gloomy room to learn that the judge was intending to withdraw the defence of insanity from the jury and direct them to enter a verdict of guilty. There was no evidence, he said, to support a finding of insanity under section 43 of the Crimes Act. Doctors Medlicott, Bennett, Stallworthy and Saville had all given evidence to the effect that, at the time they committed murder, both accused knew it was wrong in criminal law and wrong according to the standards of the community.

It was true. Medlicott and Bennett had insisted the girls were medically insane in that they were certifiable under the Mental

Defectives Act 1911 and that, because of their delusions, had believed it was right—or at least not wrong—for them to kill Pauline's mother, even though they knew it would be wrong for others to do so. It was well established that on a strict reading of section 43 such a belief, personal to themselves, did not support a defence of insanity.

Brian McClelland protested vigorously. There was evidence that, if accepted by the jury, would mean Juliet Hulme was legally insane. He would need more time to research the point. Peter Mahon, too, was strongly opposed. He firmly believed the question of the girls' guilt or innocence ought properly to be left to the jury to decide.

Mr Justice Adams was firm: the matter was his alone to decide. "In the end he said he would see us again in the morning before the court sat," McClelland remembered. "In the meantime we could think it over."

Accompanied by Mahon, McClelland disappeared to the law library in the Supreme Court to see if there were any precedents for what the judge proposed. The only case of relevance was *R v Windle*, which had been decided by the English Court of Criminal Appeal two years earlier. It was not at all helpful. The defence to murder had also been *folie à deux* insanity. Although there was evidence that the appellant suffered from a disease of the mind, medical experts on both sides were agreed that when he administered a fatal dose of aspirin to his wife he knew he was doing an illegal act. On that basis the trial judge had withdrawn the insanity defence from the jury.

The Chief Justice, Lord Goddard, in the course of the argument had said he himself had once made a similar ruling and was aware of another case where the same had been done. To decline to leave insanity to the jury, he had ruled, was a strong line for a judge to take—in most cases the effect was to condemn the prisoner to death—"but it is one he ought to take if he is convinced there is no evidence to be left to a jury on a particular issue".

Although there was good authority for the course of action the judge was threatening, McClelland was unbowed. Next morning he told Mr Justice Adams that if he ruled out insanity the defence would appeal immediately. Peter Mahon added that he would feel honour-bound to withdraw from the case. Unlike Alan Brown, Mahon was not preoccupied with winning. He thought it perfectly obvious that the girls, if not legally insane, were seriously mentally disturbed, and did not want to deny them the possibility of a sympathy verdict that might allow them to receive treatment they would not get in prison.

If the jury were not allowed to consider the defence of insanity, the kerfuffle that would create, with the world's press sitting there noting down every word, could readily be imagined. The previous day the *Christchurch Star-Sun* had boasted that not for many years had news from New Zealand received such prominence in British newspapers. Each day most were publishing at least half a column, generally on the front page. In some broadsheets the coverage was even greater. The *Mirror* and the *Daily Sketch* were giving the trial extensive space on their inside pages.

Mr Justice Adams relented. He would allow the defence to be put to the jury, subject to a careful direction. Thanks largely to Mahon, the game was still on. But the defence counsel were not at all sanguine: they were sure there would be a strong summing-up against them.

CHAPTER 28

The Jury Retires

It was the first time for many years that there had been a murder hearing on a Saturday. At nine-thirty in the morning, the upstairs public gallery in the Supreme Court was not as full as on the preceding five days but there were still a hundred spectators. Some were rugby supporters, clutching knitted woolly hats in the colours of their respective provinces. These visitors from out of town would dine out on their remembrances of the famous Christchurch murder trial for years to come.

Alec Haslam spoke first. He apologised to the jury for "a lot of repulsive evidence" that had been put before them. The intention had not been to shock, but to help them decide the question of insanity. The two accused, he said, were "lonely and withdrawn types" who had both suffered ill health in childhood, and whose friendship had quickly developed an "alarming intensity". They had become "morbidly close".

He made no attack on the psychiatric evidence called by the Crown, and did little in the course of twenty-five minutes to counter the crown prosecutor's assertion that the girls were merely "dirty-minded". Appeals to emotion were not Haslam's forte. He glossed over the crucial question of legal insanity under section 43 in the hope that if the jury felt sorry for the girls they would overlook the legal niceties. "Dr Bennett ... agreed with Dr Medlicott that the girls were suffering from paranoia with delusions of grandeur ... There was ample evidence the girls were insane in the broad general sense of the term ... Dr Bennett had said their delusion would affect their whole judgement ... They did not regard their act as morally wrong." That said, he invited the jury to bring back a verdict of not guilty on the ground of insanity.

Terence Gresson was more persuasive, but like Haslam there was not much fight in him. Dr Medlicott, he said, had arrived at a clear-cut diagnosis of paranoia with an association of *folie à deux*. The accused were certifiably insane, aware at times of wrongness and rightness, but it was so temporary they could switch from what they knew of the law to their own fantastic world at a moment's notice. Dr Bennett had arrived independently at a similar conclusion. "You have two competent, reputable doctors telling you Parker and Hulme were insane and I ask you to accept that evidence."

Dealing with the evidence of the psychiatrists from the Department of Mental Hygiene he trod carefully. The three doctors, he pointed out, all worked for the Crown. "I don't suggest they are mentally dishonest but they do come from the same stable. If they were out at Addington [Raceway] this afternoon they would have to be bracketed. It does tend to create an identity of views." He hoped jurors might grasp the point without his having to spell it out.

Then he made his final appeal to the jury. "If you had a daughter, and she displayed half the symptoms that have been enumerated in respect of these girls, would you not call a doctor? Would you not assume she was mentally touched? Is it not clear from the facts that have been proved that these girls are what is commonly called 'crackers'? I submit to you that they were incapable of forming a moral judgement on what they did. ... These girls are mentally ill, sick adolescents—not brutal criminals."

Brian McClelland knew Gresson had not made a strong enough pitch to the jury's emotions. Even Gresson's son Nico, who was sitting in court, would admonish his father for being too soft. "Why didn't you do a Marshall Hall?" he said, referring to an English barrister famous for his powerful advocacy. "It needed it."

Gresson was at heart too much the gentleman. Both he and Haslam had been content to deliver workmanlike performances. Neither had been prepared to risk alienating the judge, and perhaps making fools of themselves, with a vehement attack on the government psychiatrists, in the faint hope of winning acquittals for their unappealing clients. McClelland believed they were too keen on becoming judges themselves to risk getting offside with Mr Justice Adams.

Now it was Alan Brown's turn. Juliet and Pauline, who had been whispering and smiling to each other, fell silent as the prosecutor began to speak. The two in the dock were charged with a very dreadful crime, Brown said. One could not help pitying them for the horrible position they were in and for being such bad people. They were thoroughly depraved, but their depravity did not mean they were insane. "The evidence proved they had most unhealthy minds, but it was badness and not a question of insanity at all. I say what I said in my opening—that this was a coldly and callously planned, premeditated murder committed by two highly intelligent but precocious dirty-minded girls."

Juliet sat with her fingers in her ears. "They are not incurably insane," Brown exclaimed theatrically. "They are incurably bad!"

As he sat down he slumped forward a little, looking terribly distressed. Nico Gresson, sitting in the grand jury box, noticed and wondered what was happening to him.

Section 43 of New Zealand's Crimes Act, like the legal defence of insanity in a number of jurisdictions, was closely based on the English M'Naghten rules of 1843. Over the years various legal and medical experts, including Dr Kenneth Stallworthy, had observed that if these rules were correctly interpreted very few killers would be found not guilty by reason of insanity. This notwithstanding, it was firmly established in practice in both England and New Zealand that an accused proved to have been *medically* insane at the time of his or her crime would get an acquittal. In clear cases of insanity it was the custom of the courts, the jury, the judge, and the counsel, as Stallworthy had once written, "to connive at either ignoring the rules or paying the merest lip service to them". This was precisely the door Stallworthy and his colleagues from Sunnyside were now determined not to leave ajar for Pauline and Juliet.

The distinguished Cambridge University law professor Glanville Williams had written that the M'Naghten defence was "extremely narrow ... unless indulgently interpreted". Mr Justice Adams was a solid criminal lawyer but his approach to the law was pedantic and literal: he was not given to indulgent interpretations. The jury's task, he instructed them, was to consider coldly and calmly whether the defence of insanity had been proved beyond reasonable doubt. The case for both girls had, he said, been conducted on the basis that the evidence affecting them individually—for example, the diaries for 1953 and 1954 written by Parker—was to be considered in regard to them both. The only verdicts open were "not guilty on the ground of insanity" or "guilty".

"Insanity," the judge continued, "must of course be a question of degree. ... It may well be that you will think they suffered from some degree of mental disorder, that to some extent and in some way their minds and intelligence are abnormal. I do not think anyone could listen to the evidence in this case without forming some sort of conclusion to that effect." His words seemed a mild rebuke for the prosecution's psychiatric team, who professed to have formed no such conclusion.

At this point things got more difficult for the defence. The law, the judge explained, did not relieve persons of criminal responsibility merely because they were insane. The insanity had to be such as to render the person incapable of understanding the nature and quality of the act or omission, or of knowing that such an act or omission was wrong."

Four doctors, he reminded the jury, had said both girls knew what they had done was wrong in the eyes of the law and according to the generally accepted moral standards of the community. It was not sufficient to suggest an accused person had some private moral standard of their own: this was no defence in law. No medical man, he said, had given the evidence necessary to establish that the girls did not know the act of killing Mrs Parker was wrong for the purposes of the statute. Unless the jury could find elsewhere in the evidence any material that might support a contrary conclusion, it was their duty to convict.

Where might the jury begin to look for such evidence? The defence of insanity had been destroyed as surely as if the judge had withdrawn it. Even if they were of a mind to accept the evidence of

Medlicott and Bennett that the girls were medically insane, there would be no indulgent stretching of a legal point in their favour.

The jury retired at nineteen minutes to one. Two hours and twelve minutes later, when they filed back in and took their seats, the court had filled to capacity. The atmosphere was tense. Pauline gazed impassively ahead. Juliet briefly scanned the jurors' faces and the faint smile on her face vanished. Bill Perry placed a hand on Hilda Hulme's arm as the registrar asked the foreman for the verdict. There was no hesitation. "Guilty," he replied. The rest of the jury indicated it was the verdict of them all.

The momentary silence was broken by a young man in the upstairs gallery who yelled, "I protest! I object!"

The court crier roared, "Silence!" and two policemen propelled the interjector out of the courtroom.

There was another matter to be dealt with. Capital punishment—death by hanging—was the sentence prescribed by law for convicted murderers, but there was a proviso: where the person was under eighteen, Section 5 of the Capital Punishment Act provided that the sentence should instead be detention during Her Majesty's pleasure. That meant an indefinite term of imprisonment until the minister of justice decided to order the prisoner's release. His Honour wished to hear from counsel on the matter. Terence Gresson submitted there was clear evidence from Mrs Hulme as to her daughter's age. Alec Haslam said Mr Rieper had given similar evidence in respect of Pauline Parker. The judge was concerned to follow proper procedure: the girls' ages were questions of fact that had to be determined.

Alan Brown proposed that the evidence relevant to the ages of the prisoners be read to the jury. "He appeared upset and several times had to stop, as though he was finding it difficult to speak," *The San Francisco Examiner* reported. As he sat down again he collapsed forward, face on the table, arms stretched out in front of him, sobbing audibly. When he sat up, still weeping, he covered his face with his hands.

When Brown gained control of himself, Mr Justice Adams submitted the matter to the jury. After brief consultation in the jury box, the foreman announced that they found both prisoners to be under the age of eighteen.

Juliet and Pauline showed no sign of emotion as they were sentenced. "You both being under the age of eighteen, the sentence of the court is detention during Her Majesty's pleasure," Mr Justice Adams pronounced. "That sentence is passed upon each of you. ... The prisoners may now be removed." Pauline stared firmly ahead as they were led back to the cells upstairs. Juliet glanced sideways towards her mother but Hilda did not see her: her eyes were shut in deep despair.

Feeling sick and close to tears himself, Brian McClelland went upstairs to speak to Juliet.

"Bambi," she asked, "is it true that wig on your head is made of horsehair?"

"I'm sorry, I feel I've let you down," McClelland said.

"Don't worry. I've had a bet on it, I've read it–"

"Yes it is," he answered. "Will you see your mother?"

"I don't want to see her," she replied.

"I'll go downstairs to see her and come back," McClelland said.

On receiving the news that her daughter wouldn't speak to her, Hilda maintained her composure, as she had throughout the ordeal. "Tell her I'll do what I can to help," she said.

When McClelland went back upstairs Juliet's only concern was that he make sure she and Pauline went to the same prison. McClelland told her Dr Medlicott thought she needed his help.

"I don't mind," she said. "He was always nice to me."

Shortly before four o'clock, when most of the crowd outside had departed, the girls were driven away to start their sentences. Brian McClelland did not visit Juliet in prison and never saw her again. "Frankly," he said, "I didn't want to. There was nothing I could do. She needed a doctor, not a lawyer."

CHAPTER 29

Her Majesty's Pleasure

The despised adulterers made a handsome couple as they left the court. Hilda Hulme, arm in arm with Perry, kept her bearing. She was determined not to give the ghastly types mobbing around them the pleasure of watching her snivel. The crowd was disappointed, felt short-changed. Her behaviour wasn't natural. Some said it was a pity the girls hadn't taken *her* for a walk in Victoria Park instead of the nice mother. Even people who knew Hilda well thought her calm, dignified manner during the trial showed she was a hard woman. Almost none thought to give her credit for her courageous and steadfast support of her daughter.

One of the police officers who escorted Juliet and Pauline back to Paparua was Audrey Griffiths, the young constable who had had the job of undressing Honorah Rieper's body on the night of the murder. She would never forget Juliet's coldhearted tomfoolery. She was shocked to hear her say to Pauline in a stage whisper, "The old girl took a bit more killing than we thought." When Griffiths took her to task, Juliet turned on her, jeering, "Oh, aren't we the perfect little policewoman."

If Pauline and Juliet really were psychotic, or afflicted with some lesser mental disorder, the tragedy was that they had become individually and as a pair so odious that hardly anyone could give them a second's sympathy. A piece of paper was discovered on which they had listed all the other people they intended to kill at the first opportunity. Probably it was meant to be found. Agnes Ritchie was alarmed to be told her name and her husband's were on it. There were six other names, including Archie Tate and two or three mistresses from Girls' High, including the Latin teacher, Miss Waller.

And yet the girls were not without their admirers. There was the young man who stood up at the back of the court and shouted "I object!" as the jury returned its verdict. There was the anonymous sexual fantasist in England who posted Brian McClelland a long black evening gown and high-heeled shoes, hoping he would forward them to Juliet. And all over New Zealand—and further abroad—there were unhappy teenage girls who had no trouble imagining how they too, if only they had the resolve, might take bricks and stockings and send their mothers to kingdom come.

Then there were girls whose lives were changed by the case. One was Alison Laurie. Aged thirteen and in the third form of a girls' school in Wellington, she had found herself falling in love with girls and had a fantasy life full of romance and passion, if limited by her ignorance. Despite the best endeavours of her parents, she read about the case of Pauline and Juliet in the local newspapers. For her, it was confirmation that there were other girls who fell in love and felt for one another the way she felt for a number of girls. Many years later she would write about the case as co-author of a book, *Parker and Hulme: A Lesbian View*.

The government psychiatrists who found no evidence of mental abnormality they felt oath-bound to mention to the jury at the trial now found themselves with another part to play. The secretary for justice, Sam Barnett, consulted them before tendering a report to his minister, whose duty it was to decide where and for what duration the girls would be confined.

The editor of Wellington's *Dominion* was outraged by the process. "The accused, two thoroughly bad-minded girls, stand convicted of one of the gravest crimes in the calendar, and one which shocked the conscience of the nation," he wrote. "As we have said, the jury had no doubt of their mental state. Why then should the psychiatry issue be raised now in deciding their form of detention? Psychiatry is unwanted in this case."

As befitted a matter of such seriousness, the minister had to consult his cabinet colleagues before a decision could be announced. Meanwhile, the two girls continued to be held at Paparua, where, the superintendent announced, they were in separate cells but saw each other at exercise periods in the mornings and afternoons. No longer remand prisoners, they now wore prison clothes.

The minister's options were few. The only women prisoners Paparua held were those on remand or serving short sentences. There was Arohata Borstal and Reformatory near Porirua, a few miles north of Wellington. Borstal was a place of corrective training for juveniles who were, in the words of the Justice Department, "not yet widely experienced in crime, and might, with individual treatment, be expected to reform". At Arohata there were at any one time about thirty women and girls, whose days were spent doing laundry, gardening or sewing for other institutions. The department freely acknowledged that the Arohata inmates presented "the most difficult penal problem in New Zealand since too many of them constitute moral problems".

Auckland Prison in the suburb of Mt Eden—"the Hill" to the cognoscenti—was a dreadful old place, a damp, cold, rat-infested, foul-smelling Victorian jail built by convict labour in the 1880s from rock hewn out of its own quarry. Today it is rated too squalid, unhealthy and inhospitable to accommodate even the roughest, toughest, meanest prisoners for any length of time. Its facilities were worse in 1954. A small section was set aside for older women and "young women for whom Arohata is not suitable". These female prisoners were set to laundry work and sewing.

When the matter was submitted to the cabinet, the view of the Justice Department officers, supported by psychiatric opinion, was that the greatest punishment that could be inflicted on Parker and Hulme was to separate them. It didn't need to be said that the more severe the punishment the better: most people in New Zealand were firmly convinced the verdict was the right one.

It was decided that Juliet Hulme would be sent to Mt Eden. A few weeks later, as soon as a security compound of three escape-proof rooms was completed, Pauline Parker would go to Arohata. The justice minister, Thomas Webb, announced that this arrangement would be periodically reversed so that Parker too would have "a taste of Mt Eden". On the information available, Webb said, Hulme was the dominant personality but they did not intend to treat them differently. That commitment would be shamefully dishonoured.

As for their term of detention, "Her Majesty's pleasure" would be determined by the minister of justice. People under eighteen sentenced for a capital crime could be released at any time under conditions imposed by the minister. Webb assured the public he would keep the cases of Parker and Hulme under regular review.

On September 3, Terence Gresson's clerk Peter Penlington hurried down to the Supreme Court Registry with a document for filing. It was a deed poll changing the surname of Hilda Marion Hulme to Perry. Juliet's mother would choose to be known in years to come as Marion Perry. Five days later the tabloid *N.Z. Truth* reported that Mrs Hulme proposed leaving New Zealand within a few days. "I am distressed to leave Juliet here," she was reported as saying, "but I feel that Jonathan has a greater claim on me."

Bill Perry told the reporter that he too would be leaving New Zealand. The fact was he had little choice. Associated Industrial Consultants of London had taken a dim view of the publicity their New Zealand representative had attracted as an adulterer closely connected with a shocking and highly publicised murder case. He had embarrassed the firm to such a degree his services were no longer required.

Hilda's departure led to a falling out with Nancy Sutherland, who could not understand how her friend could skip the country, leaving her daughter in jail. Juliet refused to see her, Hilda told her. Jonathan needed her back home in England. Bill had lost his job, and could find work only in England, or with one of the international companies that recruited in England. They had no house in New Zealand. She would arrange for friends to visit Juliet in prison, and teachers to teach her. Reg Medlicott would be visiting her to give her the treatment she needed. She would come back if she were really wanted and needed. None of these arguments impressed Nancy Sutherland. Hilda's decision to leave New Zealand was, in her eyes, unforgivable.

Hilda and Bill, in gratitude for Brian McClelland's wholehearted efforts on Juliet's behalf, presented him with a fountain pen inscribed

"From W.A. and H.M. Perry". The three shared a grim little joke about it being a Parker pen. On Saturday, September 11, the couple flew out of Christchurch International Airport for Sydney, and thence to Melbourne, where they would connect with a ship for England. Only a few well-wishers were on hand to wave goodbye, among them Terence Gresson and his son, who took photographs of them walking on to the tarmac to board the aircraft.

In Sydney, Hilda gave an interview to the press. "It was not justice," she said, "to send a young girl to jail when what she needed most was love, care, attention and affection." She firmly believed Juliet was insane, a paranoiac, "although according to the M'Naghten rules she was not insane by law when she committed the murder". The rules, she said, should be revised. "Under the present rules she was guilty because she knew she was doing wrong, but in her own insane mind— which the law does not recognise—she believed she was immune to the law, that she was a god and able to break the law."

It was observed that Hilda's face was drawn and lined by the worry and anxiety she had been through. It was something, she said, she could never forget. "To do that would be to write my child off completely and no mother could do that." People had told her after the trial ended that it was all over. "How wrong they were. It is only the beginning. It will last forever." A psychiatrist was keeping her daughter under constant observation and she might return to New Zealand if Juliet made any improvement. Meanwhile, she told the Australian journalists, she was going on a trip in search of rest and peace.

N.Z. Truth was not slow to put the boot in. *The Standard*, the Labour Party newspaper, had published a front-page article deploring the fact that Mrs Perry—as she now wished to be known—had been persecuted by the press. *Truth* was indignant. "Whatever may have happened outside New Zealand, neither Dr Hulme, the father, nor Mrs Hulme, the mother, was persecuted in any way by any New Zealand newspaper. Dr Hulme's departure, although it had obvious interest, was barely reported. ... New Zealand newspapers restricted themselves to coverage of the trial itself and gave no particular emphasis to the evidence given at the trial affecting the relationship between Mrs Hulme and Perry."

The paper found Mrs Perry's concern for her daughter's welfare and the alleged unhumanity of her sentence "difficult to reconcile with the fact that she went to see the girl only occasionally after her arrest, and then only, it is understood, after a message had been passed that her daughter wanted to see her". After her conviction, Juliet had been in Paparua for a week before being moved to Auckland, the paper pointed out. During that time her mother had been in Christchurch, or staying in a bach at Port Levy about thirty miles away. Informed that an opportunity would be given her to see her daughter before the latter was transferred to Mt Eden, she had done nothing.

Truth was concerned that, with her mother's departure, Juliet Hulme would have no relatives whatever to visit her. "Any visitors she has will be officials, doctors who take an interest in the case, or official prison visitors." The headline proclaimed: "LEFT WITHOUT GOODBYE VISIT TO HER DAUGHTER".

Whatever Hilda's shortcomings as a mother, she did not deserve such a vicious attack. She would have given anything for a few words with her daughter, for whom she had lied, cheated and destroyed evidence. A few inquiries would readily have established the bitter truth: that Juliet refused to speak to her. The tone of the article reflected the hostility towards the Hulme family that hung in the air, the feeling that the manipulative daughter of degenerate upper-class Poms had led astray the honest fishmonger's girl. Although New Zealand proclaimed itself a classless society, the social and cultural divide between the Riepers and the Hulmes was seen as going a long way to explain how the churchgoing daughter of decent, hardworking ordinary folk had come to murder her own mother.

CHAPTER 30

The Presence of Evil

In 1955 Dr Maurice Bevan-Brown, a Christchurch psychiatrist who had been a colleague of Hilda Hulme on the Marriage Guidance Council, released a paper he had written on the death of Honorah Rieper. In *Adolescent Murder* he wrestled with the problem of how Juliet Hulme and Pauline Parker, children of "the educated class", could have come to commit a particularly grisly murder. He concluded the driving force had been love—"love no doubt of an immature and even infantile type and dating back to their own infantile needs; love of the best type of which they were capable, yet so egocentric as to ignore the interests of other people".

"Many people," Bevan-Brown continued, "have said the real culprits are the parents." He thought it reasonable to suggest they must indeed carry a heavy responsibility. The ultimate origin of the crime could be expressed as deprivation of love in early childhood and both Juliet Hulme and Pauline Parker had had inadequate parenting. If a child were deprived "of love and valuation, especially in the matter of tender feelings, various abnormal or morbid results will follow. One is a reaction of hate, aggressiveness, truculence and defiance, together with an unstable pseudo-independence." But this was not to condemn the girls' parents, he hastened to add. They themselves were the products of their own parents' shortcomings.

Bevan-Brown also considered the intense homosexual relationship between the girls, whether there was physical intimacy or not, to be an essential factor. Parker and Hulme, largely isolated individuals with no real friends, had found in each other a love relationship for the first time in their lives. "They mattered intensely to each other," he wrote, "and no one else in the world mattered at all or was worthy of any consideration. It was supremely important to them that they should not be separated—perhaps more important than life itself and certainly more important than anyone else's life."

Reg Medlicott, too, could not get the two girls out of his mind. The Hulme-Parker case was of such interest to the psychiatric profession that he would travel the world addressing learned gatherings. Some colleagues said, with a sniff of disapproval, that he made a career out of it. When he died in 1987, the *Bulletin of the Royal College of Psychiatrists* proclaimed that New Zealand psychiatry had lost its senior and most respected figure.

Medlicott not only remained fascinated by the case for the rest of his life, but from time to time he revised his medical opinion. In 1955 he published his first paper on the case in the *British Journal of Medical Psychology*. The outstanding thing about the girls' mood, he reported, was their "definite exaltation", which had risen to an increasing pitch in the months before the murder. "When they launched on their crucial religio-philosophical themes, the exaltation would increase to a high pitch and be accompanied by gross excitement. ... They never doubted they were outstanding geniuses far above the common herd of mankind." He had been impressed by their persistent state of exaltation, their complete lack of remorse, and their fantastic conceit, arrogance and self-inflation.

For Medlicott the diagnosis of psychosis—that is to say full-blown, systematised delusions—depended greatly on what he called the girls' "religio-philosophical" views. Juliet had told him she and Pauline had their own religion with a non-Christian god, and only twenty-five people in the whole of time had approached their level. Their god was "a nice chap", who didn't necessarily label all sin bad or evil. Sin could be good.

Medlicott was impressed that when he questioned the girls about the 4th World and *The Ones That I Worship* they gave consistent accounts, even though there was no opportunity for them to swap notes between interviews. However, given the countless hours the girls spent discussing such matters and the slavishness with which

Pauline adopted Juliet's ideas, there was probably nothing particularly remarkable about the fact their accounts tallied closely.

He considered the "Port Levy revelation" crucial evidence that the girls were paranoiac in a setting of *folie à deux*. This was open to debate. The incident had occurred less than a year after the girls became close friends. Indeed, Parker told Medlicott they had known about the 4th World six months earlier and their experience at Port Levy had simply "clarified it". If that were the case, their belief in this other world must have come into being in the early months of their friendship—an extraordinarily short time for "communicated insanity" to have developed, especially between two people not living together in isolation.

It is more likely the 4th World was just a piece of nonsense dreamed up by Juliet—perhaps dredging up vague memories of anthroposophism from Queenswood school—and committed to writing by her faithful disciple. Judging from her diary, Pauline herself had no particular interest in religio-philosophical ideas. Other than the Port Levy revelation, the only reference to religion, apart from mentioning when she went to church, was on June 14, 1953: "Juliet and I decided the Christian religion has become too much of a farce and we decided to make one up of our own." The very words "decided to make one up" made it clear the new religion would be a self-conscious invention—the antithesis of paranoiac delusional thinking. Pauline continued to attend the East Belt Methodist Church regularly until the murder in June 1954.

It is likely Juliet was spinning Medlicott a line—part of the pretence of being mad—when she told him she and Pauline had their own religion and only twenty-five people in the whole of creation had reached their level of enlightenment. The 4th World "clarified" on Good Friday 1953 at Port Levy gave frail support to Medlicott's thesis that the two girls had crossed the befogged frontier from paranoid constitutional personality into actual paranoia.

What was the medical basis of Medlicott's diagnosis? "Paranoia of the exalted type" accorded with the definition proposed by the German psychiatrist Emil Kraepelin, who in the late nineteenth century pioneered a classification system for mental illness that is the basis of systems still in use today. In the sixth edition of his *Textbook of Psychiatry*, Kraepelin recognised only two major psychoses: manic depressive illness, which was curable, and dementia praecox, now called schizophrenia, which was not. He believed paranoia was a variety of dementia praecox. Medlicott explained that although paranoia involved various kinds of delusional beliefs, intellectual functioning remained intact: "Clear and orderly thinking was preserved."

Medlicott was always well up with the play: by the 1950s Kraepelin's classification had been largely accepted by the psychiatric profession in Great Britain and the United States, even if the diagnosis of paranoia would be mostly ignored by psychiatrists until 1980, when the American *Diagnostic and Statistical Manual of Mental Disorders—Third Edition* (DSM–III) was published. Dr Kenneth Stallworthy, by comparison, appeared ignorant of a type of paranoiac psychosis whose sufferers might plan, premeditate and calculate the odds of success of a criminal act—and even feign insanity. It was unfortunate the defence lawyers had not cross-examined him on this important point.

In his paper Medlicott argued that there was nothing unusual about paranoia in its exalted form developing during adolescence. Parker and Hulme, he contended, "went into adolescence already strongly narcissistic, and each acted on the other as a resonator, increasing the pitch of their narcissism. Having their own company they were able to isolate themselves more and more from the usual outside interests of adolescent girls and the socialising experiences of group relationships".

With the onset of paranoia, subtle changes pervaded the whole personality. In particular, the girls' "defences against unconscious aggressive forces were swept away and their superegos almost silenced. … Their moral values became reversed and they embraced evil as good. These aggressive impulses were so much in ascendancy that one might have predicted their expression in a violent act even had circumstances been different".

Medlicott drew support from another of the giants of psychiatry, Eugen Bleuler, who had written in his 1924 *Textbook of Psychiatry* that paranoiacs often could not recognise or feel the rights of others.

"Their own cause is so very much the only important, I might say the only *sacred*, thing in the world. .... Like a cancer the delusion extends to ever-widening areas and there is far-reaching domination by the delusion of the entire personality in its behaviour and strivings."

In exactly that way, the girls had given no thought to Pauline Parker's mother's right to live. Medlicott reiterated his earlier conclusion: "The girls were so disturbed mentally by the time of their threatened separation they set about their murder with joyous abandon."

Like Bevan-Brown, Medlicott remained convinced that the girls' relationship was homosexual. There was no evidence that Juliet was ever interested in boys, he said, and Pauline's attempts at hetero-sexuality had ended in failure—with no evidence of real erotic involvement. Further, "all her escapades were fully discussed with Juliet ... a common feature amongst people basically homosexual in orientation". This was based on what Pauline had told him, although she may not have been entirely truthful, given the Sydney *Sun-Herald's* account of Juliet grinding her teeth and spitting silent words through rage-distorted lips when Pauline's lovemaking with Nicholas was described in court.

Despite "most incriminating evidence" both girls had denied physical homosexual relations, but Medlicott felt they were just loath to admit homosexual leanings: the choice of male partners in their acted-out love scenes with the Saints was simply a disguise.

It should be borne in mind that homosexuality was categorised as a psychiatric disorder until 1974, when it was removed from the *Diagnostic and Statistical Manual of Mental Disorders* following a referendum of the American Psychiatric Association. In 1954, even in sunny California lesbians were being given electric shock treatment to bring them to their senses.

Six years later Reg Medlicott presented a new theory. There were, he had now decided, closer parallels between Parker and Hulme and the Chicago killers Leopold and Loeb than he had been willing to acknowl-edge at the trial. Leopold and Loeb, teenage sons of millionaires, had set about a life of crime that had culminated in the murder of a schoolboy. Leopold was described as "intellectually brilliant but physically unattractive and sexually abnormal", while Loeb was "highly intelligent, good-looking". The young men had been defended by the celebrated American attorney Clarence Darrow. Realising he had no prospect of winning an acquittal on grounds of insanity, Darrow had tried to save the young men from the electric chair by persuading the judge that their legal responsibility was diminished by personality disorders. Outstanding American psychiatrists of the day gave evidence in their defence. Dr Bernard Glueck found in Loeb "the absolute absence of any signs of normal feeling". Dr William Healy said Leopold had "typical feelings and ideas of paranoiac personality ... Anything he wanted to do was right, even kidnapping and murder. There was no place for sympathy and feeling".

Medlicott had discussed the Leopold and Loeb case with Glueck and another of the defence's psychiatrists, William Alanson White. White thought that although Leopold and Loeb both unquestionably had an intellectual understanding of right and wrong "there was no adequate feeling attitude towards the wrongfulness of the act". And although the prosecution psychiatrists had testified that the boys were mentally normal, Glueck remained convinced of their "gross abnormality".

All four of these teenage killers, Medlicott now argued in the *New Zealand Law Journal*, were homosexual, had rich fantasy lives, indulged in play-acting, and saw themselves as supermen. All exhibited arrogance, feelings of omnipotence, and gross exaltation that continued after the murders and during their trials. He no longer liked his earlier diagnosis for Parker and Hulme of exalted paranoia. Paranoia was normally a disease of middle age, and the girls' grandiosity bore no similarity to that of paranoiacs whose mental faculties were in a state of deterioration. Upon reflection, he thought the cases of Parker and Hulme and Leopold and Loeb were so exceptional they demanded their own diagnostic formulation. He proposed "adolescent megalomania".

He did not expressly say whether adolescent megalomania was a psychosis or a personality disorder and made no attempt to establish what caused it, being content to state, "The natural history of adolescent megalomania is unknown." He was, nonetheless, certain that "without the continual stimulus of ... mutual reaction and with increasing age it loses its grossly psychotic nature and subsides". Adolescent megalo-maniacs recovered spontaneously in time when separated from the stimulation provided by a similarly afflicted partner. His new diagnosis seemed designed to accommodate the fact that neither Juliet Hulme nor Pauline Parker had displayed psychotic symptoms while serving their prison sentences.

Medlicott also jettisoned paranoia as such and placed narcissism at the heart of the case. Both pairs, he observed, "went into adolescence already strongly narcissistic". The individuals in each couple "acted on the other as a resonator, increasing the pitch of their narcissism".

A defect of Medlicott's analysis was that he made no attempt to distinguish Pauline and Juliet from each other, as though their thoughts, feelings and motives were at all times identical. The *folie à deux* scenario caused him to look for similarities rather than differences. Narcissism is said to be associated with inadequate development of the conscience, but the girls were quite different in this regard. Juliet Hulme seemed genuinely untroubled by conscience; a conscience was, she thought, senseless, "bred in people so that they punished themselves".

Pauline Parker, on the other hand, struggled at times to overcome feelings of guilt, deeming them unworthy of a superior being. Her diary disclosed a high degree of self-awareness: she did not have pleasant dreams on the eve of the murder; she felt "rather queer and jumpy" before setting out to rifle Dennis Brothers' safe. When, after the girls' first shoplifting expedition, she wrote, "I have come to the conclusion that I have no conscience whatsoever" it was as though she were trying to persuade herself. The more closely their cases are looked at the more obvious it becomes that, although Pauline and Juliet shared many crazy ideas, their personalities were perceptibly different.

For all his scientific analysis, Reg Medlicott never forgot that when he interviewed Pauline and Juliet at Paparua he felt he was in the presence of evil. In their grossly delusional state, he wrote, the girls had "openly embraced evil. In earlier times, one would have said they had become possessed by evil spirits". When interviewed thirty-three years later by the authors of *Parker and Hulme: A Lesbian View*, he recounted a dream in which an evil scorpion-type creature who seemed to be Juliet came crawling out of a wall.

It was certainly true that Juliet and Pauline were captivated by evil: it was glamorous and alluring, a way of proving their superiority to the lumpen mass of humanity. They worshipped evil characters such as Count Rupert of Hentzau, Black Michael, Duke of Streslau, Diello in *Five Fingers*, James Mason's Field Marshal Rommel, and Jay Robinson's Caligula. As Medlicott saw it, the two girls were both mad *and* bad.

In his 1961 article, he stepped into even more controversial territory, drawing on a 1948 paper by the noted American psychiatrist Leo Alexander to compare Parker and Hulme with the Shutzstaffel, Adolf Hitler's infamous SS. Alexander believed the SS, as an organisation, was paranoiac in nature. Medlicott wrote: "Although this may seem a far cry from these two girls, there are several very close analogies ... [specifically with] the way the SS frequently carried out crimes of sickening brutality without any sense of pity, shame or remorse, in a mood that was often frankly exultant." Pauline Parker and Juliet Hulme had approached their crime and responded to it afterwards in a similar way, he wrote.

Leo Alexander was particularly interested in what he called the "rapid perversion of the superego" achieved by SS training. Medlicott concluded: "The religious-humane cultural superego common to civilisation was replaced by an exclusively tribal one in the Nazis' case and by a narcissistic one in the girls' case. ... Reason, the main force at the disposal of the ego in repressing and sublimating primitive destructive forces of the id, was weakened. In the case of the SS, sanction by the group became the main ego support, while in the girls' case sanction one of the other provided this. With the SS there was a progressive destruction of the taboo against killing. ... Both girls came to treat death very cheaply as something of no particular concern."

These views would be mischievously misunderstood. Decades later an article in *New Zealand Listener* said that at the trial Medlicott had pronounced the girls helplessly under the sway of "evil" and had later compared them to the Nazi SS. The implication was that there was no such thing as evil, and that Medlicott was fool enough to believe the murder of Honorah Rieper on a par with the atrocities of the SS. It provided an eye-catching headline but naturally he believed no such thing.

In 1954 the capacity of human beings to commit acts of unspeakable wickedness was much in the minds not only of psychiatrists but of all thinking people. Almost the whole of Europe and a great part of Asia had recently emerged from one of the worst epochs in human history. Morality and civilisation seemed to have collapsed. There was a shocking realisation that a man of culture could preside over the extermination of thousands of his fellow humans and then go home and dine in good humour with his wife and children. How could such horror have happened? In 1954 Lord Russell of Liverpool, a member of the legal team at the Nuremberg trials, published *The Scourge of the Swastika*, which gave the English-speaking world its first detailed account of the horrors of the concentration camps and mass-extermination policies practised by the Nazis. It was a phenomenal bestseller.

In 1954, too, an English schoolmaster named William Golding published *Lord of the Flies*. This novel, which became a sensation, used the story of a group of schoolboys marooned on a desert island to explore the fragility of civilised society and the ugly violence at the heart of humanity. *The Inheritors*, published by Golding the following year, took as its theme the brute force in primeval man.

Golding came to be preoccupied with evil and original sin. Explaining his motivation, he wrote, "There was a time when I would have said we are not evil, and by the time I had found out after the Second World War what men had done to each other, what men had done to their own people, really then I was forced to postulate something which I could not see coming out of normal human nature as portrayed in good books and all the rest of it. I thought there must be some kind of principle of evil at work."

CHAPTER 31

Life in Prison

"The most outstanding defect in judgement," Reg Medlicott wrote of the two girls whose case had so much occupied his thoughts, "was their complete inability to foresee the natural outcome of their action—namely separation." Juliet had said, "Surely no one would be so illogical as to separate us?" and added, "We will behave ourselves as long as no one tries to separate us."

Inevitably her threat fell on deaf ears. Even if the girls had been found not guilty by reason of insanity, they would for therapeutic reasons have been sent to separate mental institutions. As it was, as convicted murderers they were dispatched to different institutions to compound their punishment.

N.Z. Truth assured its readers that Parker and Hulme would be kept in "full security conditions" and both girls would be subject "in every way" to the normal regime of a long-term sentence. "They will wear the ordinary prison clothes, eat the ordinary prison food, do the ordinary prison tasks set long-sentence women prisoners, and be subject to ordinary prison discipline."

Both in Arohata and Mt Eden, the work given to female prisoners was tedious and exhausting. In the laundries the only labour-saving appliances were hand-turned mangles. For work the women wore coarse jeans and a woollen cardigan—with, *Truth* was quick to point out, "plain underclothing". They were issued with a simple cotton frock to wear outside working hours.

On September 3, Juliet Hulme was airlifted to Auckland on a Royal New Zealand Air Force plane. At Whenuapai Airport she was met in person by the chief superintendent of Mt Eden prison. The women's section of Mt Eden offered grim accommodation. The fifteen year old lived in an eight-by-six-foot stone-walled cell with fourteen-foot high walls. There was only one small barred window, too high to see out of. Her furniture consisted of an iron bedstead with a straw mattress, a pillow and six blankets, a stool, a small cabinet, and a small mat on the concrete floor. No heating was provided.

Arohata, where Pauline Parker was sent as soon as its new security wing was completed, provided more pleasant quarters. It was a modern building not unlike a hospital, complete with corridors of polished linoleum. The security wing was designed to house recalcitrant or difficult inmates who, it was thought, needed to be confined apart from the other prisoners. Even the exercise yard was screened from view, and the wing had its own workroom, which looked out over green fields. Pauline had a wooden soundproof room, eight feet by ten, with a normal-sized window covered by strong meshed wire. The furnishings were a wooden bedstead and a wall-mounted table and stool. Her bedding was the same as Juliet's in Mt Eden but at Arohata the inside temperature was considerably warmer.

Convinced Juliet needed psychiatric treatment, Medlicott, supported by Hilda Hulme, sought permission to visit her. This was refused. Although Mr Justice Adams had said that no one could have sat through the trial without concluding that the two girls suffered some degree of mental disorder, *The Dominion* editorial writer who insisted "psychiatry is not wanted in this case" was in tune with the vengeful mood of the public. On December 13 Sam Barnett, the secretary for justice, was moved to deny reports in a Sydney newspaper that Juliet was receiving psychiatric treatment. All that had been done, he explained, was that her case had been studied to ascertain whether such treatment was necessary.

Barnett took personal responsibility for the two young prisoners. He was keen for them to continue their education and willing to make facilities available. He also decided who could visit and correspond with them. Many letters came from well-meaning busybodies, some of them religiously motivated, others sexual fantasists. All letters were intercepted.

As was the case with all new long-term prisoners, Juliet was kept in semi-isolation from other prisoners in the women's wing for three months. This was partly a "probation" or "settling-in" period and partly a suicide watch. After nearly two months, Barnett noted she was not showing the slightest inclination to settle down to any systematic work.

At first she was allowed visitors for half an hour on Sunday afternoons. Later, more liberal access was granted for people coming to tutor her, among them Erica Hoby, a violinist and music teacher who had taught at a private girls' school, Woodford House, in Hawke's Bay for seventeen years before becoming proprietor and headmistress of Queenswood, the Rudolf Steiner School that Juliet had briefly attended. Other dedicated visitors were Professor Kenneth Maidment, an Oxford classics don who was vice-chancellor of Auckland University, his wife Felicity Maidment, and Vivien Dixon. Although she had met Henry Hulme only weeks before the murder and did not live in Auckland, Vivien Dixon visited Juliet three times a year for the entire time she was in prison.

At the end of October 1954, in a letter to Nancy Sutherland, Felicity Maidment painted a picture of Juliet's life in prison. Juliet "talked freely and cheerfully and was animated and smiling, though none of us really knows what goes on in her mind. We bring her books to read and flowers but we are not allowed to take in anything else. … As she is considered to be a suicide risk, she is segregated from the other prisoners to a certain extent. She is taken back to her 'room' at about four and given her evening meal and then locked up until six the next morning—long hours of solitude for a little girl, which we are doing our best to help her occupy. They have even removed her looking glass—I suppose for fear she might break it and cut herself."

She reported that Juliet got up at six, had a meal, and then started work scrubbing and polishing black corridor floors. Two or three times a week she made sheets, white overalls and prison garments in the sewing room. She earned one shilling and sixpence a day, most of which she had to save. Only a few pennies were left to buy chocolate, sweets or bobby pins.

"The weekends, I should imagine, are deadly. The Salvation Army comes round and plays hymns and we are allowed to visit her for half an hour but otherwise there is nothing to relieve the tedium. ... She is apparently still doing a lot of writing, which the female superintendent calls 'sexy stuff'."

The other inmates were "a pretty crummy lot". Most were prostitutes and petty thieves in for short terms. Their conversation was "hardly edifying" and their mentality "pretty low". Quite a few had venereal disease, and most had lice, "which Juliet is nervous of catching".

To Vivien Dixon the prison was like Colditz Castle, with appalling conditions. Juliet had "awful clothes to wear, including big black boots" and had to endure "a lot of noisy Māori singing". The prisoners ate a great deal of tapioca pudding and never had eggs or fruit. Juliet had told her not to bother bringing cakes as the prison officers always broke them to see if there were drugs inside. Prisoners were allowed to shower only twice a week. Sanitary towels had to be improvised from strips of cloth. There were no doors on the lavatories, which was the thing Juliet hated most.

When Dixon complained about these conditions in a letter to Sam Barnett, he asked if she would call on him. In the event, she brought Nancy Sutherland along for moral support. The frankly spoken Sutherland got Barnett so worked up he slammed the door as they left.

In November Juliet wrote to Nancy Sutherland, thanking her for the birthday cake she had sent, and passing on the information that she would not be allowed to have it until Christmas. She was, she said, reading a great deal of poetry. "I have seventeen poetry books in my room at the moment. Seven of them have 500+ pages in them and the others, all except one, have about 250 or 300. I have 1,500 pages of Byron (complete works), 1,000 of Shelley, 500 Tennyson (lent to me, not one of my favourites), the *Rubáiyát of Omar Khayyám*, Rupert Brooke, James Elroy Flecker, *The Oxford Book of English Verse*, and of prose incidentally, and the rest are anthologies."

She had been been lent Macaulay's *History of England*, which she found very interesting although she hadn't yet got round to reading it, and was learning Italian. "I love the language, also the food, art, music and people, etc. I am nearly halfway through the course. As for my plans for the future ... I shall probably try to write. But if I could do anything I liked it would be singing. My ruling passion in life is Italian opera." Two months into her prison sentence her boastful self-confidence was undampened by the humiliating prison regime.

Three months later Henry Hulme complained in a letter to Vivien Dixon that Juliet was "still up in the clouds ... completely removed and occupied with herself and her grandiose ideas about poetry and writing, etc. I'm desperately sorry for her but it would be bad ... to sympathise in any way with her present state—she feels (as a paranoiac) that she is right and others are wrong, and Medlicott feels strongly that to encourage this would reduce the slight chances of her recovery." Although he was pleased Juliet did not seem "too unhappy", he was "very bitter about the third-rate bums in New Zealand who insist she should be treated as a criminal".

At the end of November Juliet wrote to Nancy Sutherland proclaiming that she and Pauline were marvellous opera singers. She herself was especially good, she said—a coloratura soprano! On December 15 *Truth* reported that Parker and Hulme were to be allowed to study for the University Entrance—actually School Certificate—examination. The paper added that when the girls began their prison sentences Hulme was "condescending and hoity-toity" and Parker "sulky and intractable"; neither appeared to show any obvious remorse. However, since they had been separated Hulme had apparently shown a "considerable improvement in her demeanour" and some symptoms of remorse. She had put on over a stone in weight and improved considerably in physical appearance but had "outwardly shown little interest in the fate of her friend. The two girls are not allowed to write to each other".

After Christmas Juliet informed Nancy Sutherland that her first Christmas in prison had been a very good one. "Of course there are many things one misses, but on the whole it was very nice. All sorts of people came in and gave us things." She was, she said, studying for School Certificate in English, maths, history, Latin and Italian. She was also studying Greek simply because she liked doing it, and also loved learning Italian: "The language appeals to me in every aspect and it's hardly work at all."

A strange passion had developed from her love of James Mason in *The Desert Fox*. "I'm reading Rommel at the moment and I like it so much I can't put the flaming thing down. I am very interested in and have a great liking for the German army, the North African desert, tanks, tactics and Rommel in approximately ascending order. ... I also wanted to read the memoirs of Ribbentrop but I can't get it. One of these fine days I'll finish Churchill's history of World War II. I loved it, it really was fascinating but I shall probably howl and put it down when the Germans start to get beaten."

She also loved *The Three Musketeers*. "They are right up my alley (especially Athos, Richelieu and d'Artagnan). I like Athos particularly when he spends a long time in the inn with [his servant] Grimaud." In this episode Athos, in his cups, tells d'Artagnan that as a young man he fell in love with a girl of sixteen "as beautiful as the dawn. Child as she was, she was marvellously gifted; she had not a woman's but a poet's mind; she was more than charming—she was enchanting". It was not hard to see why Juliet found this tale so appealing.

As seigneur of the district Athos could have seduced the girl, or even ravished her had he wished, but he married her and made her the first lady of the province. One day, when they were out hunting, she took a heavy fall and lost consciousness. Seeing that her tight riding habit was stifling her, Athos took a knife and slit it open as she lay on the ground, exposing her shoulder. On it was a fleur-de-lis: she was branded. "The angel was a fiend, the innocent child a thief; she'd stolen the communion plate from a church." The handsome young priest who posed as her brother was in fact her lover. Athos stripped her of the rest of her clothes, tied her hands behind her back, and hanged her. His heart was broken forever.

Nancy Sutherland must have finally found Juliet Hulme's egotism and lack of repentance hard to take. She wrote telling her she had many other commitments and could not write as regularly as she had in the past. Juliet refused to show any hurt. "I quite understand that you can't write so frequently. Oddly enough I can't either because of all sorts of restrictions and things." She enthused about her achievements as a knitter. "The red jersey—I finished that ages ago. ... I've done four more since, nearly finished a fifth, started well on a sixth and got a seventh planned. I knit and read at the same time."

She was also making prisoners' shirts. By the time she left she would, she said, be able to make all her father's shirts, as well as her mother's and her dresses, and her underwear. "I've made four pairs of brassieres since I've been here. They are rather fun. Out of unbleached calico for us, not satin, but on the same sort of principle."

Dora Sagar, charged with tutoring Juliet for School Certificate, visited regularly. One winter's day she was told Juliet could not get up because of a severe chill. A sympathetic superintendent allowed her to see Juliet in her cell. Dora later said that after seeing the conditions in which Juliet was living, she excused her all her tantrums. The building was leaking and to get to the cells she had to walk through puddles of water. The cells overlooked the laundry, the walls of which were dripping and mouldy. There was no electric light in the cell, and although it was bitterly cold Juliet wore only a cotton dress and cardigan. It was no fit place for the New Zealand government to house a young girl who had suffered most of her life from a weak chest and been discharged from a tuberculosis sanatorium only a year before. Despite the conditions, Juliet's chestnut-coloured hair looked beautiful, Sagar reported.

CHAPTER 32

A Difficult Year

While Juliet's trial was taking place Henry Hulme had taken Jonty to Brussels, where English newspapers were scarce and they could lie low. On their return to England they stayed with friends at Blackheath and Hulme got his son kitted up for boarding at a preparatory school.

With his university connections Hulme had no difficulty getting an appointment to teach mathematics at Cambridge, but by then something else was in the air. The British government had determined that if the country were to maintain its standing as a world power it needed to develop an independent thermonuclear weapon—the hydrogen bomb. The project, to be carried out at the Atomic Weapons Research Establishment, situated on an old airfield at Aldermaston in Berkshire, was put in the hands of the noted nuclear physicist William Penney, an old friend of Hulme's. By September Hulme was sufficiently certain of a job to start looking for accommodation in the area, although his pictures, books, china and other possessions salvaged from his marriage would not be arriving until the middle of October.

At Jonathan's school, parents were encouraged to visit often, Henry reported to Nancy Sutherland. Jonty was "very well" and "quite happy all the time". The boy had still not been told about Hilda and Bill. He would let him settle in at school first, and then make sure he saw a lot of the three of them together during his first school holiday. "The really upsetting part for a child is if the parents quarrel or chastise each other and I'm sure we can avoid that."

He was heartened that people in England had been "extraordinarily kind". The same could not be said of some of his former colleagues in New Zealand. Although he had been granted £900 to meet the cost of his and his family's fares to England, the executive committee of the college council, aware the family group had broken up, had resolved not to pay for Hilda's passage after all. According to the college's solicitors Dougall and Co., Mrs Hulme was no longer eligible.

The college went further. It would not meet any part of a bill for £144.12.0 Hilda had incurred shipping personal effects back to England, even though some of the effects were Henry's. Nor would it pay any of Henry's travelling expenses beyond his fare. Its solicitors had determined the college had no authority to pay travelling and removal expenses to any employee who had resigned. It had, in fact, already exceeded its authority.

In November, Hulme told Nancy that things were going reasonably well in England. Caius had made him a fellow for a year and he was spending alternate weeks at Cambridge and Aldermaston. Hilda had agreed to his having custody of Jonty. (In 1954, as an unfaithful wife, she would have had no choice.) The divorce would be going through in couple of months, "hopefully without publicity". Hilda and Bill were slowly recovering from the strain of the last few months. He himself felt very lonely at times.

He also wrote to Vivien Dixon. Hilda and Bill, he told her, did not yet have a place of their own and Bill was not finding it easy to get a job: publicity about the case had killed his chances with his old firm. Meanwhile, Jonathan had been entered for Stowe School in Buckingham in 1957. The scholarship standard there was not of the highest, he confessed, but the school was known to turn out nice people and the boys were very happy. This was a major change of attitude for Henry Hulme, who had always valued academic standards above all else.

At the end of the year Jonathan came top of his class and his teachers reported that he was very well balanced. He and his father spent Christmas day with Hilda and Bill: this was the day they had chosen to tell him they were divorcing. On Boxing Day, Henry took his son to Switzerland for a winter sports holiday. The divorce petition was heard on January 26.

*

Some time after arriving back in England Henry Hulme had met and begun a relationship with a woman called Margery Ducker. Ducker's father, Sir James Cooper, was a tycoon who held directorships of Lancashire Cotton Corporation, the vast engineering firm Vickers-Armstrongs, Goodyear Tyre and Rubber and other big companies. Margery was about the same age as Henry. She had been married twice before and had one child from each marriage, a boy aged seventeen and a girl of twelve. Henry told Nancy Sutherland that, like him, Margery been through difficult times and she had similar interests. By the time the couple married in the middle of 1955, Hulme had secured a permanent position at Aldermaston and they were hoping to buy a house in the Berkshire countryside near Reading.

In June 1955 Hulme wrote to Juliet giving her the news. His letter was intercepted by the prison authorities, who wrote back informing him they could not give his daughter such a heartless letter. He must write again showing some feelings towards her. Dora Sagar, to whom they had shown the letter, thought it "quite unbelievable", blunt and brutal. Several weeks passed before Henry wrote another letter in slightly more sympathetic terms. Nevertheless, as Vivien Dixon said, the letter knocked Juliet sideways.

Boiling with rage at Henry's callousness, Vivien went to visit Juliet. Her mood was not improved by a female warder, who sat jangling her keys and listening to every word between them. Juliet assured Vivien that, although she had been shocked at first, she was now over it. However, she felt she might have received more notice as such things didn't happen in a week—"especially to people their age". Vivien was inclined to agree that the relationship must have been going on almost from the time Juliet was sentenced.

By then Juliet had written to her new stepmother, asking her to write a few lines, but there had been no reply—"I suppose she doesn't want to own me"—although she had received photographs of her father and Margery and thought Margery very beautiful. By the end of August, however, a beautiful letter had come from Margery, and Juliet was assuring Nancy Sutherland, "You need never fear I shall be upset or resentful about the marriage. I was shocked of course but I think it is a marvellous thing—in fact the only thing."

She added a plea—probably directed more at prison authorities, who would read the letter, than at Nancy—to be left alone. "I will never look back," she wrote, "but I find it very hard because there seem to be so many people unremittingly trying to bind me down and say 'you must do this or that or the other', all of which tightens a net around me and makes me feel panicky. I will make a new character and a good one. I've learnt my lesson and I'm sorry and I'll never lose my head again. I'll rehabilitate myself, grow into a new person ... but I must do it myself without being watched over and dictated to. I must do it myself, no one can do it for me or help me."

Hilda and Bill had, in fact, been having a dreadful time. By December 1955, when Hilda belatedly replied to a letter from Nancy, they were living in Ullesthorpe, a small village in Leicestershire. "Most of this past year," she confided to her old friend, "has been too difficult.... We were so badly broke that for months we scrambled through each week as it came along, vainly hoping for something better to turn up. In the end I went to the Labour Exchange and got me a job. I'd wanted to do this first not last, but there were real reasons why I didn't. I found it almost physically impossible to talk to anyone. I had to gear myself up to do the simplest necessary shopping. I wanted to keep free to see Jonty when I could. I needed to keep Bill's courage and hope alive that a job would turn up.

"As I walked alone for miles day after day, and as the weeks passed, I suppose I became less sub-human and held on to my will to live, which at times had been non-existent. Make no mistake about my interpretation of broke. Cheap digs, no sherry to help drown my confusion."

The day after she got a job Bill Perry too found employment, with the Daimler Motor Company in Coventry. The couple had since bought a house, which they would "share with the mortgage brokers for the next twenty years! But it makes a big difference and gives us the chance to lift our heads again".

Although Hilda had been in favour of Hulme taking their son home to England while Bill Perry remained to support her in New Zealand during the trial, she was bitter that her former husband had readily found employment while Bill had struggled. "The scandal attached to the trial broke Bill's career," she wrote. "If he had left New Zealand before the trial it would have been different, but because he offered to stay instead of Henry he was too involved. On return he found he was too highly qualified for just any job he was willing to do, and the top jobs needed influence no one would give him under the circumstances." He now had a job at a quarter of the salary he should have, but it was a start. "We can live on it, just."

Henry's feet, she complained, "just don't touch the earth". No one meeting him would have a clue that anything had happened to upset him. "He seems to have some magic formula which sees to it that nothing does. If a thing may be unpleasant he turns away from it and, heigh presto, it isn't there."

She closed her long sorrowful letter saying she had written Christmas letters to others in New Zealand, where there were still "a few people left who have compassion for those in deep trouble", but there was no one else to whom she had written as freely and honestly. "On my long lonely walks I've talked to you many hours and wanted you near me. Did you ever feel this, I wonder? Or did you think I'd slid off, ridding myself of all the past and indulging in a life of careless luxury? ... It is nearly two years since you and I spent that halcyon few days at the cottage. Two years or two lifetimes. Oh Nancy, what utter tragedy. And I couldn't know, I simply couldn't guess…"

She added that her mother was coming to spend Christmas with them. "I shall like having her, though she wants to save me, naturally, for God. God help me if he can. Send me your love some time. I need it."

CHAPTER 33

A Fresh Start

Pauline Parker arrived at Arohata with her head turned by her association with Juliet Hulme and the notoriety the highly publicised murder had gained her. She could see no good reason why she should take part in prison work. "I am a special case here," she informed a staff member. She had to be reminded repeatedly that she was just another inmate.

Apart from two prison officers who shared her interests in music and literature, she treated the staff disdainfully. An observer noted that to those not on her wavelength she maintained a cool, aloof, often sarcastic disposition, and frequently an icy politeness. For a long time she refused to have any contact with her fellow prisoners, most of whom were young Māori girls with little education. Mainly they were ship girls—prostitutes who hid away on ships to service the seamen.

Beneath her defiant attitude, however, she was badly missing her beloved "Pandy", as she now nicknamed Juliet. She wrote in her diary, "I have been walking around with tears streaming down my face lately. Oh Pandy, how I miss you. I, who adored you. I, who worship you. What did I do that I should lose you?" In January 1955 it was noted in her prison file that she had developed an interest in collecting magazine and newspaper cuttings of anything pertaining to crime and terror, including overseas murder cases. She was also collecting photographs of intense love scenes cut from magazines.

Regulations allowed her to write three letters a week, each of two pages, to approved recipients. She was not permitted to write to Juliet, although there is likely to have been an underground line of communication through prisoners transferred between Mt Eden and

Arohata. According to staff notes, she wrote intelligent and amusing letters to a school friend, signing herself "Nina", "Rosemarie" and "Pauline (ugh, loathsome name)". Letters to her father, her grandmother and her sister Wendy were almost virtuously loving and understanding. She took trouble over them, once recording in her diary, "I have written to Nana and composed it very well, I think." She signed these letters "Yvonne".

Her family was less communicative. Wendy did not write until January 1955 and her father until October the same year. He visited her only once at Arohata and described the experience as depressing.

Although *N.Z. Truth* had assured its readers the girl prisoners would not escape the normal work routine on account of their studies, Pauline became increasingly involved with school work and less with sewing, laundering and floor scrubbing. Provided with text books by the Department of Justice, after a while she was virtually studying full-time. Although initially ambivalent, her attitude improved as she began correspondence lessons for School Certificate, which she passed in five subjects, before taking on University Entrance. Her hard work was rewarded with an outing: she was allowed to visit Victoria University in Wellington during the academic vacation to see what a university was like.

Prison authorities noted that as she spent less time doing work she regarded as demeaning, she became more relaxed and likeable. But she was subject to dramatic mood swings. When in an up mood, she would dismay prison officers with her lordly opinions. "I think pleasure is the only thing to live for," she once pronounced. But there were bouts of sadness. One day in March 1955 she was observed weeping, and wrote in her diary that she was lonely and felt terrible about what she had done to her father and her family. A few days later, though, she was again mixing with the other girls, "playing cards … happy, bright and cheerful".

In April she was thinking about escaping. She wrote in her diary that she could pretend to be ill: when one of the staff came in she could overpower her, grab her keys, and lock her up in the cell. The following month she began worrying about her health, thinking she was about to have a heart attack. The prison's medical officer found her heart was normal but that she was overweight and needed to go on a diet; prison had quickly cured her of bulimia. Despite trying hard she often succumbed to the temptation of cake and pudding.

Within a year of arriving at Arohata, Pauline embarked on two close relationships with fellow inmates. One would come to an unhappy end when her friend accused her of stealing her chocolate. There was a complaint from a third inmate. "Pauline keeps putting her arm around her and calling her 'dear' and 'darling'," a prison officer recorded. The staff seem not to have thought any the worse of her for it, and by the time Pauline left Arohata she was regarded as a model prisoner—polite, studious and "exemplary" in her behaviour.

Notwithstanding the secretary for justice's promise that the girls should be interchanged from time to time between the two prisons, this never happened. Although the government's psychiatric advisers believed Juliet had been the dominant character that may not have been the reason she spent most of her sentence at Mt Eden: Barnett, after all, had given his word the two would be accorded equal punishment. More likely it was a simple matter of convenience.

In August 1958 Pauline was transferred to Christchurch Prison at Paparua and Hulme to Arohata. Speaking as controller-general of prisons, Barnett assured the public that parole for the two girls had not been considered. The period of their sentences remained the same—indefinite detention. Given that both Arohata and Mt Eden prisons were less agreeable places than Paparua, Juliet Hulme was still getting the rough end of the stick. Still, at Arohata she would sometimes be given day release to travel by train to Wellington to use the Victoria University library, and she received regular visits from a psychologist, Beatrice Beeby, the wife of the director of education.

At Paparua, Pauline was regularly visited by Wendy, Rosemary, Nana Parker and her father, and by friends of the Hulmes, Professor Henry Field and his wife Helen. The Fields were ideally suited to be prison visitors. Henry Field held the chair of education at Canterbury University College and had long had an interest in the psychology of criminal behaviour and delinquency, which he had studied at Harvard under, among others, Sheldon Glueck. Helen Field was a doctor specialising in the care of mothers and children.

In October 1958 Pauline spent the first of many monthly parole weekends staying with the Fields. By then she was studying French and English for a Bachelor of Arts and, probably at Professor Field's instigation, being tutored by a Professor Sussex, head of the university's French department, and Gordon Troup, a senior lecturer in French. In December 1958 she was notified she had scored an A pass in English and a B in French. The following year she began studying Māori language and anthropology.

Pauline seemed to wage a continual internal struggle between good and evil. At Arohata the cold sarcastic young woman with a sinister fascination for murder co-existed with the polite studious model prisoner who "tried to be good", just as the dutiful sister and churchgoer had also enjoyed shoplifting, sex and revelling in "the thing called Sin". At Paparua she began taking religious instruction from a Roman Catholic priest, Father Tom Cahill, the director of Catholic Social Services. In December 1958 she attended mass for the first time at the Mount Magdala Asylum, an institution founded by the Sisters of the Good Shepherd "for the reformation of fallen women". Throughout 1959 she would attend mass at Mount Magdala once a month.

In February 1959 rumours surfaced about Juliet Hulme's future. London's *Sunday Express* claimed "the English girl who shocked the world by helping to murder her school friend's mother may soon be released from jail in New Zealand and come to England". A former inmate had told the newspaper's reporter Juliet expected to be released before her twenty-first birthday on November 28. (In fact her birthday was October 28.) Juliet had developed into an expert dressmaker, she said, and had ideas of setting up a dress shop in England. She had let it be known she never wanted to see Pauline Parker again.

Asked to comment, the minister of justice said Her Majesty's pleasure was a matter for him to advise upon and the question of Juliet Hulme's release had not been considered. The following day Sam Barnett said that the question of parole for Juliet Hulme and Pauline

Parker had not yet been before the Parole Board. Ten months later, on December 4, he confirmed that both had been released from prison a month earlier. Their release had been ordered by the Executive Council. No official announcement had been made at the time because the Justice Department wished to give them an opportunity to make a fresh start in life without being identified.

The girls had served nearly five and a half years. By today's standards, this would be considered a short period in jail for such a brutal, premeditated murder. A similar crime, committed by offenders of similar age, would be likely to result in life imprisonment with a ten- to fifteen-year minimum non-parole period.

Were prison officials confident both girls had been completely rehabilitated, Barnett was asked. He avoided a direct answer. They had been under "the closest study" during their imprisonment and had "developed in a highly satisfactory manner", he said. Both had pursued "wholesome interests". They had advanced their education and one had gone forward, with a great measure of success, towards a Bachelor of Arts degree. The parole board had concluded that individually neither would have committed the crime; it was a one-in-a-million chance that their association had been of such a nature as to lead to their planning such an outrageous act.

It has often been said, not least by Juliet Hulme herself, that a condition of the girls' release was that they were to have no further communication. This was not so. The Sydney *Sun-Herald* quoted Barnett as saying, "Miss Hulme's release is unconditional. ... Miss Parker's release is subject to general control as to her residence, employment and the like". Asked if the girls had been given, or been asked to give, an understanding to keep apart or refrain from corresponding, the secretary for justice said they had not been released on such a condition.

Juliet Hulme had already left New Zealand, Sam Barnett told the press. She had gone to Australia to make a fresh start. In Sydney, she had walked around the streets without being recognised. It was a disingenuous comment, perhaps designed to put the press off the scent. In fact the New Zealand government had provided its released prisoner with a new passport and a new identity: she was now Anne

Steward. At Wellington's Rongotai Airport she had been farewelled by the Arohata matron, who had become fond of her. Florence Howland stood waving as Juliet walked across the tarmac to the plane. Juliet did not turn around. "She never showed any remorse for her part in the murder," Howland said.

It was true that Juliet had flown to Sydney—but there she had boarded a plane for Rome.

Henry Hulme, recently promoted to chief of atomic research at Aldermaston, had arranged to meet his daughter when she arrived in Italy. He discussed his plans with Vivien Dixon, who was by then back in England. He and Margery would take the car across to France by ferry and drive to Rome, he told her. Having collected Juliet, they would make their way back to England when things had quietened down a bit.

Vivien Dixon had met Margery once and not liked her much. She was shocked Margery would be present when Henry met his daughter for the first time in nearly six years. Inevitably, the meeting was a disaster. The two women took an instant dislike to each other. Margery later told Vivien she would not have Juliet to stay in the house. She was dangerous to have around.

When she reached England, Juliet—now Anne—was lively, unabashed, and overjoyed to be reunited with her mother and Bill Perry. Her spirits seemed in no way subdued by her years in prison. She later said her mother never talked about her crime. "She felt we should leave it behind. I think, in many ways, she didn't want to feel guilty. Maybe she thought that if she'd been there for me more as a teenager this may not have happened."

After the long car journey from Rome, Margery couldn't stand the sight of her stepdaughter, but Juliet bore her father not the slightest ill will on account of his marriage. Father and daughter enjoyed each other's company, but they had to be careful about being seen together. Because of his job, Henry Hulme was fairly well known. If he were regularly seen with a young woman it would not be hard for people to work out that Anne Steward was Juliet Hulme, the murderess. Their meetings often took place at the National

Gallery or the Tate; they would wander around looking at paintings before having a quiet lunch. When her twenty-second birthday approached, Anne requested a bracelet of carnelians she had seen and admired. Henry, always careful about money, balked at the expense until she reminded him she had cost him nothing for over five years.

Anne had learnt shorthand typing in prison and found it easy to get a job as a secretary. After a couple of years, she moved into a flat and started to go out with boys. "I was always dreading the day I'd have to tell somebody what I had done," she later told a journalist who interviewed her, "but in the end I only ever felt close enough to one boyfriend to tell him." She was keen to stress her heterosexuality. Pauline Parker was "a very good friend. We had all sorts of romantic dreams. ... I like women very much as good friends but for romance it has to be a male."

Not long after arriving in England, she changed her name from Anne Steward to Anne Stewart Perry. Where the Stewart came from is a matter of conjecture. It is unlikely she chose it in honour of "Stewpot", her old headmistress at Christchurch Girls' High. It may have been from her maternal grandmother, whose middle name was Stuart. Probably, though, it was just a modification of Steward, the name supplied by the New Zealand government. As for her use of "Perry", she once remarked, "After my mother remarried, my stepfather legally adopted me so I took his name." It was an odd explanation. Why, as an adult on friendly terms with her father, would she have been legally adopted by Bill Perry? Another time she remarked that it was obvious that if she were to live with her mother and Bill Perry and "be their daughter" she should take their name.

She had not lost the urge to go to Hollywood. According to someone who heard the story from Anne herself, she went to the American embassy in London to apply for a visa and was interviewed by a consular official. Everything was going swimmingly until the last question.

"Any criminal convictions?" the official asked the beautiful, self-possessed young woman sitting in front of him.

"Oh, just something when I was fifteen," she answered airily.

"Well, I'm sure that's no problem," the official said. As she was walking towards the door, he thought to ask what it was for.

The visa was not granted.

After three years in London, Anne Stewart Perry moved to the historic market town of Hexham in Northumberland, near Hadrian's Wall. No doubt a strong part of the town's appeal was that it lay within the territory of her ancestors the Reaveleys, hereditary bailiffs of the manor of Chatton to the Earls of Northumberland.

Anne then hatched a plan. She secured a job as a stewardess for an airline that flew frequently to the United States. The airline had a block visa for its air crew, allowing members to enter for short stays. After a few return flights she told her father that next time she went to America she would not be coming back. True to her word, she jumped ship in Los Angeles and was soon working as a nanny for a Hollywood couple.

Eventually she would get the visa she had been denied in London. She later insisted she had disclosed her murder conviction to United States immigration officials, who had issued her with a full visa and work permit after studying a transcript of the trial. There is no way of knowing if this is true.

Anne Stewart Perry lived in southern California from 1967 to 1972. As she tells the story she rented a Beverly Hills apartment "on the wrong side of the tracks, in a street lined with jacarandas" and worked as a limousine dispatcher and an insurance underwriter. She had an active social life with many boyfriends but never married, although she "came near to it once or twice". According to Vivien Dixon, she was once engaged.

At the age of twenty-six, Anne became a member of The Church of Jesus Christ of Latter-day Saints. While keeping her past hidden from her everyday social contacts, she claims to have revealed her crime to the church before being baptised.

It is not difficult to see the attraction of Mormonism for the former Juliet Hulme. As a girl she had not been able to believe in the idea of hell on the grounds it was "too inartistic". In Mormonism there is no eternal hell or damnation: everyone is saved. When you reach heaven, there are three levels. The lowest and most heavily populated, the telestial kingdom, is for those who have not accepted Jesus as their saviour—including unrepentant "liars and sorcerers and adulterers and whoremongers". Above it, the terrestrial kingdom caters for essentially good people who have been led astray by the wickedness of the world and not done enough to spread the gospel of Jesus. Such people fall short of achieving "exaltation". This spirit world is located on Earth but in "another dimension". At times the veil lifts and it is possible to see the spirits.

At the top of the pyramid is the celestial kingdom where God lives. This is the highest goal for Mormons. Getting there requires baptism, faith, endurance and various rituals, including the cleansing of sins. No one can enter without the presumed consent of the church's founder, Joseph Smith. "Eternal marriage" is a prerequisite, although people who have failed to get married on Earth will get another chance after Christ's second coming. Those exalted to the celestial kingdom become gods themselves: kings and queens who dwell with God for all eternity.

No other religion could offer such an alluring prospect to a young woman who, according to her own mother, had believed herself to be a god at the age of fifteen. And the Mormon afterlife was very much like her own youthful concept of heaven for the masses and paradise for the chosen few.

Just as appealing was the church's doctrine on sin. In Mormon belief a person commits a sin only when he or she does the opposite of what they know to be right—thereby violating their conscience. Doing wrong without *knowing* it to be wrong is deemed a mere "blunder". In the words of *The Book of Mormon*, "He that knoweth not good from evil is blameless." Adam and Eve could not have committed a sin while in the Garden of Eden because knowledge of good and evil had not been given to them.

Anne Stewart Perry seems to have wholeheartedly embraced this teaching. She once explained Mormons believe that, in order to grow, Adam and Eve had to bite the apple in the Garden of Eden. "You can only learn the difference between good and evil with experience. …

I like its doctrine that you have to keep on learning, and that no one is excluded, no one is penalised. ... I don't believe that Adam and Eve sinned. We need to know about good and evil, and we need to make mistakes."

It is a short hop to the corollary: someone who "makes mistakes" —even big mistakes like helping bash someone to death—learns more about good and evil, grows more and becomes a better person than the less mistake-prone.

CHAPTER 34

Blighted Lives

Whaton she left prison Pauline Parker also changed her name. By deed poll, registered on December 1, 1959, she became Hilary Nathan. Chris Cooke, a journalist who has closely studied the Parker–Hulme case, believes that as a devout Catholic she may have chosen the name Nathan with an Old Testament story in mind. David, King of Israel, spots the beautiful Bathsheba, wife of Uriah the Hittite, bathing on the roof of her house. He has her brought to him and lies with her. Bathsheba's husband is away fighting in David's army. David arranges for Uriah to be killed, instructing his commander, Joab, to put him "in the forefront of the hottest battle, and retire ye from him, that he may be smitten and die". God sends Nathan to David to inform him of his wrath at David's despicable act. When the king admits he has sinned, Nathan tells him he is forgiven: "The Lord also hath put away thy sin."

Cooke was told by a Catholic priest that a person who chose the name Nathan would be indicating they had repented of their sins. This theory overlooks the fact that Nathan was God's messenger, not a repentant sinner. A more mundane possibility, also suggested by Cooke, is that Pauline had been fond of a social worker at Arohata whose surname was Nathan.

As it had been a condition of Parker's release that she be under the supervision of the Department of Justice, in February 1960 she was ordered to report to the probation office in Auckland. She resumed her studies towards a Bachelor of Arts degree at Auckland University, supporting herself with manual work, which included washing bottles in a hospital. At the time she graduated in 1963, her probation officer expressed concern that she was mixing with lesbians.

Sometime after leaving university, Hilary decided to become a nun. She entered a convent as a novice, but after a short time was found unsuited to life in an enclosed order. She would have to find salvation in the outside world. By 1964 she was living in a cottage in Lyall Bay, a Wellington seaside suburb, and attending the New Zealand Library School. Cooke, writing in the *New Zealand Woman's Weekly*, told readers that Hilary's fellow students found her mysterious and secretive; she made sure she was absent on the day of the class photograph. Someone who claimed to be a close friend at the time said she had had no idea who Hilary Nathan was. "There was something from her past she kept well hidden."

In 1965 she moved back to Auckland, where she worked as a librarian at Auckland University. In time the Justice Department decided she no longer needed to be on probation and her release from prison became unconditional. Soon afterwards she left her job at the university and disappeared, her whereabouts known to only a very few.

Pauline Parker's murder of her mother blighted many other lives: she had every reason to "feel terrible" about what she had done to her family. As well as emotional torture, the Riepers suffered dire financial consequences. They had relied on income from boarders, but without Nora that business came to an end. Bert Rieper struggled to pay off the legal fees for his daughter's defence. In 1957, when Alec Haslam was appointed a judge of the Supreme Court, he learned his fees were still causing the family hardship and generously waived the large outstanding balance.

There were also legal complications. The house at 31 Gloucester Street was registered in Nora's name, as was Nana Parker's home, an attractive two-storied Victorian house near the Avon River off Bealey Avenue. The arrangement had almost certainly been set up to make it easier for the family to secure mortgage finance through Eric Cleland's firm where Nora worked and—on the reasonable assumption that Nora would outlive her mother—avoid future death duties. Now death duties were payable. And there was another matter to be resolved. Pauline was a beneficiary under her mother's will but Bert was determined she would not benefit from her crime. More legal fees were incurred sorting out the estate.

For the first few years after the murder, Nana Parker lived with Bert and Wendy in Gloucester Street, where the three of them were able to look after one another. It is possible the Public Trust, as Nora's executor, collected much-needed rental income from Nana Parker's house in Churchill Street while the estate was being wound up. The house was finally sold in 1957.

Bert Rieper saw little of Pauline. Although he drove her grandmother and sisters to see her after she was transferred to Paparua, he himself paid few visits and wrote few letters. Not a churchgoing man, he had little to say to her and never forgave her. On learning she had been released he reportedly said, "It still doesn't make up for robbing a person of their life. It was evil between them that did it, pure evil."

Two things happened to alleviate a little of the sadness in Bert's life: his unmarried sister, Rhoda, came from Tasmania to take care of him, and as a result of the publicity about the trial his sons Ken and Andre got in touch. Over the years they and their families would visit him when they came to the South Island, apparently bearing him no resentment for having abandoned them as children. In later years Bert lived in a sad little flat in Upper Riccarton. Wherever he went for the rest of his life he was an object of pity, with people pointing at him and whispering. He died of a respiratory condition in 1981.

Pauline's sister Wendy, seventeen at the time of the murder, would say it was the worst thing that could ever have happened to her. A serious boyfriend whom she had hoped to marry was put off by the scandal that enveloped her family. In the circumstances she was extraordinarily loyal to her sister. "I can't believe what's happened. I don't want to accept this," she wrote to Pauline in prison. The alternative, she said, was to hate her for the rest of her life for taking her mother away. Pauline's reply was matter-of-fact."It just all got out of hand," she wrote. "I don't know what happened and I just want to keep in touch with you."

Although Wendy married and had children, when she looked back she felt her life had been unhappier than her sister's. While Pauline had been able to escape New Zealand with a new identity, she had had to stay and deal with the situation. "There are thousands of people out there who will look and say, 'Oh, you know who she is, don't you?'" she told a journalist. "I have to live with that and I'm very sensitive to it."

Over the years the sisters kept in touch. "I loved her and she still loves me," Wendy said. It would be thirty-three years before they were able to discuss the murder. Pauline reminded Wendy she had always been an extremist. Even as a little girl she would go overboard when things went against her, she said.

Wendy believes her sister understood what she was doing and had intended to kill their mother, but had not fully understood the finality of death. "After it happened, she was very sorry about it. It took her about five years to realise what she had done."

CHAPTER 35

A Secret Past

All Anne Stewart Perry ever wanted to do was write. There was, she once said, no plan B. In Hexham, in Los Angeles, and later in England, where she returned in 1972 after Bill Perry became seriously ill, she wrote steadily. By 1978 she had produced several historical novels, all of which had been rejected by publishers. She was living in the small Suffolk town of Saxmundham when by a stroke of luck the house next door was bought by a writer. Through this connection Anne met a literary agent, Meg Davis, and showed her her latest novel. *The Cater Street Hangman* was a murder mystery set in Victorian London; the idea had come from a conversation with Bill Perry about Jack the Ripper. The book was quickly accepted for publication in the United States and became a commercial success. Anne shortened her name to the crisper "Anne Perry". She was now forty-one and a very attractive-looking woman.

In *The Cater Street Hangman* five young women are murdered by a serial killer, who garrottes them with a cheese wire and disfigures their breasts with knife wounds. The killer turns out to be the crazed wife of a vicar, to whom the victims had been a temptation to fleshly lust. The language is at times florid. "You creature of the devil," the murderer raves. "You tempted me with your white arms and your flesh but you shan't win! The Lord said better you should not have been born than you should have tempted and brought to destruction one of these, my little ones, and brought them to sin. ... I know how your body burns, I know your secret lusts, but I shall destroy you all, till you leave me alone in peace. Satan shall never win!"

It is all too much for wide-eyed Charlotte Ellison, soon to marry Inspector Pitt and become the heroine of the series. "I didn't even know women could feel like that—about other women," she gasps, echoing Juliet Hulme's reply to Dr Bennett twenty-four years earlier when he asked her about homosexual practices.

While living in Saxmundham, Anne also met a woman who would become her lifelong companion. Meg MacDonald was in the throes of divorce, and like herself had little money. "We didn't have a penny," Meg remembered, "but we did have some good times."

Early in their friendship, Meg MacDonald learned of her friend's secret past. She had begun to suspect something when they were studying the bible together. Anne "was irrationally against King David sending Uriah the Hittite into battle so he could have Bathsheba. We were discussing the idea of deliberately killing someone and it just came out". It is an astonishing coincidence that the catalyst for Anne Perry's confession was the biblical story that might have inspired Pauline Parker's choice of a new name.

The murder was a bogey that had always haunted her friend, Meg MacDonald said. "She is very, very insecure. She looks confident, but underneath there's a lost little girl." Anne would get into "a right tiswas" whenever the subject of capital punishment came up. This was hardly surprising. Five hangings had taken place at Mt Eden during her time there. The whole prison knew there was to be a hanging when a tarpaulin was rigged up over the exercise yard in the punishment block. The prisoners would hear a loud clang as the trapdoor of the gallows flew open.

Many more books followed *The Cater Street Hangman*. There seemed to be, at least for a time, a literary collaboration between Anne and Meg. According to MacDonald, "We think about names and characters. Then Anne writes it out in longhand a chapter at a time. Anne will read the chapter to me, and we'll go through it with a red pen. We're always thinking of new things. We went to the Canary Islands and worked on eight books we chapterised and characterised for two weeks."

In 1988 Meg MacDonald moved north to Invernesshire in the Scottish highlands and Anne followed. "I came to visit Meg," she explained, "and I fell in love with the place." Portmahomack is a picturesque fishing village of around five hundred inhabitants on Dornoch Firth, fifty miles north of Inverness. Meg found her a cottage on the outskirts of the village, which she bought sight unseen.

A few years later an old stone barn next to the cottage, with planning permission for conversion into a motorcycle repair shop, came on the market. Not wanting a motorcycle repair shop next door, Anne bought the barn. With royalties from her books now rolling in, she converted it into what one visitor described as "an elegantly renovated, pseudo-Italian mansion and garden". Although the exterior was dour, inside, a journalist reported, was "a riot of faux Tuscan reds and yellows and lime greens". There were Italian chandeliers and gold taps in the guest bathroom. An ornamental fountain formed the centrepiece of a courtyard that had started life as a pigsty. A Jaguar and a sports car were sitting in the garage. Here Anne wrote six days a week, attended by two part-time secretaries, a full-time assistant, three gardeners and a housekeeper. On Sundays she worshipped for three hours at the nearest Mormon temple in Invergordon on Cromarty Firth.

Her books gained a huge following, particularly in the United States and Germany. By 1994 she had sold more than three million copies in America and had a one-million-dollar contract for eight new ones. The books were replete with ethical and moral messages, some trite in the extreme ("If you love someone, you should be prepared to let them go"). Others might be seen as personally revealing ("If you are rejected enough, it hurts so much you lash out wherever you can. You pick the vulnerable people, not necessarily the ones that attacked you"). A certain unworldliness was occasionally visible ("Come for us when the chef is ready, Blunstone. And get me some of that claret again, same as last time. The Bordeaux was awful").

A writer for *The Times* saw her work as "one long debate between good and evil, and the grey areas between". Anne Perry claimed, "There are so many understandable motives for crime—social ills, injustices, many of which are with us today."

An interesting aspect of the earlier Anne Perry books is the attitude to murder and murderers. In *Bethlehem Road* two members of parliament are murdered in fairly quick succession on Westminster Bridge. Both are found strung up to street lamps by their white silk evening scarfs with their throats cut. Inspector Thomas Pitt investigates and suspicion immediately falls on Florence Ivory, a well-known suffragist, and Miss Africa Dowell, the friend she lives with. Both murder victims had been instrumental in depriving Florence of the custody of her daughter.

Florence, while having "no bosom to speak of" and shoulders that are "square and a trifle bony", is "not unfeminine", with large wide-set eyes and a "husky, sweet and completely unique" voice. When she thinks of the injustice done to her, "hatred twists her face and mouth that a moment before were mobile, soft and intelligent". Africa Dowell is younger and bigger, with "a delicate bosom, rounded arms", and a "face like a Rossetti model crowned with a cloud of auburn hair". Inspector Thomas Pitt notices the way she puts her arm protectively around Florence's slender frame, and directs anger at him on her friend's behalf.

Willingness to commit murder is depicted as admirable, even heroic. Florence has been heard to say there are occasions when violence is the only response to incurable wrongs. Pitt reports to his superior that she "certainly has the imagination and intelligence to do it, and the willpower". He believes that when it comes to murder she will not be stopped by "fear or convention, risks to herself or other people's doubts or beliefs ... she was capable of it both emotionally and physically with Africa Dowell's help".

Charlotte Pitt is of the same opinion. She takes one look at Florence and concludes that "a woman with a face like this could assuredly have loved and hated enough to do anything". And Africa, with her ashen, Pre-Raphaelite face, would be prepared to defend what she loved—both the woman and the ideal. "It was a dreamer's face, the face of one who would follow her vision and die for it."

Anne Perry spells it out: "Pitt liked murderers. ... It was the petty sinners, the hypocrites, the self-righteous that he could not bear." It turns out the killer is someone else entirely. Pitt's admiration for murderers of the right type had thrown him off the scent.

In *Brunswick Gardens* Miss Unity Bellwood plummets to her death down a staircase in the house of Reverend Ramsay Parmenter, a distinguished theologian. Even in death, this young woman, a brilliant student of languages, fluent in Greek and Aramaic, and a believer in free love, is "extremely handsome in a wilful and sensuous fashion". She is found to be three months pregnant and suspicion falls on two young men, the startlingly handsome Dominic Corde and the Reverend Parameter's son, who is studying for the Catholic priesthood. When the Reverend Parmenter attacks his wife Vita, a "most striking woman" with "very large wide-set eyes" and "very handsome shoulders and bosom", suspicion falls on him as well.

Once again, murder is the moral preserve of the passionate, the caring and the bold. Pitt—now a superintendent—agrees with wise old Lady Vespasia that people killed "because they cared about something so fiercely they lost all sense of reason and proportion. For a time their need eclipsed everyone else's, even drowned out their own sense of self-preservation".

In Anne Perry's other crime series, Inspector Monk, like Pitt, regards the capacity to commit murder as a test of character. In *A Dangerous Mourning* he ruminates that "to care for any person or issue enough to sacrifice greatly for it was the surest sign of being wholly alive. What a waste of the essence of a man that he should never give enough of himself to any cause, that he should always hear the passive, cowardly voice uppermost which counts the cost and puts caution first. One would grow old with the power of one's soul untested…"

Similar sentiments are uttered by a cook in one of the households. It is impossible, she thinks, that the maidservants could have done it. One is "too afraid of what'd happen to her, apart from anything else", another is "far too mild to do anything so passionate" and a third "wouldn't 'ave the courage either".

It seems only the most miserable, shallow and gutless of beings—uncaring of anyone or anything—would *not* commit murder if the circumstances called for it. It is a point of view completely in accordance with the fifteen-year-old Juliet Hulme's declaration to Dr Bennett that "the best people are those who fight against all obstacles in the pursuit of happiness".

"Even murder?" Bennett had asked.

"Oh yes," she replied, "if necessary."

CHAPTER 36

A Lesbian View

The murder of Honorah Rieper took an extraordinary hold on the popular imagination. Accounts of the case were published in many anthologies of crime, among them *The World's Worst Murderers, Greatest Criminals of All Time, The Deadly Innocents: Portraits of Children Who Kill, Queens of Crime, Murderous Innocents, Killer Couples: Terrifying True Stories of the World's Deadliest Duos,* and *The World's Wickedest Women.*

At least three novels appeared. *The Evil Friendship* by American Marijane Meaker, writing under the pseudonym Vin Packer, and *Obsession* by Tom Gurr and H.H. (Harold) Cox, two of the Australian reporters who had covered the trial, were both published in 1958. Inspired by newspaper reports of the case, English novelist Beryl Bainbridge completed *Harriet Said* that same year, but did not find a publisher until 1972. One of the rejection letters said the author had made the two central characters "repulsive almost beyond belief".

In 1991 a serious book-length study of the case appeared. *Parker and Hulme: A Lesbian View* was written by Julie Glamuzina, a tutor in information technology, and Alison J. Laurie, a lecturer in women's studies at Victoria University of Wellington. Laurie had come out as a lesbian when she was sixteen, and according to an article in *New Zealand Listener* "began a long search for others like herself". Signs on her noticeboard at Victoria University read, "Grow your own dope, plant a man" and "The more I know about men, the more I like my dog".

Glamuzina and Laurie set out to write about the murder from a pro-lesbian, feminist point of view. Laurie later explained, "I sympathised with the girls and thought that they must have had some stronger provocation for committing such a deed than was apparent from the newspaper stories." The result sometimes makes for uncomfortable reading. Laurie believes Parker and Hulme were made such public monsters that for thirty-five years it was difficult for any lesbians to come out in New Zealand.

In 1995, an updated edition of the book, published in America, included an introduction by B. Ruby Rich, a cultural scholar and film critic. Rich claimed that in Christchurch lesbianism was, at the time of the murder, as taboo as matricide. It's not surprising she would think so. Glamuzina and Laurie confront their readers with a vision of New Zealand in the 1950s that is alarmingly black. There is rigorous censorship of films and publications. Films reinforce a "romantic, hetero-sexual model of life". Māori are oppressed and exploited by the white majority, whose racism is also directed against Chinese, Yugoslavs, Jews, Indians and Lebanese. Persons of Indian origin are not allowed the best seats in picture theatres. At a South Auckland primary school, Māori boys are made to use segregated toilet facilities. This last piece of information, astounding news to anyone who attended a state primary school in the 1950s, came from a Communist Party newspaper, *People's Voice*, as did other illustrations of the evils of the time.

It did not end there. Racially offensive words such as chink, chow, nigger, dago, wop and wog were, Glamuzina and Laurie claimed, used conversationally. Many jobs were advertised in gender-specific terms. Sex outside marriage was frowned on, especially for women—although many broke the sexuality codes. Divorced women and unmarried mothers were reviled as loose and immoral. Women were unwelcome in public bars. Canterbury itself was a "deeply stratified society" and the city of Christchurch "conservative ... reflecting its origins as a white, class-conscious, Anglican settlement".

In the 1995 edition of the book the authors quoted Fay Weldon, who lived in Christchurch as a child and briefly attended Girls' High. Weldon said it did not surprise her that two girls from her old school had taken one of their mothers and battered her to death. Post-war New Zealand was "repressive and repressed". In fact Weldon had left New Zealand forever in 1946 at the age of thirteen, eight years before the murder.

Glazumina and Laurie had little doubt of one thing. "Did Pauline and Juliet have a lesbian relationship? In our view they did, although there are difficulties involved in using the term 'lesbian' for women and girls in the past who may not have defined themselves in this way." The fact is that Juliet Hulme—Anne Perry—has never defined herself as lesbian. More than fifty years later, she still adamantly denies she is, or ever was, lesbian.

Parker and Hulme: A Lesbian View championed the normality of the two girls and took issue with anything that might amount to criticism of them. There was nothing odd, the authors insisted, about the girls calling each other—and demanding that others called them—Deborah and Gina. "We think it is common that teenage girls experiment with names and identities this way." Similarly, Pauline's diary entry about the Port Levy revelation, rather than evidence of paranoia, could, they asserted, be an actual record of a religious experience, experimental writing, over-romantic prose describing a beautiful setting, or a reference to an "emotional physical encounter" between the two girls.

From Glamuzina's and Laurie's perspective, the girls' talents were "unjustly devalued by agents of the dominant culture". Pauline's poem *The Ones That I Worship*, far from showing a lack of talent, contained "some interesting lines, with a lively use of language and some sense of rhythm". And many women had, like these girls, dreamed of publishing poetry and novels that were unlikely to find publishers "because of oppressive publishing controls and dismissive male critics". Nor did the girls' plans to travel overseas and publish their writings show a neglect of reality. In Glamuzina and Laurie's eyes, the steps taken by the girls to achieve their travel goals, such as Pauline visiting shipping companies and collecting money "by various means, including stealing", were practical ones.

Even bolder was the claim that Parker and Hulme probably had little idea of the permanence of death or what it meant. Many found this hard to believe. While very young children sometimes have difficulty comprehending the permanence of death, Pauline and Juliet clearly understood that killing Nora Rieper meant she would be dead forever, as evidenced by the past tense in Juliet's chilling words, "There's nothing in death. After all, she wasn't a very happy woman."

Glamuzina and Laurie argued that Juliet and Pauline were not in any way mentally abnormal. "Psychiatrisation"—the supposed presumption that females who commit crimes must be mentally ill—was no more than the hostile prejudice of a male-dominated world. They deplored Reg Medlicott's belief that there could be a connection between homosexuality and paranoia. "Medlicott's diagnosis had been rejected, not only in the legal sense, but also in medical terms, at the Supreme Court trial. Psychiatrists for the prosecution had clearly refuted the concept of *folie à deux* and had explicitly denied that there was any connection between paranoia and homosexuality." Indeed, any hypothesis that might reinforce negative attitudes about lesbianism was unthinkable. The jury's verdict rejecting insanity as a defence was, in their view, the end of the matter.

Convinced the girls were not insane, Glamuzina and Laurie pondered whether the family circumstances of the Rieper or Hulme families could help answer the question "Why was Honora Parker killed?" There were, they pointed out, secrets and stresses in both households; both "contained many unresolved conflicts". The relationship between Juliet and her mother, for example, had "conflicts typical of a culture which encouraged children to see the absence of a mother as neglect". Even so, they rejected the idea that dysfunctionality within the Rieper or Hulme families might supply an answer: "The suggestion that some families are 'dysfunctional' implies the existence of a 'functional' family, a concept we reject."

Their conclusion was that Hulme and Parker had found an "extreme solution" to the problem they faced, and by using violence had stepped outside expected gender patterns. "Pauline chose to kill her mother as the solution to the conflicts. Juliet chose to help her, possibly as a substitute for killing her own mother, or perhaps she simply wanted to help Pauline."

Alison Laurie would later suggest to a *New Zealand Listener* journalist that there were extenuating circumstances. "They were absolutely isolated as young lesbians. They undoubtedly felt that if they were separated they would never meet anyone else again—so they were desperate."

"These days," she continued, "we would hope that two young lesbians in that position could ring up Lesbian Line and get advice and support."

Alison Laurie and Julie Glamuzina had a wilder theory to throw into the mix. As evidence in court showed, before dawn on Good Friday 1953 Pauline and Juliet had walked up a hill behind the Hulmes' bach at Port Levy. Here, Pauline recorded in her diary, they had found a gateway through the clouds using an extra part of their brains possessed by only ten others, and looked into the beautiful 4th World where they would go when they died.

Port Levy—Koukourarata—is a place of ancient Māori habitation, rich in sites of spiritual, cultural and historical significance for the Ngāi Tahu people. On the advice of Māori friends who read Pauline's diary, Glamuzina and Laurie had consulted a local tohunga—a priestly expert. Far from the incident being, as Dr Medlicott had thought, evidence of paranoia, the tohunga believed it was an actual occurrence and the girls *had* entered another dimension. "A gateway through the clouds," he said, might be a way to ascend to other worlds.

He explained that mauri was the physical life force that came from the solar system and was controlled by kaitiaki, or guardians. Once a person knew where mauri was, karakia—prayers or incantations—or waiata tawhito—ancient songs—could get that person into another dimension. It was possible to enter this other dimension only twice a year, just before and after certain planets came into alignment. One of the times was at Easter. Pauline and Juliet appeared to have stumbled on this accidentally.

The tohunga thought the fact the girls were so young and that Pauline was menstruating—as mentioned in her diary—made them especially vulnerable. It was possible, he thought, that the Saints were gatekeepers to the 4th World. Sexual symbolism was a key to what had happened: the girls' "experiments" may have triggered a spiritual experience; their frequent bathing would have "provided an opportunity for forces to go through them and to be received".

When it came to the question posed by Glamuzina and Laurie— "Why was Honorah Parker killed?"—the tohunga believed Pauline and Juliet had been near several wāhi tapu—sacred, forbidden places. Today these places are still known and feared by local Māori, as is a giant red octopus, or wheke, which residents of Port Levy say they have seen lurking off the eastern end of Horomaka Island, guarding it.

The most tapu place is on the hillside climbed by the girls: the sacred red rocks of Te Ngarara. When the Port Levy reserve was being surveyed in 1849, the surveyor, Octavius Carrington, reportedly caused an uproar by standing on these rocks, and Māori still steer well clear of them. In the past the rocks were a tuahu—shrine—where tohunga performed rituals, and offerings were made to atua, the gods or spirits. The dead were laid to rest in caves among the rocks and lethally tapu items, such as the unwanted garments and food baskets of high-ranking chiefs and tohunga, were discarded there. The tuahu, like others of its kind, stood at a safe distance from dwellings.

Airini Grennell's grandfather Teone Taare Tikao, a highly learned man who lived in Port Levy from 1880 to 1889, had once said the sanctity of the tuahu was so great that any Māori who trespassed, even accidentally, on its immediate surroundings died. He did not need to be put to death: the shrine's tapu killed him.

Anyone walking up the hill behind the Hulmes' bach would soon come to these sacred red rocks. Pauline and Juliet probably went there: it was a perfect place to look down over the bay and Horomaka Island. The tohunga told Glamuzina and Laurie that local Māori would be protected against such violations of tapu by their spiritual guardians. People in the know could protect themselves by taking cooked food; without it a disaster could happen. If it did the guardians would have to be placated with cooked food or blood. If blood was required, the person killed would have to be of that person's own group.

The tohunga concluded that the spiritual effect on the girls of this experience could have been the cause of the killing of Honorah Parker. As Glamuzina and Laurie wrote in their book, "Honorah's death could be seen as a sacrifice."

Most people versed in such matters would challenge the notion that Pakeha-European New Zealanders could, by inadvertently violating a wāhi tapu, find themselves unconsciously programmed to kill a blood relation. The authors of *Parker and Hulme: A Lesbian View*, however, found the tohunga's insights "compelling and helpful".

CHAPTER 37

Stripped Naked

Nineteen ninety-one was an eventful year for those following New Zealand's most notorious murder case. Not only was the Glamuzina-Laurie book published, but in October a play based on the murder opened at the Court Theatre in Christchurch. *Daughters of Heaven* was written by a young American-born playwright, Michelanne Forster. Since 1989 Forster had been interviewing everyone she could find who had known Juliet Hulme or Pauline Parker, or had any personal knowledge of the case. Information had not been given lightly. "Women tended to voice the same bewildered sentiment: 'How could this have happened here in Christchurch?' Most men were even more reticent. "It was a long time ago," they would say. "I don't recall. The girls were punished ... what's to be gained from talking about it now?"

Despite having to prise information out of unwilling subjects, Forster had created brilliantly convincing characterisations of Pauline and Juliet that pulled audiences into the girls' strange world. The production was a sensational success, proving particularly fascinating to people born after 1954. The following year the play was staged in Wellington, where critics praised its "gripping theatre" and "diamond-hard production".

Michelanne Forster was not the only person to have seen the strong dramatic potential in the story. At least two screenplays had already been written: *Fallen Angels* by Australian playwright Louis Nowra in 1987 and *The Christchurch Murder* by English writer Angela Carter in 1988. Neither would be produced, pipped at the post by a young Wellington film-maker, Peter Jackson, and his wife and collaborator Fran Walsh.

Jackson and Walsh had a name among aficionados as auteur-directors of splatter movies but were little known to mainstream film audiences. Researching and writing the screenplay for their film, *Heavenly Creatures*, they were, like Michelanne Forster, having difficulty getting people to open up.

"I can understand the reluctance of some people to talk with us, but it is very frustrating," Jackson complained. "After all, the film is happening—nothing can stop it—and we're trying so hard to make a good job of it. In a year it will all be over, and any information or thoughts people have held back will be of no use to us. Some people tell us, 'You shouldn't make the film until everyone involved has died.' But what's the use of that? How could it possibly be accurate if there's no one left to talk to?"

Nevertheless, he felt squeamish about the project. "I feel a bit guilty making a film about the death of someone's mother," he said. "It's not the sort of thing I would want made about me." He and Walsh also worried they would be accused of exploiting the girls or glamourising the crime.

Jackson struggled—excessively perhaps—to justify the decision to go ahead. In New Zealand the case was "an open wound that has never healed," he said. Interest had never gone away. He knew of five or six prospective films. Fellow New Zealand film-maker Jane Campion and Dustin Hoffman's production company were just two who had shown interest. Given that someone was going to make a film, Jackson and Walsh reckoned they could do the best job. "What was important to us was to make the film as fairly as possible, not taking sides in any way. ... Deciding to do the film when we did may at least have stopped something more unsympathetic being made." It came across as an odd aspiration: to make a film about a horrific murder in a manner sympathetic to the murderers.

The evening Jackson and Walsh attended the opening party of Michelanne Forster's *Daughters of Heaven* at Wellington's Downstage Theatre there was lots of talk about Pauline Parker and Juliet Hulme. What had become of them? It was rumoured that Pauline was working in a Catholic bookshop in Auckland. A former classmate of the two girls at Christchurch Girls' High let it slip that Juliet was now a writer named Perry living in Scotland. This morsel was picked up by Lin Ferguson, a journalist for the Wellington tabloid *Sunday News*.

In July 1994, three months before Jackson and Walsh's film was to be released, Ferguson decided to try and track down Juliet Hulme. It proved amazingly easy. There was an entry for an Anne Perry in the reference work *Contemporary Authors*. Perry's date of birth was given as October 28, 1938, Juliet Hulme's birthday. Her mother was listed as H. Marion Perry (née Reaveley) and her father as Walter Perry. It was well known that Walter Perry had been Hilda Hulme's lover and that Hilda had changed her name to Perry. It was all very obvious. A recent photograph of Anne Perry closely matched photographs of Juliet Hulme at the time of the trial.

Ferguson agonised about whether to go with the story. "I knew I was going to blow up this woman's life after forty years." Before going public she phoned Peter Jackson, who spent an hour trying to persuade her not to run the story. "They're not Nazi war criminals," he argued. "They don't deserve to be hunted down."

It was Anne Perry's career as a writer of murder-mysteries that finally overcame Ferguson's qualms. Towards the end of July she rang Perry's literary agent, Meg Davis, in London. Davis noticed the journalist phoning from New Zealand was in a great state of excitement. She wanted to know if Davis had heard of the Parker–Hulme murder or the film *Heavenly Creatures*. One of the murderers, Juliet Hulme, she contended, was now Anne Perry, the writer.

"Hand on my heart, I think you've got the wrong woman," Davis said. Her next thought was that she must immediately instruct lawyers to get an injunction in New Zealand before the *Sunday News* went to print. She needed Anne's authority to do this.

It was the telephone call Anne Perry had been dreading for thirty-five years. "There's a ridiculous rumour going around in New Zealand. There's a film being made about a murder. They say you're Juliet Hulme, one of the… We must put it to rest."

"You can't," Perry said. "It's the truth."

They both knew the news would soon hit Britain. Perhaps it would be in the papers next day. "It was an absolute unqualified nightmare," Anne Perry would remember. "All I could think about was that my life would fall apart and it might kill my mother. ... I thought I might lose my career, my home ... It seemed so unfair. Everything I had worked so hard to achieve as a decent member of society was threatened."

Hilda was eighty-two, and according to Perry had a serious heart condition, but it was she who came up with a plan. "We must speak to the postmistress," she announced firmly. "She is the heart of the village." If they told the postmistress, the news would come from them and nobody else.

Perry summoned the postmistress to her house and told her of her true identity. "It was the first time in years I had told anyone my secret," she said. "It was one of the hardest things I've ever had to do." Then she phoned all the people she cared about. "That was absolutely bloody."

The story broke in the *Sunday News* on July 31 under the headline "MURDER SHE WROTE! BEST-SELLING BRITISH AUTHOR'S GRISLY KIWI PAST REVEALED". Two days later it was picked up by the Scottish paper *The Daily Record*, and by August 5 English journalist Sarah Gristwood had been granted an interview with Anne Perry and produced a long sympathetic piece for *The Daily Telegraph*. According to Gristwood, Perry had been "literally half-fainting with distress" when they met. The story was headlined "When murder catches up with you".

The news then went global. For Anne Perry it was "a very painful business being stripped naked in front of the world". Reporters laid siege to her house and camped on her mother's lawn. Her companion Meg MacDonald snapped and snarled, trying to keep them at a distance. But at least the Rosshire Mormons and the villagers of Portmahomack had been forewarned.

If it were a personal crisis for Anne Perry, it was a commercial opportunity for her publishers. If it were handled carefully, the discovery that the author of their extremely popular murder mysteries was writing from personal experience might not be a bad thing.

Peter Jackson's worst fears had been realised: because the exposure of Anne Perry as the former Juliet Hulme was a publicity coup for his film, many felt he must be behind it. He was at pains to deny any responsibility. He had had no contact with either Anne Perry or Hilary Nathan, he said. "The last thing I [wanted] to happen was for them to be found out and exposed." He insisted that by 1992 Anne Perry's identity had, anyway, been an open secret among New Zealand literati.

Jackson and Walsh had received a good deal of help with their screenplay from Hilda's old friend Nancy Sutherland and had established a warm relationship with her. They were quick to write and assure her they had had no part in revealing Juliet's new identity. Meanwhile, Hilda had received reports on Jackson's film from, among others, a New Zealand friend, Brian Easton, who told her how helpful Nancy Sutherland had been to the film-makers. She wrote to thank Nancy. "Brian tells us you played a large part in putting an entirely different perspective on the events, more sensitive to the human frailties of them and their personal integrity. He speaks of you with affection and admiration. And now, because he has shared this with us, I can write to you again, for Anne as well as myself, and say a heartfelt 'thank you'. We shall NOT be seeing the film, but have heard from many who have, around the world, much of its flavour etc, and now we know that you had a large part in this we want you to know how deeply and sincerely we appreciate your time and efforts."

In 1994 Sarah Gristwood met Peter Jackson at the Venice Film Festival, where *Heavenly Creatures* won a Silver Lion. She found him "rumpled, worried, friendly ... Above all guilty". He was still defending himself. The film, he said, might have been made less sympathetically by someone else, and he would never have made it had he known Anne Perry's mother was still alive.

He worried far too much. Anne Perry would say of her outing, "It was the best thing that could ever have happened because now I feel free. There's nothing to be afraid of any more in the middle of the night." Later on her website she would briskly dismiss the film that launched Peter Jackson's international career. "I have been asked questions occasionally about the film *Heavenly Creatures*, but I cannot answer them. Neither I nor my family and friends knew anything about it until the day before it was released, and I have preferred not to see it, or comment on the accuracy or otherwise of any part of it. I am very grateful to that vast majority of generous people who allow me to move on and leave that grief behind."

After the world learned that the international bestselling crime writer Anne Perry had, in an earlier life in distant New Zealand, been Juliet Hulme, convicted murderer, she received, so she told Sarah Gristwood, "the most incredible support. ... No one has turned away. Everybody has said, 'You were a child, this was forty years ago, we are right with you.' I didn't know there were so many compassionate, honourable people around."

To the *Daily Mail* she said, "People didn't point. They didn't stare, and I didn't lose one single friend once my identity was out." Someone had pushed a note under her door saying: "Don't worry. We know you. We take you as you are, not as you were." Even the Mormon Church supported her. She asked a senior figure if her membership would be affected—an odd question, given her stated position that the church knew about the murder before she became a member. "Your calling comes from God and He knows," the elder assured her. It was all perhaps a little too perfect to be the absolute truth.

Perry claimed to be surprised that the media were still so interested in her past. In an interview with *The Times* in March 2006 she complained, "Why do they all bring up something that happened fifty-two years ago?" She was being disingenuous: she and her publishers were well aware of the publicity value of her story. That particular interview had been arranged to promote her latest book, *The Sins of the Wolf*.

The *Times* writer spelled out the big selling point. "Perry has an insight that few crime writers can boast of. Perry committed murder, in 1954. Her name back then was Juliet Hulme, played by Kate Winslet in the film *Heavenly Creatures*." A bold sub-headline informed readers, "Her intimate knowledge of good and evil has brought literary acclaim".

The endless rehashing of Anne Perry's past proved exceedingly good for sales. Up until August 1994, when Lin Ferguson blew her cover, her books had sold three million copies in America, her biggest market. By March 2006, according to *The Times*, twenty million had sold worldwide. In the intervening period Perry had retailed a version of her early history to, among others, *The Daily Telegraph*, *The Times*, *The Guardian*, *USA Today* and the *Daily Mail*. To publicise *Weighed in the Balance*, Robert McCrum of *The Guardian: Weekend* had been granted an interview extending over several days.

Many of the interviews were reprinted in other newspapers and magazines, and formed the basis of many more articles published around the world. Perry was interviewed for United States television by Jamie Gangel of NBC and Bob Brown of ABC. She also appeared in *The Poisoned Pen* series, on which specialist bookstore owner Barbara Peters interviewed crime writers. The videoed six-part interview was readily available online.

On British television there was a prime-time interview with an uncomfortable Ian Rankin, the Scottish crime writer. It was clear from Perry's comments to the creator of the Inspector Rebus series that a new line in mitigation had emerged. "I was an ... accessory," she murmured. "I was involved ... there was no time to find a better solution." Rankin lobbed a gentle question about redemption. "Redemption comes when you decide you want to become the person you want to be," Perry replied.

There was yet another interview when *The Cater Street Hangman* was dramatised for television by Ardent, the production company owned by Prince Edward. Perry was obviously pleased with the royal connection. "He [Prince Edward] said to me he could see the headlines in print about us teaming up together—he actually came up with a few choice headlines himself," she told British journalist Louise Gannon. "But he said he didn't care, and that as far as he was concerned he was behind this project one hundred percent."

In 2007 Anne Perry consented to a documentary about her being made by Dana Linkiewicz, a young German film-maker. Linkiewicz and her crew followed their subject to an international writers' conference in Vancouver and then spent six weeks at her home in Portmahomack.

The film, *Anne Perry Interiors*, gave the world a rare window into the writer's everyday life. It was shot in mid winter. The wind whips, as Robbie Burns would say, "snell an' keen" into Dornoch Firth off the North Atlantic. An air of misery hangs about the place. There is no laughter. Reclining in a La-Z-Boy with pen and foolscap pad, Perry churns out novels relentlessly, not even allowing herself time to walk the dogs across the frosty corn stubble. There is a Rolls-Royce—or is it a Bentley?—in the garage, but for all the accoutrements of wealth it seems a life few would envy.

Anne Perry rules a little principality. Her mood determines the mood of the people around her. "Anne's emotions change us," her sad-eyed companion Meg MacDonald says. "If Anne's happy, we're happy." Anne does not seem to be happy all that often. When the woman typing Anne's latest book exclaims to the camera, "Never a dull moment!" it seems like ironic despair.

Meg lives in the cottage next door to Anne's converted barn. It seems she no longer travels to places like the Canary Islands to help Anne plan her new books. Instead she keeps an eye on the barn and feeds the cats and dogs when Anne is away in America on month-long book tours. Jonathan Hulme, retired from medical practice, lives in Portmahomack and helps his sister with her research. He appears bored and a little uncertain of his place in the scheme of things. "I have to be mature and not push my ego over this," he says. There is a faint hint that his ego takes a pounding from time to time.

There are odd comments about Anne's marital prospects. Jonathan comments, "She'd be happy if there was a man in her life, but her personality and intelligence would make it rather awkward." There is a curious monologue by Meg as she and Anne drive along in a car. "When you meet the right person," Meg intones, "it'll be the right person. You have to move out of your comfort zone. ... There's nobody here. You've been in the comfort zone too long." What the dickens is she talking about? Is Anne Perry, aged over seventy and never married, still searching for Mr Right? Or is this a subliminal message to the world that she is not lesbian? Is this important after all these years?

In pre-publicity for the documentary, Dana Linkiewicz revealed that the initial cut presented to Perry after half a year of editing had taken a rather critical stance. Clearly, this had not been acceptable. "They all agreed it was a good film. In the end, however, the final version turned out to be much more affectionate." You can't help wondering what has been added to, or subtracted from, the first cut of Linkiewicz's film to make it less critical, more "affectionate".

Despite being painfully slow-moving, *Anne Perry Interiors* contains some memorable sound bites.

Anne Perry: "I'm in the right place. I quite like myself. I'm not looking at myself too closely."

Meg MacDonald: "Anne doesn't talk much about her childhood—she doesn't believe she had a childhood."

Perry: "I grew up taught to show self-control."

MacDonald: "She's got to make time for fun as well—a walk on the beach or a walk in the fields."

Perry: "No one talks about it. ... My friends don't want me to talk about it. They find it distressing. They don't want me to be hurt."

MacDonald: "I wish she could trust other people with her life. Until she does she is not going to be free..."

Perry: "My family never talked about it. I assumed that other people wouldn't."

MacDonald: "Anne ... I love you so much I want people to know the real you."

Perry (in tears): "Mother was going with Bill. I was going to South Africa. When Pauline heard, her world fell apart. I really thought she would take her life. She had bulimia. She was throwing up after every meal. ... I knew it was stupid. I felt trapped. I knew it was wrong. I knew it was stupid. I knew I would have to pay for it. I didn't see any other way. I couldn't go to my mother or father. I couldn't walk away. I did something stupid I'll regret for the rest of my life. I can't undo it..."

There was nothing like penitence or contrition in the letters Juliet Hulme wrote as a sixteen year old from prison. Nearly five months after the murder, Henry Hulme complained his daughter was "still much the same as she was immediately after the event. Completely removed and occupied with herself ... she feels that she is right and others are wrong". After being in prison a year, she defiantly told Nancy Sutherland, "I'll rehabilitate myself and grow into a new person ... but I must do it myself without being ... dictated to". On her release, not even Sam Barnett, the Secretary for Justice, was prepared to claim she was a reformed character. Florence Howland, who saw her off at the airport, said she never showed any remorse.

Now as Anne Perry the crime writer she talks a good deal about redemption, and in interviews with international media has regularly related a colourful tale of repentance and redemption. "Once I was in prison alone I had to come to terms with it and I did," she told Bob Brown of the ABC. "You get on your knees and you say to God, 'I was wrong. No excuses. I am sorry.' As long as you make excuses for yourself, blame others, somebody else, you are still not here." She claimed this dark night of the soul came during three months in solitary confinement at the beginning of her stay in Mt Eden.

More details appeared in an interview with Amanda Cable of the *Daily Mail*: "Finally, after I'd been there for three months and was at my lowest, I knelt by my bed and prayed. I just begged for forgiveness. I said sorry again and again and I meant it."

The story was reprised for Dana Linkiewicz and the German film crew. "The first three months I was frozen ... then I cried and cried and cried again. ... After that I never cried again."

She spoke with pride to Angela Neustatter of *The Guardian* about being the youngest inmate by years in the toughest prison in the southern hemisphere. "I went down on my knees and repented ... That is how I survived my time while others cracked up. I seemed to be the only one saying, 'I'm guilty and I am where I should be'." To some this read more like a profession of moral superiority than actual remorse. She boasted to Sarah Gristwood, "I have had people say that my work is studied in ethics classes for its compassion and humanity."

Being sorry did not meant beating your breast all the time, she informed Deirdre Donahue of *USA Today*. Far from beating her breast, as she repeatedly told interviewers, she had blocked the murder from her mind. "I'm not amnesiac, for Pete's sake," she told Robert McCrum. "I just don't choose to remember certain things."

Most revealing of all was her exchange with Amanda Cable of the *Daily Mail* in 2006. Did she ever, as those dark Scottish nights drew in, think back to the murder, Cable asked.

"No," Perry said, "I would just torment myself and that wouldn't help anybody."

Did she ever think of her victim?

"No. She was somebody I barely knew."

CHAPTER 38

A Piece of Fiction

What was the real explanation for the killing of Honorah Rieper that sunny winter's afternoon in 1954? Why did two intelligent adolescent girls commit an almost unimaginably savage murder—and just as important, how were they able to bring themselves to do it? As with Leopold and Loeb, the enduring interest in Parker and Hulme has come about in large part because no answers have ever seemed completely satisfactory.

The issues that preoccupied the trial—the girls' possible insanity and their sexual relationship—ultimately shed little light on the crime. The girls were not psychotics of the sort who receive messages from God or their television set telling them to kill people. They were in love, certainly, but throughout history untold millions have been passionately in love and threatened with separation without resorting to murder. Lesbian couples are no more likely to commit acts of violence than heterosexual couples. And while many teenage girls may entertain thoughts of killing their mother, very few actually do so. Matricide is the rarest of crimes. A 2009 American study showed that of murders where the victim and offender were known to each other, fewer than two percent were matricides. In most of these cases the mothers were killed by their adult sons. When a daughter was the killer, they were almost always over eighteen years of age, and most were single middle-aged women living at home with their mother. To this day it is extremely rare for girls of fifteen or sixteen, the ages of Juliet Hulme and Pauline Parker respectively at the time of the murder, to commit or be a party to matricide.

What was it, then, that led Juliet and Pauline to leave their world of fantasy, put a half-brick in one of Pauline's old school stockings, and swing it at Pauline's mother's head?

In the seventeen years since the release of *Heavenly Creatures*, intense public interest has meant numerous opportunities for both women to tell their stories. Pauline Parker—Hilary Nathan—has chosen to remain silent, but Anne Perry has told and retold her version of events many times. Amanda Cable summed up her media appeal: "With her neatly tailored suit, bobbed hair and immaculate make-up, Anne exudes success. As a top-selling crime writer she has made a fortune writing fifty novels over the past four decades. ... It's hard to look at her perfectly manicured nails and know these same hands once bludgeoned a woman to death."

More than once Perry has complained that, as a minor, she was not permitted to testify in her own defence. Sarah Gristwood faithfully reported in *The Daily Telegraph*: "At the trial she found that a fifteen year old had the worst of both worlds—compelled to be present but not allowed to say a word." The truth was quite different. The law of New Zealand did not prevent a minor from testifying. It was Juliet Hulme's defence lawyers who were against her doing so. They were convinced that if she gave evidence her overweening arrogance and condescension would destroy whatever chance they had of a defence of insanity, her only hope of an acquittal.

Perry established her basic storyline soon after Lin Ferguson's exposé. After she was taken out of school with chest problems, she told Sarah Gristwood, she had a lonely time, relieved only by the friendship of another girl, Pauline Rieper. "I don't want in any way to implicate or blame her ... but she wished me to join her in this act and I believed that if I did not she would take her own life. ... We were going to leave the country. I felt I was deserting Pauline. We would have taken her with us, but her mother wouldn't let her go. She felt her mother was the only thing stopping her from leaving a situation she felt was intolerable.

"I believed at that time her survival depended upon her coming with us. I sincerely believed that her life was in the balance. Crazy as this sounds, I thought it was one life or the other. I just couldn't face the thought of being responsible for her dying. And I made a very foolish choice."

Reading this one might feel sympathetic. Far from being a cold-blooded killer, Juliet Hulme had been put in an impossible situation by her only friend, who felt pressed to kill her mother and had threatened to commit suicide if Juliet did not help her. With hindsight it was foolish, but she was only fifteen and acting under extreme moral duress. Wasn't it entirely understandable? And wasn't there something rather commendably loyal about her not wishing to blame or implicate the friend who put her in this moral bind?

Reading on, you learn she had been receiving treatment using drugs that had "since been withdrawn because they tend to warp judgement". Although the normal course of treatment was three months, she had been given these drugs for nine months. How could anyone blame her, especially when she was prepared to square up and admit to having been "an accomplice … a party to this act, and I never pretended otherwise". Didn't you really have to admire her?

The story was on its way. A couple of weeks later the respected writer Sebastian Faulks wrote in *The Guardian* that Juliet, "confused by high doses of medication, provided a brick with which Pauline killed her mother". It seemed Anne Perry had played only a very minor part in the thing.

NBC's Jamie Gangel tried hard to pin her down on the details, but by now the story had grown. "[Pauline] felt her mother was the one thing standing between her coming with us, which to her seemed to represent safety, warmth, happiness, a chance to be the kind of person she wanted to be, and I didn't have the strength to say, 'No, this is wrong no matter what' and to just walk away."

"I don't remember the events very much," she added.

"You have blocked it out?"

"Yes, I have."

Gangel persisted. "Let me give you a description … about what happened based on the court documents, and also your admission to the police. What it says is you gave half a brick to your friend Pauline, that she put it in a stocking and, at the deserted area of a local park, first she repeatedly hit her mother over the head, then you did the same. Then one of you held her down while the other one repeatedly hit her and there was a great deal of blood and she died within a few minutes. Did that sound to you like what happened? Do you think that was a fair account of what happened?"

"Probably," Perry said. "I certainly hope it was a few moments," she added.

It was often mentioned that Juliet Hulme had been taking medication. *USA Today*, America's largest-circulation national newspaper, reported, "While Perry makes no excuses for herself, she does point out she was on a medicine that was eventually taken off the market for its judgement-altering qualities." She repeated this in the *Daily Mail*. "At the same time I'd also been taking strong experimental drugs for tuberculosis which were later found to be hugely mood-altering. … They can't have helped."

Then there was the question of her friend's state of health. Not only had Pauline threatened to take her own life, Juliet feared she was about to die of malnutrition. She was literally wasting away. "I was afraid that she was seriously ill to the point where she might not survive. … She was vomiting after every meal and losing weight all the time. I am sure now she was bulimic. I really believed she would take her own life and I couldn't face it."

By the time Perry was interviewed for Dana Linkiewicz's documentary there was another layer of detail. Pauline had been "throwing up after every meal. She was a bag of bones. Her skin was very pale. If you put a sticking plaster on it, it used to suppurate."

The most comprehensive account was to Amanda Cable. Her one constant friend, Anne Perry said, was her classmate Pauline Parker. It was an obsessive friendship on Pauline's part. Her parents suddenly announced they were divorcing and she—Juliet—would be returning to England within days. When Pauline's mother refused to let Pauline accompany her, Pauline got into a murderous rage.

On the morning of the murder, Perry said, she felt as you would if you were going to jump out of a plane with a parachute—"that awful sickening 'Am I going to jump or am I not?'"

In the space of a few days her whole life had fallen apart. "I adored both my parents and I hadn't a clue the marriage was in trouble. My own safe, happy little world was destroyed overnight. I was devastated … We were such a close family and now I didn't have a clue what the future would hold…

"I felt I had an immense obligation to my friend," she continued. "She was the only person who had written to me during the months I had been in a sanatorium recovering from TB. She had shown me such loyalty and now I must return it. She was bulimic—she had an eating disorder—and I truly believed that she would take her own life and it would be my fault if I didn't do what she suggested. My debt to her just had to be paid, no matter how horrific. …

"I remember feeling real nerves beforehand. I was horrified even as the attack was happening, but I felt it was a debt and I had to continue. It was as if I was a completely different person."

Within hours, she was being questioned on her own in a police cell. "I was utterly terrified. There was no solicitor or adult there to represent me. … When the case came to court I stood there alone and I remember them discussing hanging. I knew then my life was hanging in the balance. I wasn't allowed to give my side of the story—to try to explain my desperation or the events leading up to it. … We were never lesbians. That was made up and I was unable to speak out."

Of the numerous ways in which these stories deviate from reality, three stand out. First, there was no possibility of Juliet being under the influence of judgement-warping medication at the time of the murder. As Reg Medlicott said at the trial, she had received both isoniazid and streptomycin during her stay at the sanatorium, but there was no evidence either drug produced psychological changes. Both were antibiotics commonly used to treat tuberculosis. Neither was experimental or later withdrawn from the market. Furthermore, Juliet had left the sanatorium nine months before the murder.

Secondly, although it seems likely that Pauline Parker was bulimic, there is no evidence the disease had reached a life-threatening stage, or that Juliet believed her friend was at risk of dying. Pauline's mother believed her daughter was starting a new job the following week, and allowed her to stay away from home for eight nights with her friend. She had been well enough on her return to energetically help her mother with housework. When the family had lunch on the day of the murder she was lively and sparkling—and there is no denying the physical energy she displayed in the afternoon.

Both when she was a remand prisoner and later, when she served her sentence, there was no indication that her life was in danger, or even that special treatment was required because of an eating disorder that was causing her to waste away. In April 1955 the medical officer at Arohata found she was overweight and needed to diet.

Thirdly, there is no possibility that Juliet took part in the murder of Honorah Rieper only under moral duress. All the contemporaneous evidence points to her being a willing participant. While on April 28, nearly two months before the murder, Pauline recorded a moment of depression when she "quite seriously considered committing suicide" as "life seemed so much not worth living", this had quickly turned into active hatred. "Anger against Mother boiled up inside me as it is she who it one of the main obstacles in my path. Suddenly a means of ridding myself of this obstacle occurred to me. If she were to die," she wrote in her diary.

By Saturday, June 19 they were "both thrilled by the idea. … Naturally we feel a little nervous [but] the pleasure of anticipation is great". Hilda Hulme said Juliet looked "radiantly happy" as she left the house on the day of the murder; afterwards she was elated and jubilant. "Neither of them showed the slightest remorse," Medlicott said, and Dr Bennett would never forget Juliet's insistence that not only was Mrs Rieper's murder justified, but further murders might be justified of anybody else who threatened their friendship.

It seems Anne Perry, consciously or unconsciously, has reworked the raw facts in her imagination to such an extent as to create a piece of fiction. The writer Anaïs Nin once remarked, "We see things not as they are but as we are." For all Perry's lip service to "no excuses" and not blaming others, she admits to nothing more than a youthful error of judgement in highly extenuating circumstances involving the death of a virtual stranger.

Whether real repentance can come from this is a subject worthy of discussion in one of the ethics classes said to use Anne Perry novels as teaching materials. Perry herself believes, "I have done everything I can to live as good a life as I know how since. To the best of my belief I am doing nobody any harm and as much good as I am able."

CHAPTER 39

The Other Girl

With Anne Perry unmasked, attention shifted to finding "the other girl". Peter Jackson told the media he was determined Pauline Parker would not suffer the same fate as Juliet Hulme. *The Guardian* reported that the film-maker would not release any details about her, except to say that "she apparently lived a life of great regret and not a very happy life either". It is doubtful Jackson knew any more about her than the widespread rumour she was working in a bookshop in Auckland.

It was generally believed Pauline had lived in England for some years but had since returned to New Zealand. After the release of *Heavenly Creatures*, representatives of the world's press unsuccessfully staked out Auckland's two Catholic bookshops hoping to spot her. Robert McCrum wrote in *The Guardian: Weekend* that she was proving difficult to track down. "Those who protect her will speak only on condition of anonymity, but her presence in New Zealand has helped keep the story alive." The last official reference to Parker, under her new name Hilary Nathan, had been in February 1967, he said, when she had been reported teaching in an English girls' school. By the 1970s she had become a figure of mystery, although McCrum assured readers she was known to have returned to New Zealand and taken a new name. She had kept in touch with her family, but from a distance, and had pursued a number of different careers, including work with the mentally handicapped.

"Reports of her state of health and mind vary," McCrum wrote. "Some say she is 'troubled', 'sad', even 'suicidal'. Others indicate a more robust condition, pointing out that she has been adept at covering tracks." There were other reports that she had married and was living in a rural town in New Zealand with children of her own who did not know her true identity.

The journalist Chris Cooke was not convinced Pauline had returned from England. He learned from someone who had attended the New Zealand Library School at the same time as her that after going to London in 1966 she had worked at the Wandsworth Town Library. By clever detective work he found she had a close companion called Joan Nathan, known as Jo, and since 1985 had been living in the village of Hoo St Werburgh on the Medway Estuary in Kent. Once he got that close he found her name in the telephone directory. Her address was the Abbots Court Riding School.

Hoo St Werburgh may have once been a pretty place, but it was now a straggly village of mostly ugly post-war pebbledash houses. One of the few he could find who knew Hilary Nathan was the local librarian. Miss Nathan, she told him, spent many hours in the library reading.

The headquarters of the Abbots Court Riding School turned out to be an old, semi-detached, red brick farm-worker's cottage, run-down and half-choked with ivy, with stables behind. What must have once been a pleasing view over cornfields to the Medway, beneath towering clouds worthy of Constable, was now marred by power stations and pylons.

Cooke knocked on the door and asked the woman who answered if he could talk to her about certain events in New Zealand in 1954. She refused to speak to him, insisting "I've never had another name. I'm sorry, you've got the wrong person." She was, he said, "a wiry, fit figure, decked in moleskins and gumboots, with a broad, rural accent". He managed to take some photographs before making his departure.

Cooke had the news the world was waiting for and the media were quick to grab hold of it. On January 8, 1997 Wellington's *Dominion* reported that Miss Nathan had refused to comment, but a friend claimed to be negotiating on her behalf to sell her story to Britain's *Daily Mail* and other publications. The friend, Joan Nathan, described as having lived near Hilary Nathan for thirty years, said she had never detected anything sinister in Hilary's background. "She is a thoroughly nice person and I'm very sorry this has all surfaced again."

Chris Cooke was granted an interview with Hilary's sister Wendy, who said Hilary had authorised her to speak to the press in New Zealand in the hope this would extinguish media interest. Her sister was not like Anne Perry, Wendy said. She had no interest in giving interviews but was prepared to allow New Zealanders to learn of her new life. She asked that once they had heard her story she be left alone to continue her quiet existence.

Wendy explained that Hilary lived as a recluse in a village where no one knew of her secret past. Although she had failed to become a nun, she was now "a nun in her way. She's living in solitude. She's deeply religious. … She leads a very unusual existence. She doesn't have a TV or a radio so would never have heard what Anne Perry had to say and she wouldn't care." She had not seen and did not want to see *Heavenly Creatures*. "She doesn't have any contact with the outside world. She's a devout Roman Catholic and spends much of her time in prayer."

It had been her sister's childhood dream to own a place in the country and have a stable of horses. Now she had achieved that lifestyle she was a much more contented person. "She has led a good life and is very remorseful for what she's done. She committed the most terrible crime and has spent forty years repaying it by keeping away from people and doing her own little thing."

The most highly paid New York public relations consultant could not have done a better job of explaining Hilary's present way of life and her attitude to the crime she had committed. There were no excuses.

The discovery of Pauline Parker was the lead item on television news in New Zealand. A reporter from TV One had got hold of some locals who said they were surprised to learn of Miss Nathan's past but would rally around and give her whatever support she needed. TV3 had secured hidden-camera footage of the Abbots Court Riding School.

In England the *Express* and *Daily Mail* made their own inquiries and published stories, seemingly without Hilary Nathan's cooperation. "SWEET SPINSTER WHO IS ONE OF THE WORLD'S LOST KILLERS" was the *Express*'s arresting headline. The newspapers revealed that she had been a teacher of mentally handicapped children at Abbey Court Special School in nearby Strood, and risen to deputy headmistress before retiring three years earlier to establish her riding academy. "It will come as a shock to the whole school," a so-called source close to Abbey Court Special School said. "Nobody knew anything about it." She was, the source said, well-liked but strange, "often turning up for classes in wellies and battered black sunglasses". It was noticed that when school photographs were taken she was never in the picture.

Reporters thought it odd there was no television, radio or even an oven in Nathan's three-bedroom cottage. Odd also that the living room was full of dolls and there was a large rocking horse standing inside the front door. The former Pauline Parker kept ten ponies and an Arab stallion. Each weekend, it was said, half a dozen young girls from the village would come to muck out the stables. When the "small sprightly woman" had been ambushed by the press while feeding and grooming her ponies, she insisted she had absolutely no comment to make.

Villagers dished up slivers of information. Miss Nathan was very eccentric. She kept herself very much to herself. She lived on a diet of sandwiches and currant buns. She attended the English Martyrs Roman Catholic Church in Strood every day without fail. To one informant she seemed "quite childish in a way": at gymkhanas she would take part in children's events such as the sack race. Joyce Hopkins, her next-door neighbour, said she seemed very nice and clearly loved children. Miss Nathan never said anything about her past, Hopkins remembered. "We didn't even know she was from New Zealand."

The press more or less left Hilary Nathan alone after that, but now she had been exposed to the world as one of the infamous New Zealand teenage murderers it was time for her to move on. Her cottage, stables, land, stables and all appurtenances were put on the market.

The buyers were a local man, Andrew Ayres, and his wife. The Ayres liked Hilary Nathan. "She was very direct," Ayres said. "We hit it off very well."

After an unconditional contract was signed, Nathan wanted to bring forward the completion date. She had learned that *Heavenly Creatures* was to be shown on prime-time television across Britain on Saturday, June 27. She wished to be out of the house before then and Ayres was happy to oblige. He noted that, despite what the newspapers had said, Nathan had a television set.

An interesting feature of Hilary Nathan's house was a mural on a wall of the upstairs front bedroom, which Ayres was sure had been painted by Nathan herself. Encompassing a number of different styles, the work consisted of dream-like vignettes making up a composite whole. At its heart a girl with dark curly hair—surely Pauline herself—sat, head bowed, under a blighted tree in a post-apocalyptic landscape. The figure was painted in a crude expressionist style, its tremulous brushstrokes suggesting an artist in the grip of severe depression. Below it, another image depicted the dark-haired girl as a fallen angel imprisoned in a bird cage. Her wings were dirty and bedraggled, her body stooped and naked. Nearby, another naked Pauline figure was desperately diving to submarine depths to grab hold of an image of the Virgin Mary.

In a striking scene a blonde girl was seated on a horse, leaping skywards, while a dark-haired girl struggled on the ground to bridle the horse, attempting to keep both it and the rider on terra firma. Another depicted two girls, one dark-haired and the other blonde, as two flowers blooming on one plant but cruelly sundered by the stroke of a large heavy axe. More enigmatically, figures were entombed in utero, and there were corps de ballet of fairies or sprites.

At the centre top of the mural, a beautiful blonde Juliet figure, rendered in comic-strip style, was mounted on a winged horse. Arms outstretched, jubilant, the girl shimmered and shone like a goddess. If the mural was indeed the work of Hilary Nathan, it was clear she was deeply troubled by her past and had not been able to put Juliet Hulme and the horror of their parting out of her mind.

During the years the Ayres lived in the cottage a steady succession of inquisitive visitors came to the door, hoping to meet the notorious murderer face-to-face, but Pauline Parker had moved far away, to Orkney in the far north of Scotland, as isolated and secret a place as she could find.

One of those fascinated by the Parker–Hulme murder was Alexander Roman, a young American film-maker. Roman's interest having been aroused by *Heavenly Creatures*, he decided to make a dramatised documentary about the case. From the internet he learned that Hilary Nathan was living on a Scottish island. A private investigator he employed unearthed more specific information about where she could be found. Roman sent her a letter by FedEx, inquiring about the paintings found on the bedroom wall at Abbots Court, which he wanted to reproduce in his documentary. There was no reply.

Roman decided to pay Hilary Nathan a visit. At Easter 2010 he flew from Los Angeles to Scotland and made his way to the island on which she lived. The local taxi driver, who doubled as the publican, was otherwise engaged but a helpful person volunteered to drive him from the main town to the incomer's house.

It was raining a fine drizzle as Roman travelled the short distance across the island. He noticed the scenery was beautiful in a bleak, barren way; trees obviously struggled to grow in the face of the Atlantic gales. The stone house and farm buildings stood looking out to sea at the end of a long uphill drive. The driver waited while Roman had a look around. There was a herd of goats, and a white horse that kept bumping Roman's hand affectionately. The barn door was decorated with a huge painting of a tree, an artistic touch incongruous in such an austere place. The dark house had a "broken-hearted" look. A cat lay morosely on a windowsill beside a line-up of small dolls. There was a Roman statue of some sort in the porch, and a small conservatory tacked on to the house.

Roman had come prepared. In his bag were small gifts from Los Angeles and a copy of his script, which he intended to present to Nathan. While he was snooping about, she drove out of the barn on a huge tractor and jumped down. Fair-skinned, with rich dark-brown hair, she was, he observed, thin and tough-looking.

She glared at him as he muttered something about the documentary he was making and handed her the bag of gifts. "You have the wrong person. This is the wrong place," she insisted firmly. "Go immediately." She pushed him into the waiting car. As it moved off she ran after it trying to return the bag, but it was too late.

Back at his hotel, Roman felt disappointed about the way things had gone. He had handled it badly. He had travelled a long way to meet Pauline Parker and got nothing out of it. By next morning the rain had stopped. He had left some battery packs for his camera in the bag he had given Nathan and wanted them back. He decided to have one more try at talking to her. Fortunately the taxi driver was free to take him. Easter Sunday was possibly the worst day he could have chosen to invade the sanctuary of a devout and reclusive Roman Catholic, but that thought did not cross his mind. In any event, his schedule was tight.

On the long unsealed driveway the taxi overtook a pretty young girl who was on a moped, maybe on her way to have a riding lesson. Roman got out of the car and walked towards the house. He was nervously patting a small dog when Hilary Nathan suddenly appeared, striding towards him. He recognised the look on her face, the angry, protruding lower lip, from her police mug shot.

She was extremely angry. "Get out!" she yelled.

He hurriedly mentioned the battery packs he had left in the bag. Could he please have them back?

"I burned them!" she shouted. "I burned everything!"

"Where did you do that?" he asked gently. "Might I have a look?"

"I don't know where," she snarled. She waved towards a pile of rubbish. "You can rummage through that if you like."

The taxi driver, realising there was some sort of altercation going on, wandered over. "Is there something wrong?" he asked.

"There is something *seriously* wrong," Hilary Nathan said. "This man is harassing me. Take him away at once."

"I wouldn't allow a woman like that in my pub," the driver remarked as he and Roman headed back to town.

CHAPTER 40

What the Heck Was It?

Psychiatry has moved a long way since 1961, when Reg Medlicott suggested that Pauline Parker and Juliet Hulme were suffering from "adolescent megalomania". Perhaps out of respect for Hilda Hulme and the dead Honorah Rieper, he had shied away from delving into the possible causes of their condition. Today, however, it is common to see a connection between emotional neglect in infancy or early childhood and psychoses and personality disorders later in life.

It is now well understood that a young child has a deep need to be lovingly attached to a reliable mother figure, whose unconditional adoration and physical warmth supplies emotional security. Children deprived of this are likely to become emotionally frozen or insecure, lack ego-control, and have a low sense of self-worth, even if this is well camouflaged. Natural feelings of affection for the mother are overwhelmed by rage, and this may be turned inward to become self-loathing: people who hate their mothers invariably hate themselves as well. The wounds of maternal abandonment remain for life. The unloved or under-loved child becomes ever more unlovable.

Both Juliet Hulme and Pauline Parker experienced difficulties with their mothers, although these were different in nature. Juliet's parents cared for her in a material sense and seemed fond of her, if in a somewhat cool and offhand way, but her upbringing was characterised by frequent and prolonged separations from her family in infancy and childhood. Later, when Hilda Hulme took a lover, she had less and less time to give to her difficult daughter, and Henry Hulme, while proud of Juliet, had little clue about human relationships, as witnessed by the letter he wrote her in prison—a letter so cold prison staff refused to deliver it to her.

Such an upbringing can be expected to produce an "avoidant attachment" character style. "Avoidants", as they are called, have shut down their emotions to defend themselves against further injury. They cannot be warmly affectionate, and come across as arrogantly self-sufficient, seeing themselves as perfect, and incapable of admitting faults of any kind. They can be shy loners who get sick a lot. For all their self-sufficiency in childhood, when they become adolescents avoidants often find themselves longing for a soulmate. In adulthood they may become workaholics, addicted to power or absorbed by other ambitions.

Avoidant attachment is known to be at the heart of narcissistic personality disorder, the diagnostic criteria for which are a grandiose sense of self-importance; preoccupation with fantasies of unlimited success, power, brilliance and beauty; the belief the person is "special" and "unique"; excessive need for admiration; arrogance and haughtiness; sense of entitlement; lack of empathy for others; and exploitation of others for selfish needs—all factors that seem to square with the young Juliet's personality. While, beneath their grandiosity, narcissists have a fragile sense of self-esteem, it doesn't show: they have succeeded in burying their insecurities.

Psychopathic traits are closely related to narcissism: doctors often refer to the "narcissist-psychopath type". Psychopaths are often articulate and charming. They lie glibly and convincingly. In some types, violent behaviour is likely to be premeditated rather than impulsive. Fearlessness and lack of conscience and remorse are common.

Such an individual has an advantage over the majority of the population when it comes to not remembering an act that would leave most people guilt-ridden for the rest of their lives—namely dissociation, the ability of the mind to hide a memory, a feeling, or a body sensation for a short or a long time. Meg MacDonald's statement that "Anne doesn't talk about her childhood—she doesn't believe she had a childhood" is revealing. Anne Perry may have blocked out not only the memory of Pauline's mother's death, but most of her childhood with it.

*

Although both girls were insecurely attached to their mothers, Pauline Parker had a distinctly different psychological profile from Juliet. From the outside, apart from a spell of serious illness her childhood appeared to be relatively normal. But there were tensions and secrets within the family. Her father had abandoned his first wife and children, and he and her mother had started a new life in the South Island. They were not married, something seen as intensely shameful in 1950s New Zealand. They struggled financially and endured the stress of a baby's death and later of raising an intellectually handicapped child. Pauline was seen as the difficult daughter and her mother's behaviour towards her fluctuated wildly.

In terms of character Pauline was "anxious ambivalent". Rather than being unwilling to become emotionally close to others, the ambivalent is desperate to have close relationships—although, for fear no one would want to get close to them, they can act in a superior, stand-offish way. Ambivalents' inner feelings of self-worth are sometimes so lacking they see themselves as loathsome, unclean, and even poisonous. While drawn to relationships with others, they handle them incompetently: friendships can be destroyed by eruptions of irrational rage. Jealousy and clinginess often drive away friends and potential partners.

It is believed that in ambivalents the character-shaping trauma occurred later in life than it did for avoidants, and that their mothers were less rejecting. It has been said that ambivalents result from partial maternal deprivation rather than drastic separation.

Whereas avoidants learn to disguise their inner hurt and anger, ambivalents do not develop protective indifference and are obviously full of rage. Where Juliet had an icy contempt for humanity, Pauline had open anger and animosity. She neatly captured the distinction herself in *The Ones That I Worship*: "Hatred burning bright in the brown eyes with enemies for fuel / Icy scorn glitters in the grey eyes, contemptuous and cruel."

The mothers of ambivalents blow hot and cold. Emotional, or even physical, cruelty followed by kindness is a familiar picture. The child may become hooked on the mother's unpredictability. Now and then the mother will deliver the emotional warmth desperately wanted and the child will become more addicted than ever. As one expert, Jude Cassidy, professor of psychology at the University of Maryland, explains, "Nothing makes a laboratory rat push the pedal more furiously than an inconsistent reward."

The relationship between ambivalents and their mothers is always complicated: the anger and aggression mingle with an anxious neediness. This conflict probably explains Pauline's intervals of "being good". Eating disorders like hers are also common: self-starvation can be a way for a child to punish their mother. In teenage years and later, ambivalents may attempt to satisfy a sense of emptiness and need for love with overeating, alcohol or drugs.

While Pauline was not strongly narcissistic, her behaviour might be seen as satisfying the criteria for the disorder "borderline personality", which, like all personality disorders, has a narcissistic component. "Borderlines" have much in common with the ambivalent character type and the two often coincide. Most borderlines have been at times physically or emotionally abused by a mothering figure who at other times was adequate and nurturing. Not surprisingly, the borderline child hates and loves her vacillating mother at the same time: a book on the disorder has the title *I Hate You—Don't Leave Me.*

Borderlines grow up with an unstable self-image and acquire a history of stormy personal relationships. At the heart of the personality lies a profound feeling of emptiness and a weak sense of self. "Unable to figure out who or what they are ... they glom on to others so as if to acquire an identity by osmosis," was how Jerrold Maxmen and Nicholas Ward expressed it in their 1994 work *Essential Psychopathology and Its Treatment.* Their moods oscillate wildly: "inappropriate intense anger" is one of the defining symptoms. Relationships with friends and lovers are all-consuming, characterised by "overidealisation" that usually ends in deep disappointment. As with other personality disorders, the borderline has low tolerance of frustration, grief and threats of abandonment: the first of the American Psychiatric Association's criteria is "frantic efforts to avoid real or imagined abandonment". Borderlines are also known to have "transient delusions"—brief psychotic incidents—which might explain Pauline's Port Levy "revelation".

Dr Phil Brinded, a Christchurch psychiatrist familiar with the case, questions whether the label "borderline" is appropriate for Pauline Parker in light of her later history. As Hilary Nathan, Parker has shown deep remorse, embracing Catholicism to the extent of wanting to become a nun, devoting herself to special needs children, and avoiding the public glare. She seems to have had a stable long-term relationship and none of the violence, self-mutilation and drug-dependency typical of someone with borderline personality disorder.

A recent development in psychology has been the identification of the "symbiotic" character, or personality. Symbiotics are thought to have been excessively corrected by their parents at a young age, overdisciplined to conform to the parents' expectations. They have a weak sense of self and often "borrow" an identity from someone else, conforming to this person's tastes and interests and even being invaded by their moods. This is accompanied by a deep-rooted fear that the person will abandon them. The symbiotic personality experiences extremely hostile fantasies and dreams, and has difficulty modulating aggressive impulses. People who compulsively overeat are often found to have issues of symbiosis. It is not hard to see evidence of the symbiotic character in Pauline and her relationship with Juliet.

Mental illness may also have had a part in shaping the destinies of Pauline Parker and Juliet Hulme. Bipolar disorder, or manic depressive illness, was recognised in 1954 but little understood until the 1970s. Today DSM–IV—the American Psychiatric Association's Diagnostic and Statistical Manual of Mental Disorders, Fourth Edition—defines manic episodes as periods of "abnormally and persistently elevated, irritable or expansive mood, accompanied by symptoms such as inflated self-esteem, non-delusional grandiosity, decreased need for sleep, flight of ideas, and excessive involvement in pleasurable activities. Sufferers overvalue their beauty, talents, achievements, brilliance, and other qualities.

During the manic phase the person will feel euphoric, see humour in everything, and have an increased interest in sex. Racing thoughts and rapid speech are characteristic. Abnormal beliefs, such as grandiose delusions, are found in nearly half of bipolar patients in manic phase. Manic depressives in general are narcissistic and temperamentally hyper-excitable. It has often been observed that sleep deprivation triggers manic episodes, and in full flight sleep is impossible, as it often was for Juliet and Pauline during April, May and June of 1954.

During manic episodes there may also be "somatic" delusions—bizarre beliefs about the body. An example in psychiatric literature is a German judge who one night found himself wondering what it would be like to be a woman having sexual intercourse. This developed into the delusion that he was changing sex. Something like this might explain Pauline's diary for Good Friday, April 16, 1954: "We had the most intriguing conversation about what her parents would think if they concluded that [Juliet] had changed into a male. It would have explained a great many things extraordinary to them"? The girls' belief they had an extra part to their brain might also be seen as a somatic delusion.

While psychiatry offers these tantalising explanations and insights, another factor at least as potent factor was at work: neurochemistry. The two girls were wildly enamoured with each other. In the throes of love the body experiences chemical changes. Dopamine, a neurotransmitter, increases in parts of the brain, including the *nucleus accumbens*, a region associated with reward, motivation and addiction. It then drives up testosterone levels—in women as well as men—increasing the sexual drive. And dopamine metabolises into norepinephrine, a hormone and neurotransmitter that stimulates wild flights of imagination and increased energy. When you can think of nothing except your beloved, sleep and food are unnecessary.

These psychiatric and neurological theories go some way to explaining the strange and ultimately criminal behaviour of Pauline Parker and Juliet Hulme, but there is still one last question. As one of Pauline and Juliet's classmates at Christchurch Girls' High said, "There was definitely some attraction between them, but what the heck was it?"

Brian McClelland, who saw a good deal of Juliet before and during the trial, thought Juliet loved only herself. The Hulmes' housekeeper, Mrs Grinlaubs, went further. She believed Juliet's main consideration was to completely take over someone such as Pauline Parker as "a shadow person". Nancy Sutherland, too, remarked that when Pauline first started appearing at Ilam she was always in a servile role, waiting on Juliet much as Juliet's little brother had until then.

How true was this? After she was released from the sanatorium Juliet seemed besotted with her friend. In his written statement for the crown prosecutor, Bill Perry said that when Pauline left Ilam after staying there Juliet would collapse, take to her bed for two or three days, and mope until her next visit. When Pauline went home she would get on with life in a way that seemed quite impossible for Juliet.

Pauline wanted to be like Juliet, and Juliet was more than willing to colonise her, transplanting her thoughts, opinions, tastes in music, films, literature and everything else. The dynamics of narcissistic relationships such as this were studied by Heinz Kohut in the late 1960s. He found that ambivalents want to merge with people who have desirable characteristics they feel they lack. Someone who inwardly feels ugly seeks to merge with someone beautiful. A person who feels unintelligent wants to merge with someone perceived as particularly intelligent. This was true of Pauline. Juliet, for her part, needed another person to help maintain her inflated self-image; the twinship relationship served her narcissistic needs because Pauline was willing to adopt all her likes, dislikes, ideas and philosophies.

Kohut called this "twinship transference". The more alike the two people become, the more they love each other. He, and others who followed him, observed that some of the great romances in history had nothing to do with love in the mature selfless sense but were, in essence, narcissistic, based on self-love.

It has been suggested—by a Canterbury historian, Stevan Eldred-Grigg, among others—that two key factors in the murder of Honorah Rieper were sex and class. The first is indisputable: whatever the girls' long-term sexual orientation, their fascination with each other found a homoerotic expression pleasurable to both, and this bound them even closer in a relationship increasingly detached from reality.

But what of "class"? It is part of the mythology surrounding the case that, because of the Hulmes' superior social standing and cultural sophistication, Pauline, "the girl from the fish shop", was swept off her feet, dazzled by the glamour of life at Ilam, and became enslaved to Juliet. It makes a good story but the truth is more complex. Certainly, the Hulmes lived in a house that was grand by New Zealand standards and mixed easily with the Anglophile upper tier of Christchurch society. And certainly Pauline, with her limited social experience, was impressed by their life and sometimes fantasised about being a Hulme herself: she even taught herself to speak as they did. Yet her adoration of Juliet went far beyond admiration for a social superior. And her seething anger, self-loathing and intermittent hatred of her mother did not spring from dissatisfaction with her social mileu and envy of Juliet's: these feelings had started long before she met Juliet Hulme. No one could say the social cleft between the Riepers and the Hulmes had nothing at all to do with the girls' fatal friendship, but if Pauline had been the daughter of well-off educated parents closer to the Hulmes in social class the same events would probably have occurred. Nathan Leopold and Richard Loeb were, after all, both sons of Jewish millionaires from the affluent suburbs of Chicago.

CHAPTER 41

Separate Lives

Are Anne Perry and Hilary Nathan in contact with each other? Has there been a *Heavenly Creatures* reunion? Do these girlhood friends, now in their early seventies, get together from time to time to reminisce? Speculation has been driven by the fact that for years both women have lived in Scotland, only about one hundred miles apart. Surely this is too much of a coincidence? It is such an intriguing thought some are convinced the women must have met. Their imaginary reunion is even the premise of a play, *Folie à Deux*, by Canadian playwright Trevor Schmidt, first staged in Edmonton in March 2010.

There are several reasons for thinking that, for all the theatrical possibilities of such a meeting, it has probably never occurred. Juliet and Pauline could not have met in New Zealand after their release: Juliet was whisked out of the country while Pauline was still in prison. In 1966, when Pauline went to England, Anne was living there, although very soon afterwards she moved to California, where she remained until 1972. Even if such a meeting would have been possible before her departure, or after she later returned to England, the odds are against it. Assuming the girls' friendship served narcissistic needs that were particularly strong in adolescence, it can be expected to have long outlived its usefulness.

Anne Perry has made abundantly clear her lack of feeling for Hilary Nathan and laid the blame for the murder squarely on her former friend. Chris Cooke revealed that this allegation had given rise to considerable sympathy for Parker, not least from the girls' former classmates, who remembered Juliet Hulme "as a girl who didn't do anything she didn't want to". If Hilary Nathan ever made a public statement she might well challenge Anne Perry's version of events. Perhaps this was what Perry meant when she told Robert McCrum, "My worst fear about all this is that you will find Pauline."

Two weeks after Hilary Nathan was discovered living in England, Perry told readers of *Woman's Day*, "I hope things go well for Pauline. That is my hope for everyone. There is no one I wish any harm to."

She insisted to NBC's Jamie Gangel that since being sent to prison she had not seen, or had any communication with or about, Hilary Nathan.

"No contact at all?" Gangel asked.

"Until the story broke, when I heard she is a private person and apparently doing quite well and I hope it remains that way."

To Bob Brown on America's ABC television, she said, "I don't think we have anything to say to each other now, honestly. I wish her well. I wish her well but I think it is best we keep our separate lives." Amanda Cable wrote in the *Daily Mail*, "When asked if she ever thinks of Pauline ... Anne will not be drawn, but her icy response—and the fact she will refer to Pauline only as 'she'—seems to speak volumes about her feelings."

Anne Perry finished with Pauline Parker a very long time ago. The last thing in the world she would want is some sort of emotional reconnection. Nor would Hilary Nathan—struggling to run her island croft, communing with God, and battling the elements and the occasional journalist or film-maker intent on invading her privacy—conceivably be eager to reestablish contact with Juliet Hulme, who proved so dangerous to know all those years ago. Would either want to be reminded of the time when Gina and Deborah believed themselves goddesses, heavenly creatures, the two most glorious beings in creation?

Epilogue

S ome of the police officers and lawyers involved in the investigation of Honorah Parker's murder and the trial of Pauline Parker and Juliet Hulme would be profoundly affected. One of the first was the crown prosecutor, Alan Brown. It was clear to everyone at the trial that Brown was at times extremely distressed, and noticeable to some that his cross-examination, particularly of Dr Francis Bennett, often galloped out of control. Dr Reg Medlicott was no doubt smarting about his own cross-examination by Brown when he told Brian McClelland that the crown prosecutor was certifiable— "off his head"—and would be his patient within two years. Medlicott was wrong: Alan Brown was in Ashburn Hall, where Medlicott was medical superintendent, within weeks.

He had clearly suffered what was then called a "nervous breakdown". After the trial his behaviour, which included very heavy drinking, was soon alarming his partners and colleagues. The problem landed in the lap of Derek Round, the most junior member of Raymond, Donnelly and Brown. Round, then a law clerk and part-time law student, would go on to become a distinguished foreign correspondent and editor for the New Zealand Press Association, but in July 1954 he was nineteen years old and, as he is first to admit, wet behind the ears.

Brown refused to talk to his law partners, Peter Mahon and Jack McKenzie, but often spoke to Round, who became increasingly worried. While the exact details are unclear, there is a story that Brown dumped a load of legal files into the Avon, and another that he removed a painting from the Canterbury Officers' Club.

Of particular concern to Derek Round was a relationship Brown had formed with an unusual couple who frequently visited him at his office. Round was not sure whether they were clients or friends, but thought the man, from his appearance, was Indian or from the West Indies. The woman was conspicuous by her outlandishly large hats. The pair claimed to have a silver mine in which they wanted Brown to invest. The man was in possession of a shotgun, which he carried with him much of the time, fearing someone was trying to steal the map locating the mine. Round remembers seeing him come up the stairs one day carrying a leather gun-case, presumably with the gun in it.

The final straw came when Brown was said to have wandered up to Cathedral Square with a rifle and started taking his clothes off. Round went to Ted Taylor, the Christchurch coroner, who was a good friend of Brown's, and told him everything he knew and had heard. Taylor asked Round to apply to have Brown committed under the Mental Health Act.

Feeling "acutely embarrassed and uncomfortable", Round went to see the magistrate Rex Abernethy S.M. and an arrangement was made to have Brown examined by the police surgeon. Round made a sworn statement in front of Abernethy, who then signed the order for Brown's committal. Round felt so uneasy about his part in the proceedings he hoped Brown's wife would not learn it was he who had made the application.

Ted Taylor and another close friend of Brown's, Colin Urquhart, who later became the commissioner of police, found Brown at the Canterbury Club and drove him to Dunedin, where he became the inmate and patient of the man to whom he had given a public mauling at the trial.

Shortly after Brown's committal, at Medlicott's request Derek Round drove down to Ashburn Hall. Brown received him cordially and introduced him to a number of his fellow patients. Medlicott told Round that Brown was suffering from a pre-existing mental disorder that had been brought to the fore by the stresses of the trial. He did not name the disorder but Round guessed it was manic-depression. Medication with lithium was then unknown.

On one occasion Brown phoned the country's solicitor-general, complaining he was being held against his will. Eventually he rang Brian McClelland and said, "For God's sake, you're a friend, get me out." McClelland went to Dunedin to see him and talk to Reg Medlicott. Medlicott, McClelland observed, "lived like the Rajah of Bong", drinking only the best brandy and being waited on by his wife Nan, who believed the great man needed to rest his brain, and never expected him to lift a finger. He found Alan Brown hoeing the rose garden.

McClelland persuaded Medlicott to release Brown on condition he never drank again. The crown solicitor did not return to his post: in 1957 Peter Mahon was appointed to replace him. As an act of kindness a fellow lawyer, Ralph Thompson, gave Brown a job in his firm, Charles S. Thomas, Thompson and Hay. When Brown died in 1961 at the age of sixty-four, his obituary described it as "a less exacting position". It was a sad end for a man of his many talents.

Mr Justice Adams, by then Sir Francis, surprised everyone by marrying his associate the day before he retired; the happy timing meant the new Lady Adams would be eligible for a judicial pension when he died. After retiring he enjoyed some good productive years, parked at the end table in the Supreme Court library beavering away on revisions to *Adams on Criminal Law*. He was always willing to share his encyclopaedic knowledge of the law with young lawyers stuck on a difficult point. One afternoon Nico Gresson came across Sir Francis and Lady Adams taking tea in the United Service Hotel. Seizing the moment, he asked Sir Francis what he had thought of his father's defence of Juliet Hulme. "Absolute poppycock, my boy," he replied.

Terence Gresson was appointed a judge of the Supreme Court in 1956. He was forty-two, one of the youngest judges ever appointed, but his life was to end in tragedy when eleven years later, on November 14, 1967, he was found dead. He had put his head in a gas oven. He had planned his death meticulously, even remembering to leave gifts for his godson and others. He was said to have been under financial pressure, and many friends wished they had had some hint of his problems. They would have been only too willing to help, but he was a proud man. He was greatly missed.

Alec Haslam was appointed to the Supreme Court in 1957, when it was recorded that he was "notable among his friends and contemporaries for his unusual combination of mental and physical vigour, enlivened by frankness in speech, and governed by courtesy in behaviour". He may have been courteous in a social setting, but lawyers who appeared before him in court were more likely to remember him as one of the most dyspeptic judges they ever encountered.

Jimmy Wicks' future career surprised those who knew him as a student and young practitioner of the law. Although less obviously gifted than any other counsel in the Parker–Hulme trial, he was appointed a magistrate in 1961, and by 1978 was senior stipendiary magistrate. Given a knighthood that year, he was appointed Wanganui Computer Centre privacy commissioner, a position he held until 1983.

Brian McClelland's part in the Parker–Hulme trial led to a long and successful career. Speaking of himself and his much-loved wife Phyll, he said, "We were young [and] proud of the fact I was in the trial. It was marvellous, a wonderful experience—even though we got done." As one of the governors of Christ's College McClelland was at the heart of the Canterbury establishment, yet he was worshipped by the hundreds of trade union members for whom he had acted in personal injury claims. Appointed Queen's Counsel in 1977, he never fully retired. Not long before his death he lamented the change in criminal court work. Once, he said, he had appeared for "unarmed, skilled criminals" such as safe-blowers. "Now it's drugs and gangs. ... That doesn't interest me greatly." He always had a photograph of Terence Gresson beside his desk.

Peter Mahon, too, would have a distinguished career. In 1962 he resigned as crown solicitor to take up practice as a barrister sole. In 1971 he was appointed Queen's Counsel and became a judge of the Supreme Court. He was an outstanding judge. Calm and patient, even if often bored, he produced beautifully written judgements notable for their humanity and a determination to see justice done. In 1980 he was appointed to chair a Royal Commission of Inquiry into an air disaster in which an Air New Zealand sightseeing plane to Antarctica had crashed into Mount Erebus, killing all 257 passengers and crew.

Mahon's 166-page report contained the words: "I am forced reluctantly to say that I had to listen to an orchestrated litany of lies." The fatal phrase reflected his conviction that the senior management of Air New Zealand had conspired to falsely blame the pilot for the accident.

Air New Zealand persuaded the Court of Appeal that making such a finding without giving the airline an opportunity to refute it amounted to a miscarriage of justice. Mahon was stung by the finding, which he believed called into question his competence and sense of justice, and resigned as a judge. The Crown appealed to the Privy Council in London to overthrow the Court of Appeal's decision but was unsuccessful. Mahon, with good cause, was extremely bitter. Sadly, he came to believe old and dear friends were snubbing him in the street.

The most tragic story is Archie Tate's. The police officer who played a leading part in the Honorah Parker murder investigation and ensuing trial was described by one of the members of a rugby team he coached as "quite a refined sort of bloke for a cop in those days. You never heard Archie swear or use coarse language". Tate's daughter Lesley told journalist Chris Cooke that the murder and trial had deeply upset her father. "What really got to him was that not only were they the same age as me but they appeared to be two normal girls."

Like Alan Brown he seems to have had a breakdown of sorts, but terrified of showing weakness and perhaps ruining his career he soldiered on. By January 1964 he was a detective chief inspector stationed in the northern city of Hamilton. Towards the end of that month he was ordered to take charge of a murder investigation. David Rowe, chief steward of the *New Zealand Star*, had been found dead while the ship was at sea. Tate and two other detectives boarded the vessel at Napier to investigate. Within twenty-four hours they had arrested John Vincent, a seaman.

When the *New Zealand Star* sailed for Lyttelton on Sunday, February 2, Tate and the two detectives remained on board to continue their inquiries. Later that night Tate was found hanging in his cabin. There were, the police announced, "no suspicious circumstances".

What had made him do it? Derek Round heard from a police source that a case in which Tate had given evidence was weighing heavily on his mind. He had come to believe that the man against whom he had given evidence had been wrongly convicted. It had all got too much for him. He was forty-nine years old.

Henry Hulme's time at Canterbury University College was just a blip in an otherwise successful career. As head of nuclear research in Britain and a first-rate theoretical physicist, Hulme would get much of the credit for the well-planned programme that saw Britain explode its first thermonuclear bomb in the Christmas Islands in 1957. It is rumoured he refused a knighthood.

Not everyone was thrilled about the bomb. Aldermaston became the destination for an annual protest. Every self-respecting pacifist, beatnik and left-wing intellectual in London would march on the atomic weapons research facility bearing "Ban the Bomb" placards. Vivien Dixon once asked Hulme how he felt about this. "Couldn't care less," he replied.

As it happened, much of his most important work was in the field of test-ban verification. Statistical and probability methods were used to determine the number of on-site inspections needed to distinguish underground bomb-testing from volcanic eruptions and other seismic activity. In 1960 he proposed that the three nuclear powers—Britain, America and the Soviet Union—set up a joint programme of seismological research and agree to suspend nuclear testing for several years. It was a fine idea, derailed when a United States U-2 spy plane was shot down over Soviet airspace, the pilot captured, and the United States forced to admit he had been on a surveillance mission.

In his private life Hulme collected English watercolours, scouring auction houses and antique dealers to make acquisitions. He was also said to be clever with stocks and shares. Although his second wife Margery never got on with Juliet, and Henry had little affection for his stepchildren, the couple had a happy marriage.

Henry Hulme died in Hampshire in January 1991. His obituary in *The Telegraph* described him as "a level-headed communicator and a good critic ... greatly liked and respected by his colleagues at Aldermaston, for whom he was always ready with advice and encouragement". He was "a kindly, charming man with a Rabelaisian sense of humour".

There was a building called Black Nest connected to Aldermaston. Hulme's subordinates remembered with affection that he would call at Black Nest most evenings on his way home, "compose himself flat on his back and, eyes closed, … swap ideas and unprintable stories … always new and never repeated". Such eccentricity would not have gone down well at Canterbury University College.

After Bill Perry died in 1986, Hilda—living in the Midlands and long since known as Marion Perry—took a job as a voluntary tutor at a college of further education, helping teach English as a second language, and remedial English to slow learners and stroke victims. She did not retire from this fulfilling work until she was eighty, when she moved to Portmahomack to be near her daughter. She bought a fisherman's cottage with glorious views over Dornoch Firth to the mountains of Sutherland and came to love the wild beauty of the place.

By then she was suffering from arthritis and her eyesight was failing, but she still walked two or three miles a day and enjoyed pottering in her garden, feeding the seagulls that nested in her shed, and making new friends among the villagers. A visitor from New Zealand described her as "still charming and lively". She missed her son Jonathan, who lived in Zimbabwe where he practised as a doctor, but he visited regularly and wrote to her often. It was a shock to her when he married a Chinese woman, but their two beautiful grandchildren became a great joy. She died in 2004 at the age of ninety-one.

Select Bibliography

All Shook Up: The Flash Bodgie and the Rise of the New Zealand Teenager in the Fifties, Redmer Yska: Penguin Books, Auckland, 1993

The Battle of the Atlantic, Andrew Williams: BBC Books, London, 2002

Brief Encounters: Some Uncommon Lawyers, Glyn Strange: Clerestory Press, Christchurch, 1997

A Concise Encyclopaedia of Māori Myth and Legend, Margaret Orbell: Canterbury University Press, Christchurch, 1998

Fendall's Legacy: A History of Fendalton and North West Christchurch, Frieda Looser: Canterbury University Press, Christchurch, 2002

The Film Encyclopaedia: The Complete Guide to Film and the Film Industry (6th edition), Ephraim Katz, revised by Ronald D. Nolen: Collins Publishers, New York, 2008

The Gardens of Canterbury: A History, Thelma Strongman: A.H. & A.W. Reed, Wellington, 1994

The Historic Story of the Coronation, Ceremony and Ritual, Laurence E. Tanner: Pitkins, London, 1952

A History of the University of Canterbury, 1873–1973, W.J. Gardner, E.T. Beardsley, T.E. Carter: University of Canterbury, Christchurch, 1973

The Longest Night, 10–11 May 1941: Voices from the London Blitz, Gavin Mortimer: Phoenix, London, 2005

The Manhattan Project: The Birth of the Atomic Bomb in the Words of its Creators, Eyewitnesses, and Historians, Cynthia C. Kelly, ed.: Black Dog and Leventhal Publishers, New York, 2007

My Father's Shadow: Portrait of Justice Peter Mahon, Sam Mahon: Longacre Press, Dunedin, 2008

Oxford Dictionary of National Biography: Oxford University Press, Oxford, 2004–8

Parker & Hulme: A Lesbian View, Julie Glamuzina and Alison J. Laurie: New Women's Press, Auckland, 1991

Parker & Hulme: A Lesbian View, with introduction by B. Ruby Rich, Julie Glamuzina and Alison J. Laurie: Firebrand Books, Ithaca, New York, 1995

The Port Hills of Christchurch, Gordon Ogilvie: A.H. & A.W. Reed, Wellington, 1970

The Prisoner of Zenda, Anthony Hope: Penguin Books, London, 2007

Rudi Gopas: A Biography, Chris Ronayne: David Ling Publishing, Auckland, 2002

Test for Greatness: Britain's Struggle for the Atom Bomb, Brian Cathcart: John Murray Publishers, London, 1994

Tikao Talks: Ka Taoka O Te Ao Kohatu, Treasures of the Ancient World of the Māori, Herries Beattie: Penguin Books, Auckland, 1990

Te Wai Pounamu, The Greenstone Island: A History of the Southern Māori during the European Colonisation of New Zealand, Harry C. Evison: Aoraki Press, Wellington, 1993

Tolkien's Gown and Other Stories of Great Authors and Rare Books, Rick Gekoski: Constable and Robinson, London, 2005

Young Voices: British Children Remember the Second World War, Lyn Smith: Penguin Books, London, 2008

Works on abnormal psychology

Abnormal Psychology (13th edition), James N. Butcher, Susan Mineka, Jill M. Hooley: Pearson Education, Boston, 2007

Becoming Attached, Robert Karen: Oxford University Press, Oxford, 1994.

Character Styles, Stephen M. Johnson: Norton, New York, 1994

Essential Psychopathy and its Treatment (2nd edition), Jerrold S. Maxmen, Nicholas G. Ward: Norton, New York, 1995

Madness Explained, Psychosis and Human Nature, Richard P. Bentall: Penguin Books, London, 2004

The Restoration of the Self, H. Kohut: International Universities Press, New York, 1997

Selected magazine, newspaper and journal articles

"Murder Without Remorse", Neil Clarkson: *The Press: Weekend*, October 5, 1991

"When Murder Catches Up With You", Sarah Gristwood: *The Daily Telegraph*, August 5, 1994

"Solved: The mystery of Juliet Hulme": *The Press*, August 6, 1994

"Past Imperfect", Sebastian Faulks: *The Guardian*, August 25, 1994

"Hulme describes plot to kill friend's mother": *The Press*, September 20, 1994

"Anne Perry, forced to relive her own murder story", Deirdre Donahue: *USA Today*, September 23, 1994

"The Most Disturbing Story of All", Sarah Gristwood: *You*, January 15, 1995

"Slaughter by the innocents", Louise Chunn; "A happy ending?", Sarah Gristwood: *The Guardian*, January 30, 1995

"Whatever happened to Pauline Parker?", Chris Cooke: *New Zealand's Woman's Weekly*, January 13, 1997

"Parker–Hulme Probe: Anne Finally Talks about Pauline": *Woman's Day*, January 20, 1997

"Heavenly creature", Angela Neustatter: *The Guardian*, November 12, 2003. Reprinted in *New Zealand Listener*, January 24, 2004

"Doctors 'drugged' Hulme", Sean Scanlon: *The Press*, March 6, 2006

"Willing to pay the fare": *The Press*; March 11, 2006

"I'm the Heavenly Creatures murderer", Amanda Cable: *Daily Mail*, September 28, 2006

"Delving into a closed book", James Croot: *The Press*, April 16, 2010

"Matricide: A Critique of the Literature", Kathleen M. Heide and Autumn Frei: *Trauma, Violence & Abuse*, January 2010

Archives

Alexander Turnbull Library, Wellington (James McNeish papers)

Canterbury Museum

Christchurch City Libraries

Macmillan Brown Library, University of Canterbury (Nancy Sutherland papers and James Logie papers)

National Archive, Christchurch

Newspaper and periodical records

The Press, Christchurch

N.Z. Truth, Wellington

Star-Sun, Christchurch

The Express, London

Daily Mail, London

New Zealand Law Journal, Wellington

Internet resources

"Pauline Parker Found":
http://www.adamabrams.com/hc/faq2/library/7.9.5.html

"The Norasearch Diary", Andrew Conway: http://reocities.com/Hollywood/Studio/2194/faq2/norasearch/index.html

New Zealand Archives, http://archway.archives.govt.nz

Christchurch City Libraries, http://www.christchurchcitylibraries.com/Heritage/Digitised/ParkerHulme/

Acknowledgements

There is a list of those to whom I owe gratitude and thanks. The playwright Michelanne Forster is a good starting point. When doing research for her play *Daughters of Heaven*, Michelanne interviewed numerous people, including Brian McClelland and several academics and their wives who had known Henry and Hilda Hulme. Another of her interviewees was Mrs Grinlaubs, the Hulmes' Latvian housekeeper. It was extremely generous of her to send me all her notes and papers with authority to make whatever use I wished of them.

I also owe a good deal to my friend Christopher McVeigh QC, who made an application to the High Court on my behalf seeking access to the official manuscript of the trial of Pauline Parker and Juliet Hulme, and a subsequent application to view and copy a typescript of Pauline's 1954 diary. This was by no means a formality and I much appreciate Chris's kind and capable handling of these matters and other help he has given.

I must also thank Oliver Sutherland and his sisters Diony Young, Julia Sutherland and Jan Oliver. They kindly gave me permission to use their mother Nancy Sutherland's papers, deposited in the Macmillan Brown Library at Canterbury University, and also supplied useful information about the Hulme family and their mother's friendship with Hilda. The correspondence which forms a large part of these papers gave me several anecdotes and insights without which the book would have been much the poorer.

Sam Mahon, too, was generous in allowing me access to his father Peter Mahon's personal papers relating to the case. This file contained some valuable information, for example Herbert Rieper's statement to the police about his first marriage, his non-existent accountancy practice in Feilding, and his wife's allegedly dying of cancer. There were other interesting items in the Crown's proofs of evidence that had not come out at trial: witnesses do not always say everything counsel leading them hope and expect they will.

I wish to also record my thanks to Donalda and Alan Beattie, who could not have been more kind and hospitable on my visit to the Scottish Highlands. Many others gave help and supplied useful information. In no particular order I would like to thank Wallace Colville, Chris Cooke, Joan Livingstone, Barbara Cox, Jock Phillips, Derek Round, Peter Penlington, James Walshe, Vivien Dixon, Gerald Lascelles, Peter Champion, Fred Shaw, Jeff Field, Barry Tait, Bill Sheate, Tim Beaglehole, Helen Beaglehole, Simon Acland, Anna Burbery, Marina Hughes, Mike Norris, Gerald Hensley, Juliet Hensley, Alexander Roman, Jenny Carlyon, Phil Brinded, Nicholas Gresson, Simon Rowley, Pip Hall, Jimmy Wallace, Prue Lowry, Laura Cairns, Matt McClelland, Robin Laing, Rosemary Heaphy, Colin Bennett, John Ritchie, Caroline Maze and Rachel McAlpine. I have omitted the names of a few informants whom I know or feel would not wish to be mentioned. Thanks to them as well.

I also give praise and thanks to the charming and capable Emily Hewitt, who served as my personal assistant. I commend her to any writer—if such a person exists—as inept as myself at word processing. I am grateful to Mary Varnham, publisher at Awa Press, whose editorial skill and a lot of hard work pulled this book together. Thanks, too, to Sarah Bennett of Awa Press for her industrious and effective photo research, and to *N.Z. Truth* and the *Christchurch Star-Sun* for their assistance.

And finally I thank Annabel Graham for her extraordinary patience and support over what has been a long haul.

P.G.
Dunsandel
September 2011

Index

continued over

continued over